Lay Flat Binding

We have bound this manual using a new *lay-flat* binding technology. This type of binding allows you to open a soft cover book so that it "lays flat" on a table without creasing the binding.

In order to make the book lay flat properly, you need to "crack" the binding. To do this, divide the book into two sections and bend it so that the front and back covers meet. Do not worry; the pages are glued to the binding, and will not fall out easily. The outer cardboard binding itself is designed so that it will not break or crease as an ordinary paperback binding will. Bend the book several times in this manner, dividing it in a different place each time and pressing the pages flat and open. With use, the binding will become flexible and the pages will lay flat without needing to be pushed or held down.

Texinfo

The GNU Documentation Format
Edition 2.20, for Texinfo Version Three
February 1995

by Robert J. Chassell and Richard M. Stallman

Copyright © 1988, 1990, 1991, 1992, 1993, 1995 Free Software Foundation, Inc.

This is the second edition of the Texinfo documentation,
and is consistent with version 2 of '`texinfo.tex`'.

Published by the Free Software Foundation
675 Massachusetts Avenue,
Cambridge, MA 02139 USA
Printed copies are available for $15 each.
ISBN 1-882114-63-9

Permission is granted to make and distribute verbatim copies of this manual provided the copyright notice and this permission notice are preserved on all copies.

Permission is granted to copy and distribute modified versions of this manual under the conditions for verbatim copying, provided that the entire resulting derived work is distributed under the terms of a permission notice identical to this one.

Permission is granted to copy and distribute translations of this manual into another language, under the above conditions for modified versions, except that this permission notice may be stated in a translation approved by the Free Software Foundation.

Cover art by Etienne Suvasa.

Short Contents

Texinfo Copying Conditions		1
1	Overview of Texinfo	3
2	Using Texinfo Mode	15
3	Beginning a Texinfo File	31
4	Ending a Texinfo File	47
5	Chapter Structuring	51
6	Nodes	59
7	Menus	67
8	Cross References	71
9	Marking Words and Phrases	81
10	Quotations and Examples	91
11	Making Lists and Tables	99
12	Creating Indices	107
13	Special Insertions	113
14	Glyphs for Examples	119
15	Making and Preventing Breaks	123
16	Definition Commands	127
17	Footnotes	141
18	Conditionally Visible Text	143
19	Format and Print Hardcopy	149
20	Creating an Info File	159
21	Installing an Info File	167
Appendix A	@-Command List	171
Appendix B	Tips and Hints	187
Appendix C	A Sample Texinfo File	193
Appendix D	Sample Permissions	195
Appendix E	Include Files	199
Appendix F	Page Headings	205
Appendix G	Formatting Mistakes	211
Appendix H	Refilling Paragraphs	221
Appendix I	@-Command Syntax	223
Appendix J	How to Obtain TeX	225
Appendix K	Second Edition Features	227
Command and Variable Index		235
Concept Index		239

Table of Contents

Texinfo Copying Conditions 1

1 Overview of Texinfo 3
   1.1 Info files 4
   1.2 Printed Books 5
   1.3 @-commands 6
   1.4 General Syntactic Conventions 7
   1.5 Comments 8
   1.6 What a Texinfo File Must Have 9
   1.7 Six Parts of a Texinfo File 10
   1.8 A Short Sample Texinfo File 10
   1.9 Acknowledgements 13

2 Using Texinfo Mode 15
   2.1 The Usual GNU Emacs Editing Commands 15
   2.2 Inserting Frequently Used Commands 16
   2.3 Showing the Section Structure of a File 18
   2.4 Updating Nodes and Menus 19
      2.4.1 Updating Requirements 22
      2.4.2 Other Updating Commands 23
   2.5 Formatting for Info 24
   2.6 Formatting and Printing 25
   2.7 Texinfo Mode Summary 26

3 Beginning a Texinfo File 31
   3.1 Sample Texinfo File Beginning 31
   3.2 The Texinfo File Header 33
      3.2.1 The First Line of a Texinfo File 33
      3.2.2 Start of Header 33
      3.2.3 @setfilename 34
      3.2.4 @settitle 34
      3.2.5 @setchapternewpage 35
      3.2.6 Paragraph Indenting 36
      3.2.7 End of Header 37
   3.3 Summary and Copying Permissions for Info 37
   3.4 The Title and Copyright Pages 38
      3.4.1 @titlepage 38
      3.4.2 @titlefont, @center, and @sp 39
      3.4.3 @title, @subtitle, and @author 40
      3.4.4 Copyright Page and Permissions 40

		3.4.5	Heading Generation	41
		3.4.6	The `@headings` Command	42
	3.5	The 'Top' Node and Master Menu		43
		3.5.1	Parts of a Master Menu	44
	3.6	Software Copying Permissions		45

4 Ending a Texinfo File 47

4.1	Index Menus and Printing an Index	47
4.2	Generating a Table of Contents	48
4.3	`@bye` File Ending	49

5 Chapter Structuring 51

5.1	Tree Structure of Sections	51
5.2	Types of Structuring Command	52
5.3	`@top`	53
5.4	`@chapter`	53
5.5	`@unnumbered`, `@appendix`	53
5.6	`@majorheading`, `@chapheading`	53
5.7	`@section`	54
5.8	`@unnumberedsec`, `@appendixsec`, `@heading`	54
5.9	The `@subsection` Command	55
5.10	The `@subsection`-like Commands	55
5.11	The 'subsub' Commands	55
5.12	`@raisesections` and `@lowersections`	56

6 Nodes 59

6.1	Node and Menu Illustration	59
6.2	The `@node` Command	61
	6.2.1 How to Write an `@node` Line	62
	6.2.2 `@node` Line Tips	63
	6.2.3 `@node` Line Requirements	63
	6.2.4 The First Node	64
	6.2.5 The `@top` Sectioning Command	64
	6.2.6 The 'Top' Node Summary	65
6.3	Creating Pointers with `makeinfo`	65

7 Menus 67

7.1	Writing a Menu	68
7.2	The Parts of a Menu	68
7.3	Less Cluttered Menu Entry	69
7.4	A Menu Example	69
7.5	Referring to Other Info Files	70

8 Cross References 71
8.1 Different Cross Reference Commands 71
8.2 Parts of a Cross Reference 72
8.3 `@xref` 73
8.3.1 `@xref` with One Argument 74
8.3.2 `@xref` with Two Arguments 74
8.3.3 `@xref` with Three Arguments 75
8.3.4 `@xref` with Four and Five Arguments 76
8.4 Naming a 'Top' Node 77
8.5 `@ref` 78
8.6 `@pxref` 79
8.7 `@inforef` 80

9 Marking Words and Phrases 81
9.1 Indicating Definitions, Commands, etc. 81
9.1.1 `@code{`*sample-code*`}` 82
9.1.2 `@kbd{`*keyboard-characters*`}` 83
9.1.3 `@key{`*key-name*`}` 84
9.1.4 `@samp{`*text*`}` 84
9.1.5 `@var{`*metasyntactic-variable*`}` 85
9.1.6 `@file{`*file-name*`}` 86
9.1.7 `@dfn{`*term*`}` 86
9.1.8 `@cite{`*reference*`}` 87
9.2 Emphasizing Text 87
9.2.1 `@emph{`*text*`}` and `@strong{`*text*`}` 87
9.2.2 `@sc{`*text*`}`: The Small Caps Font 88
9.2.3 Fonts for Printing, Not Info 88
9.2.4 Customized Highlighting 89

10 Quotations and Examples 91
10.1 The Block Enclosing Commands 91
10.2 `@quotation` 92
10.3 `@example` 92
10.4 `@noindent` 93
10.5 `@lisp` 94
10.6 `@smallexample` and `@smalllisp` 95
10.7 `@display` 95
10.8 `@format` 96
10.9 `@exdent`: Undoing a Line's Indentation 96
10.10 `@flushleft` and `@flushright` 96
10.11 Drawing Cartouches Around Examples 97

11 Making Lists and Tables 99
- 11.1 Making an Itemized List 100
- 11.2 Making a Numbered or Lettered List 101
- 11.3 Making a Two-column Table 103
  - 11.3.1 `@ftable` and `@vtable` 104
  - 11.3.2 `@itemx` 104

12 Creating Indices 107
- 12.1 Making Index Entries 107
- 12.2 Predefined Indices 107
- 12.3 Defining the Entries of an Index 108
- 12.4 Combining Indices 110
  - 12.4.1 `@syncodeindex` 110
  - 12.4.2 `@synindex` 111
- 12.5 Defining New Indices 111

13 Special Insertions 113
- 13.1 Inserting '`@`', Braces, and Periods 113
  - 13.1.1 Inserting '`@`' with `@@` 113
  - 13.1.2 Inserting '`{`' and '`}`' with `@{` and `@}` ... 113
  - 13.1.3 Spacing After Colons and Periods 114
- 13.2 `@dmn{`*dimension*`}`: Format a Dimension 114
- 13.3 Inserting Ellipsis, Dots, and Bullets 115
  - 13.3.1 `@dots{}` 115
  - 13.3.2 `@bullet{}` 115
- 13.4 Inserting TeX and the Copyright Symbol 116
  - 13.4.1 `@TeX{}` 116
  - 13.4.2 `@copyright{}` 116
- 13.5 `@minus{}`: Inserting a Minus Sign 116
- 13.6 `@math`: Inserting Mathematical Expressions 116

14 Glyphs for Examples 119
- 14.1 ⇒: Indicating Evaluation 119
- 14.2 ↦: Indicating an Expansion 119
- 14.3 ⊣: Indicating Printed Output 120
- 14.4 `error` : Indicating an Error Message 120
- 14.5 ≡: Indicating Equivalence 121
- 14.6 Indicating Point in a Buffer 121

15 Making and Preventing Breaks 123
- 15.1 @*: Generate Line Breaks 123
- 15.2 @w{*text*}: Prevent Line Breaks 124
- 15.3 @sp *n*: Insert Blank Lines 124
- 15.4 @page: Start a New Page 124
- 15.5 @group: Prevent Page Breaks 125
- 15.6 @need *mils*: Prevent Page Breaks 125

16 Definition Commands 127
- 16.1 The Template for a Definition 127
- 16.2 Optional and Repeated Arguments 129
- 16.3 Two or More 'First' Lines 129
- 16.4 The Definition Commands 130
  - 16.4.1 Functions and Similar Entities 130
  - 16.4.2 Variables and Similar Entities 131
  - 16.4.3 Functions in Typed Languages 132
  - 16.4.4 Variables in Typed Languages 134
  - 16.4.5 Object-Oriented Programming 136
  - 16.4.6 Data Types 138
- 16.5 Conventions for Writing Definitions 139
- 16.6 A Sample Function Definition 139

17 Footnotes 141

18 Conditionally Visible Text 143
- 18.1 Using Ordinary TeX Commands 143
- 18.2 @set, @clear, and @value 144
  - 18.2.1 @ifset and @ifclear 144
  - 18.2.2 @value 146
  - 18.2.3 @value Example 147

19 Format and Print Hardcopy 149
- 19.1 Format using `tex` and `texindex` 149
- 19.2 Format using `texi2dvi` 150
- 19.3 Shell Print Using `lpr -d` 151
- 19.4 From an Emacs Shell 151
- 19.5 Formatting and Printing in Texinfo Mode 151
- 19.6 Using the Local Variables List 153
- 19.7 TeX Formatting Requirements Summary 154
- 19.8 Preparing to Use TeX 154
- 19.9 Overfull "hboxes" 155
- 19.10 Printing "Small" Books 156
- 19.11 Printing on A4 Paper 156

  19.12 Cropmarks and Magnification 157

20 Creating an Info File 159
  20.1 Running `makeinfo` from a Shell 159
  20.2 Options for `makeinfo` 159
  20.3 Pointer Validation 162
  20.4 Running `makeinfo` inside Emacs 162
  20.5 The `texinfo-format`... Commands 163
  20.6 Batch Formatting 164
  20.7 Tag Files and Split Files 164

21 Installing an Info File 167
  21.1 Listing a New Info File 167
  21.2 Info Files in Other Directories 168

Appendix A @-Command List 171

Appendix B Tips and Hints 187

Appendix C A Sample Texinfo File 193

Appendix D Sample Permissions 195
  D.1 'ifinfo' Copying Permissions 196
  D.2 Titlepage Copying Permissions 196

Appendix E Include Files 199
  E.1 How to Use Include Files 199
  E.2 `texinfo-multiple-files-update` 199
  E.3 Include File Requirements 200
  E.4 Sample File with `@include` 201
  E.5 Evolution of Include Files 202

Appendix F Page Headings 205
  F.1 Standard Heading Formats 205
  F.2 Specifying the Type of Heading 206
  F.3 How to Make Your Own Headings 207

Appendix G Formatting Mistakes 211
- G.1 Catching Errors with Info Formatting 211
- G.2 Catching Errors with TeX Formatting 213
- G.3 Using `texinfo-show-structure` 215
- G.4 Using `occur` 216
- G.5 Finding Badly Referenced Nodes 216
  - G.5.1 Running `Info-validate` 217
  - G.5.2 Creating an Unsplit File 217
  - G.5.3 Tagifying a File 218
  - G.5.4 Splitting a File Manually 218

Appendix H Refilling Paragraphs 221

Appendix I @-Command Syntax 223

Appendix J How to Obtain TeX 225

Appendix K Second Edition Features 227
- K.1 New Texinfo Mode Commands 227
- K.2 New Texinfo @-Commands 229

Command and Variable Index 235

Concept Index 239

Texinfo Copying Conditions

The programs currently being distributed that relate to Texinfo include portions of GNU Emacs, plus other separate programs (including **makeinfo**, **info**, **texindex**, and 'texinfo.tex'). These programs are *free*; this means that everyone is free to use them and free to redistribute them on a free basis. The Texinfo-related programs are not in the public domain; they are copyrighted and there are restrictions on their distribution, but these restrictions are designed to permit everything that a good cooperating citizen would want to do. What is not allowed is to try to prevent others from further sharing any version of these programs that they might get from you.

Specifically, we want to make sure that you have the right to give away copies of the programs that relate to Texinfo, that you receive source code or else can get it if you want it, that you can change these programs or use pieces of them in new free programs, and that you know you can do these things.

To make sure that everyone has such rights, we have to forbid you to deprive anyone else of these rights. For example, if you distribute copies of the Texinfo related programs, you must give the recipients all the rights that you have. You must make sure that they, too, receive or can get the source code. And you must tell them their rights.

Also, for our own protection, we must make certain that everyone finds out that there is no warranty for the programs that relate to Texinfo. If these programs are modified by someone else and passed on, we want their recipients to know that what they have is not what we distributed, so that any problems introduced by others will not reflect on our reputation.

The precise conditions of the licenses for the programs currently being distributed that relate to Texinfo are found in the General Public Licenses that accompany them.

1 Overview of Texinfo

Texinfo[1] is a documentation system that uses a single source file to produce both on-line information and printed output. This means that instead of writing two different documents, one for the on-line help or other on-line information and the other for a typeset manual or other printed work, you need write only one document. When the work is revised, you need revise only one document. (You can read the on-line information, known as an *Info file*, with an Info documentation-reading program.)

Using Texinfo, you can create a printed document with the normal features of a book, including chapters, sections, cross references, and indices. From the same Texinfo source file, you can create a menu-driven, on-line Info file with nodes, menus, cross references, and indices. You can, if you wish, make the chapters and sections of the printed document correspond to the nodes of the on-line information; and you use the same cross references and indices for both the Info file and the printed work. *The GNU Emacs Manual* is a good example of a Texinfo file, as is this manual.

To make a printed document, you process a Texinfo source file with the TeX typesetting program. This creates a DVI file that you can typeset and print as a book or report. (Note that the Texinfo language is completely different from TeX's usual language, PlainTeX, which Texinfo replaces.) If you do not have TeX, but do have `troff` or `nroff`, you can use the `texi2roff` program instead.

To make an Info file, you process a Texinfo source file with the `makeinfo` utility or Emacs's `texinfo-format-buffer` command; this creates an Info file that you can install on-line.

TeX and `texi2roff` work with many types of printer; similarly, Info works with almost every type of computer terminal. This power makes Texinfo a general purpose system, but brings with it a constraint, which is that a Texinfo file may contain only the customary "typewriter" characters (letters, numbers, spaces, and punctuation marks) but no special graphics.

A Texinfo file is a plain ASCII file containing text and *@-commands* (words preceded by an '@') that tell the typesetting and formatting programs what to do. You may edit a Texinfo file with any text editor; but it is especially convenient to use GNU Emacs since that editor has a special mode, called

---

[1] Note that the first syllable of "Texinfo" is pronounced like "speck", not "hex". This odd pronunciation is derived from, but is not the same as, the pronunciation of TeX. In the word TeX, the 'X' is actually the Greek letter "chi" rather than the English letter "ex". Pronounce TeX as if the 'X' were the last sound in the name 'Bach'; but pronounce Texinfo as if the 'x' were a 'k'. Spell "Texinfo" with a capital "T" and write the other letters in lower case.

Texinfo mode, that provides various Texinfo-related features. (See Chapter 2 [Texinfo Mode], page 15.)

Before writing a Texinfo source file, you should become familiar with the Info documentation reading program and learn about nodes, menus, cross references, and the rest. (See Info file `info', node `Top', for more information.)

You can use Texinfo to create both on-line help and printed manuals; moreover, Texinfo is freely redistributable. For these reasons, Texinfo is the format in which documentation for GNU utilities and libraries is written.

1.1 Info files

An Info file is a Texinfo file formatted so that the Info documentation reading program can operate on it. (`makeinfo` and `texinfo-format-buffer` are two commands that convert a Texinfo file into an Info file.)

Info files are divided into pieces called *nodes*, each of which contains the discussion of one topic. Each node has a name, and contains both text for the user to read and pointers to other nodes, which are identified by their names. The Info program displays one node at a time, and provides commands with which the user can move to other related nodes.

Each node of an Info file may have any number of child nodes that describe subtopics of the node's topic. The names of child nodes are listed in a *menu* within the parent node; this allows you to use certain Info commands to move to one of the child nodes. Generally, an Info file is organized like a book. If a node is at the logical level of a chapter, its child nodes are at the level of sections; likewise, the child nodes of sections are at the level of subsections.

All the children of any one parent are linked together in a bidirectional chain of `Next' and `Previous' pointers. The `Next' pointer provides a link to the next section, and the `Previous' pointer provides a link to the previous section. This means that all the nodes that are at the level of sections within a chapter are linked together. Normally the order in this chain is the same as the order of the children in the parent's menu. Each child node records the parent node name as its `Up' pointer. The last child has no `Next' pointer, and the first child has the parent both as its `Previous' and as its `Up' pointer.[2]

The book-like structuring of an Info file into nodes that correspond to chapters, sections, and the like is a matter of convention, not a requirement. The `Up', `Previous', and `Next' pointers of a node can point to any other

---

[2] In some documents, the first child has no `Previous' pointer. Occasionally, the last child has the node name of the next following higher level node as its `Next' pointer.

Chapter 1: Overview of Texinfo

nodes, and a menu can contain any other nodes. Thus, the node structure can be any directed graph. But it is usually more comprehensible to follow a structure that corresponds to the structure of chapters and sections in a printed book or report.

In addition to menus and to 'Next', 'Previous', and 'Up' pointers, Info provides pointers of another kind, called references, that can be sprinkled throughout the text. This is usually the best way to represent links that do not fit a hierarchical structure.

Usually, you will design a document so that its nodes match the structure of chapters and sections in the printed output. But there are times when this is not right for the material being discussed. Therefore, Texinfo uses separate commands to specify the node structure for the Info file and the section structure for the printed output.

Generally, you enter an Info file through a node that by convention is called 'Top'. This node normally contains just a brief summary of the file's purpose, and a large menu through which the rest of the file is reached. From this node, you can either traverse the file systematically by going from node to node, or you can go to a specific node listed in the main menu, or you can search the index menus and then go directly to the node that has the information you want.

If you want to read through an Info file in sequence, as if it were a printed manual, you can get the whole file with the advanced Info command **g* RET**. (See Info file '`info`', node '`Expert`'.)

The '`dir`' file in the '`info`' directory serves as the departure point for the whole Info system. From it, you can reach the 'Top' nodes of each of the documents in a complete Info system.

1.2 Printed Books

A Texinfo file can be formatted and typeset as a printed book or manual. To do this, you need TeX, a powerful, sophisticated typesetting program written by Donald Knuth.[3]

A Texinfo-based book is similar to any other typeset, printed work: it can have a title page, copyright page, table of contents, and preface, as well as chapters, numbered or unnumbered sections and subsections, page headers, cross references, footnotes, and indices.

You can use Texinfo to write a book without ever having the intention of converting it into on-line information. You can use Texinfo for writing

---

[3] You can also use the `texi2roff` program if you do not have TeX; since Texinfo is designed for use with TeX, `texi2roff` is not described here. `texi2roff` is part of the standard GNU distribution.

a printed novel, and even to write a printed memo, although this latter application is not recommended since electronic mail is so much easier.

TeX is a general purpose typesetting program. Texinfo provides a file called '`texinfo.tex`' that contains information (definitions or *macros*) that TeX uses when it typesets a Texinfo file. ('`texinfo.tex`' tells TeX how to convert the Texinfo @-commands to TeX commands, which TeX can then process to create the typeset document.) '`texinfo.tex`' contains the specifications for printing a document.

Most often, documents are printed on 8.5 inch by 11 inch pages (216 mm by 280 mm; this is the default size), but you can also print for 7 inch by 9.25 inch pages (178 mm by 235 mm; the `@smallbook` size) or on European A4 size paper (`@afourpaper`). (See Section 19.10 [Printing "Small" Books], page 156. Also, see Section 19.11 [Printing on A4 Paper], page 156.)

By changing the parameters in '`texinfo.tex`', you can change the size of the printed document. In addition, you can change the style in which the printed document is formatted; for example, you can change the sizes and fonts used, the amount of indentation for each paragraph, the degree to which words are hyphenated, and the like. By changing the specifications, you can make a book look dignified, old and serious, or light-hearted, young and cheery.

TeX is freely distributable. It is written in a dialect of Pascal called WEB and can be compiled either in Pascal or (by using a conversion program that comes with the TeX distribution) in C. (See section "TeX Mode" in *The GNU Emacs Manual*, for information about TeX.)

TeX is very powerful and has a great many features. Because a Texinfo file must be able to present information both on a character-only terminal in Info form and in a typeset book, the formatting commands that Texinfo supports are necessarily limited.

See Appendix J [How to Obtain TeX], page 227.

1.3 @-commands

In a Texinfo file, the commands that tell TeX how to typeset the printed manual and tell `makeinfo` and `texinfo-format-buffer` how to create an Info file are preceded by '@'; they are called *@-commands*. For example, `@node` is the command to indicate a node and `@chapter` is the command to indicate the start of a chapter.

Please note: All the @-commands, with the exception of the `@TeX{}` command, must be written entirely in lower case.

The Texinfo @-commands are a strictly limited set of constructs. The strict limits make it possible for Texinfo files to be understood both by TeX and by the code that converts them into Info files. You can display Info files

Chapter 1: Overview of Texinfo

on any terminal that displays alphabetic and numeric characters. Similarly, you can print the output generated by TeX on a wide variety of printers.

Depending on what they do or what arguments[4] they take, you need to write @-commands on lines of their own or as part of sentences:

- Write a command such as `@noindent` at the beginning of a line as the only text on the line. (`@noindent` prevents the beginning of the next line from being indented as the beginning of a paragraph.)
- Write a command such as `@chapter` at the beginning of a line followed by the command's arguments, in this case the chapter title, on the rest of the line. (`@chapter` creates chapter titles.)
- Write a command such as `@dots{}` wherever you wish but usually within a sentence. (`@dots{}` creates dots ...)
- Write a command such as `@code{`*sample-code*`}` wherever you wish (but usually within a sentence) with its argument, *sample-code* in this example, between the braces. (`@code` marks text as being code.)
- Write a command such as `@example` at the beginning of a line of its own; write the body-text on following lines; and write the matching `@end` command, `@end example` in this case, at the beginning of a line of its own after the body-text. (`@example` ... `@end example` indents and typesets body-text as an example.)

As a general rule, a command requires braces if it mingles among other text; but it does not need braces if it starts a line of its own. The non-alphabetic commands, such as `@:`, are exceptions to the rule; they do not need braces.

As you gain experience with Texinfo, you will rapidly learn how to write the different commands: the different ways to write commands make it easier to write and read Texinfo files than if all commands followed exactly the same syntax. (For details about @-command syntax, see Appendix I [@-Command Syntax], page 225.)

1.4 General Syntactic Conventions

All ASCII printing characters except '@', '{' and '}' can appear in a Texinfo file and stand for themselves. '@' is the escape character which introduces

---

[4] The word *argument* comes from the way it is used in mathematics and does not refer to a disputation between two people; it refers to the information presented to the command. According to the *Oxford English Dictionary*, the word derives from the Latin for *to make clear, prove*; thus it came to mean 'the evidence offered as proof', which is to say, 'the information offered', which led to its mathematical meaning. In its other thread of derivation, the word came to mean 'to assert in a manner against which others may make counter assertions', which led to the meaning of 'argument' as a disputation.

commands. '{' and '}' should be used only to surround arguments to certain commands. To put one of these special characters into the document, put an '@' character in front of it, like this: '@@', '@{', and '@}'.

It is customary in TeX to use doubled single-quote characters to begin and end quotations: `` and ''. This convention should be followed in Texinfo files. TeX converts doubled single-quote characters to left- and right-hand doubled quotation marks, "like this", and Info converts doubled single-quote characters to ASCII double-quotes: `` and '' to ".

Use three hyphens in a row, '---', for a dash—like this. In TeX, a single or even a double hyphen produces a printed dash that is shorter than the usual typeset dash. Info reduces three hyphens to two for display on the screen.

To prevent a paragraph from being indented in the printed manual, put the command `@noindent` on a line by itself before the paragraph.

If you mark off a region of the Texinfo file with the `@iftex` and `@end iftex` commands, that region will appear only in the printed copy; in that region, you can use certain commands borrowed from PlainTeX that you cannot use in Info. Likewise, if you mark off a region with the `@ifinfo` and `@end ifinfo` commands, that region will appear only in the Info file; in that region, you can use Info commands that you cannot use in TeX. (See Chapter 18 [Conditionals], page 143.)

> **Caution:** Do not use tabs in a Texinfo file! TeX uses variable-width fonts, which means that it cannot predefine a tab to work in all circumstances. Consequently, TeX treats tabs like single spaces, and that is not what they look like.
>
> To avoid this problem, Texinfo mode causes GNU Emacs to insert multiple spaces when you press the `TAB` key.
>
> Also, you can run `untabify` in Emacs to convert tabs in a region to multiple spaces.

1.5 Comments

You can write comments in a Texinfo file that will not appear in either the Info file or the printed manual by using the `@comment` command (which may be abbreviated to `@c`). Such comments are for the person who reads the Texinfo file. All the text on a line that follows either `@comment` or `@c` is a comment; the rest of the line does not appear in either the Info file or the printed manual. (Often, you can write the `@comment` or `@c` in the middle of a line, and only the text that follows after the `@comment` or `@c` command does not appear; but some commands, such as `@settitle` and `@setfilename`, work on a whole line. You cannot use `@comment` or `@c` in a line beginning with such a command.)

You can write long stretches of text that will not appear in either the Info file or the printed manual by using the `@ignore` and `@end ignore` commands. Write each of these commands on a line of its own, starting each command at the beginning of the line. Text between these two commands does not appear in the processed output. You can use `@ignore` and `@end ignore` for writing comments. Often, `@ignore` and `@end ignore` is used to enclose a part of the copying permissions that applies to the Texinfo source file of a document, but not to the Info or printed version of the document.

1.6 What a Texinfo File Must Have

By convention, the names of Texinfo files end with one of the extensions '`.texinfo`', '`.texi`', or '`.tex`'. The longer extension is preferred since it describes more clearly to a human reader the nature of the file. The shorter extensions are for operating systems that cannot handle long file names.

In order to be made into a printed manual and an Info file, a Texinfo file **must** begin with lines like this:

```
\input texinfo
@setfilename info-file-name
@settitle name-of-manual
```

The contents of the file follow this beginning, and then you **must** end a Texinfo file with a line like this:

```
@bye
```

The '`\input texinfo`' line tells TeX to use the '`texinfo.tex`' file, which tells TeX how to translate the Texinfo @-commands into TeX typesetting commands. (Note the use of the backslash, '`\`'; this is correct for TeX.) The '`@setfilename`' line provides a name for the Info file and the '`@settitle`' line specifies a title for the page headers (or footers) of the printed manual.

The `@bye` line at the end of the file on a line of its own tells the formatters that the file is ended and to stop formatting.

Usually, you will not use quite such a spare format, but will include mode setting and start-of-header and end-of-header lines at the beginning of a Texinfo file, like this:

```
\input texinfo   @c -*-texinfo-*-
@c %**start of header
@setfilename info-file-name
@settitle name-of-manual
@c %**end of header
```

In the first line, '`-*-texinfo-*-`' causes Emacs to switch into Texinfo mode when you edit the file.

The `@c` lines which surround the '`@setfilename`' and '`@settitle`' lines are optional, but you need them in order to run TeX or Info on just part of the file. (See Section 3.2.2 [Start of Header], page 33, for more information.)

Furthermore, you will usually provide a Texinfo file with a title page, indices, and the like. But the minimum, which can be useful for short documents, is just the three lines at the beginning and the one line at the end.

1.7 Six Parts of a Texinfo File

Generally, a Texinfo file contains more than the minimal beginning and end—it usually contains six parts:

1. Header   The *Header* names the file, tells TeX which definitions' file to use, and performs other "housekeeping" tasks.

2. Summary Description and Copyright

   The *Summary Description and Copyright* segment describes the document and contains the copyright notice and copying permissions for the Info file. The segment must be enclosed between `@ifinfo` and `@end ifinfo` commands so that the formatters place it only in the Info file.

3. Title and Copyright

   The *Title and Copyright* segment contains the title and copyright pages and copying permissions for the printed manual. The segment must be enclosed between `@titlepage` and `@end titlepage` commands. The title and copyright page appear only in the printed manual.

4. 'Top' Node and Master Menu

   The *Master Menu* contains a complete menu of all the nodes in the whole Info file. It appears only in the Info file, in the 'Top' node.

5. Body   The *Body* of the document may be structured like a traditional book or encyclopedia or it may be free form.

6. End   The *End* contains commands for printing indices and generating the table of contents, and the `@bye` command on a line of its own.

1.8 A Short Sample Texinfo File

Here is a complete but very short Texinfo file, in 6 parts. The first three parts of the file, from '`\input texinfo`' through to '`@end titlepage`', look more intimidating than they are. Most of the material is standard boilerplate; when you write a manual, simply insert the names for your own manual in this segment. (See Chapter 3 [Beginning a File], page 31.)

Chapter 1: Overview of Texinfo

In the following, the sample text is *indented*; comments on it are not. The complete file, without any comments, is shown in Appendix C [Sample Texinfo File], page 195.

Part 1: Header

The header does not appear in either the Info file or the printed output. It sets various parameters, including the name of the Info file and the title used in the header.

```
\input texinfo   @c -*-texinfo-*-
@c %**start of header
@setfilename sample.info
@settitle Sample Document
@c %**end of header

@setchapternewpage odd
```

Part 2: Summary Description and Copyright

The summary description and copyright segment does not appear in the printed document.

```
@ifinfo
This is a short example of a complete Texinfo file.

Copyright @copyright{} 1990 Free Software Foundation, Inc.
@end ifinfo
```

Part 3: Titlepage and Copyright

The titlepage segment does not appear in the Info file.

```
@titlepage
@sp 10
@comment The title is printed in a large font.
@center @titlefont{Sample Title}

@c The following two commands start the copyright page.
@page
@vskip 0pt plus 1filll
Copyright @copyright{} 1990 Free Software Foundation, Inc.
@end titlepage
```

Part 4: 'Top' Node and Master Menu

The 'Top' node contains the master menu for the Info file.
Since a printed manual uses a table of contents rather than
a menu, the master menu appears only in the Info file.

```
@node      Top,         First Chapter, (dir),     (dir)
@comment node-name, next,              previous, up

@menu
* First Chapter::    The first chapter is the
                     only chapter in this sample.
* Concept Index::    This index has two entries.
@end menu
```

Part 5: The Body of the Document

The body segment contains all the text of the document, but not the indices
or table of contents. This example illustrates a node and a chapter containing
an enumerated list.

```
@node     First Chapter, Concept Index, Top,    Top
@comment node-name,     next,          previous, up
@chapter First Chapter
@cindex Sample index entry
```

This is the contents of the first chapter.
@cindex Another sample index entry

Here is a numbered list.

```
@enumerate
@item
This is the first item.

@item
This is the second item.
@end enumerate
```

The @code{makeinfo} and @code{texinfo-format-buffer}
commands transform a Texinfo file such as this into
an Info file; and @TeX{} typesets it for a printed
manual.

Chapter 1: Overview of Texinfo

Part 6: The End of the Document

The end segment contains commands both for generating an index in a node and unnumbered chapter of its own and for generating the table of contents; and it contains the `@bye` command that marks the end of the document.

```
@node     Concept Index,      , First Chapter, Top
@comment  node-name,       next,   previous,      up
@unnumbered Concept Index

@printindex cp

@contents
@bye
```

The Results

Here is what the contents of the first chapter of the sample look like:

This is the contents of the first chapter.

Here is a numbered list.

1. This is the first item.
2. This is the second item.

The `makeinfo` and `texinfo-format-buffer` commands transform a Texinfo file such as this into an Info file; and TeX typesets it for a printed manual.

1.9 Acknowledgements

Richard M. Stallman wrote Edition 1.0 of this manual. Robert J. Chassell revised and extended it, starting with Edition 1.1.

Our thanks go out to all who helped improve this work, particularly to Francois Pinard and David D. Zuhn, who tirelessly recorded and reported mistakes and obscurities; our special thanks go to Melissa Weisshaus for her frequent and often tedious reviews of nearly similar editions. Our mistakes are our own.

2 Using Texinfo Mode

You may edit a Texinfo file with any text editor you choose. A Texinfo file is no different from any other ASCII file. However, GNU Emacs comes with a special mode, called Texinfo mode, that provides Emacs commands and tools to help ease your work.

This chapter describes features of GNU Emacs' Texinfo mode but not any features of the Texinfo formatting language. If you are reading this manual straight through from the beginning, you may want to skim through this chapter briefly and come back to it after reading succeeding chapters which describe the Texinfo formatting language in detail.

Texinfo mode provides special features for working with Texinfo files:

- Insert frequently used @-commands.
- Automatically create @node lines.
- Show the structure of a Texinfo source file.
- Automatically create or update the 'Next', 'Previous', and 'Up' pointers of a node.
- Automatically create or update menus.
- Automatically create a master menu.
- Format a part or all of a file for Info.
- Typeset and print part or all of a file.

Perhaps the two most helpful features are those for inserting frequently used @-commands and for creating node pointers and menus.

2.1 The Usual GNU Emacs Editing Commands

In most cases, the usual Text mode commands work the same in Texinfo mode as they do in Text mode. Texinfo mode adds new editing commands and tools to GNU Emacs' general purpose editing features. The major difference concerns filling. In Texinfo mode, the paragraph separation variable and syntax table are redefined so that Texinfo commands that should be on lines of their own are not inadvertently included in paragraphs. Thus, the M-q (`fill-paragraph`) command will refill a paragraph but not mix an indexing command on a line adjacent to it into the paragraph.

In addition, Texinfo mode sets the `page-delimiter` variable to the value of `texinfo-chapter-level-regexp`; by default, this is a regular expression matching the commands for chapters and their equivalents, such as appendices. With this value for the page delimiter, you can jump from chapter title to chapter title with the C-x] (`forward-page`) and C-x [(`backward-page`) commands and narrow to a chapter with the C-x p (`narrow-to-page`) command. (See section "Pages" in *The GNU Emacs Manual*, for details about the page commands.)

You may name a Texinfo file however you wish, but the convention is to end a Texinfo file name with one of the three extensions '.texinfo', '.texi', or '.tex'. A longer extension is preferred, since it is explicit, but a shorter extension may be necessary for operating systems that limit the length of file names. GNU Emacs automatically enters Texinfo mode when you visit a file with a '.texinfo' or '.texi' extension. Also, Emacs switches to Texinfo mode when you visit a file that has '-*-texinfo-*-' in its first line. If ever you are in another mode and wish to switch to Texinfo mode, type `M-x texinfo-mode`.

Like all other Emacs features, you can customize or enhance Texinfo mode as you wish. In particular, the keybindings are very easy to change. The keybindings described here are the default or standard ones.

2.2 Inserting Frequently Used Commands

Texinfo mode provides commands to insert various frequently used @-commands into the buffer. You can use these commands to save keystrokes.

The insert commands are invoked by typing `C-c` twice and then the first letter of the @-command:

`C-c C-c c`
`M-x texinfo-insert-@code`
>Insert @code{} and put the cursor between the braces.

`C-c C-c d`
`M-x texinfo-insert-@dfn`
>Insert @dfn{} and put the cursor between the braces.

`C-c C-c e`
`M-x texinfo-insert-@end`
>Insert @end and attempt to insert the correct following word, such as 'example' or 'table'. (This command does not handle nested lists correctly, but inserts the word appropriate to the immediately preceding list.)

`C-c C-c i`
`M-x texinfo-insert-@item`
>Insert @item and put the cursor at the beginning of the next line.

`C-c C-c k`
`M-x texinfo-insert-@kbd`
>Insert @kbd{} and put the cursor between the braces.

`C-c C-c n`
`M-x texinfo-insert-@node`
>Insert @node and a comment line listing the sequence for the 'Next', 'Previous', and 'Up' nodes. Leave point after the @node.

Chapter 2: Using Texinfo Mode

`C-c C-c o`
`M-x texinfo-insert-@noindent`
> Insert `@noindent` and put the cursor at the beginning of the next line.

`C-c C-c s`
`M-x texinfo-insert-@samp`
> Insert `@samp{}` and put the cursor between the braces.

`C-c C-c t`
`M-x texinfo-insert-@table`
> Insert `@table` followed by a SPC and leave the cursor after the SPC.

`C-c C-c v`
`M-x texinfo-insert-@var`
> Insert `@var{}` and put the cursor between the braces.

`C-c C-c x`
`M-x texinfo-insert-@example`
> Insert `@example` and put the cursor at the beginning of the next line.

`C-c C-c {`
`M-x texinfo-insert-braces`
> Insert `{}` and put the cursor between the braces.

`C-c C-c }`
`C-c C-c ]`
`M-x up-list`
> Move from between a pair of braces forward past the closing brace. Typing `C-c C-c ]` is easier than typing `C-c C-c }`, which is, however, more mnemonic; hence the two keybindings. (Also, you can move out from between braces by typing `C-f`.)

To put a command such as `@code{...}` around an *existing* word, position the cursor in front of the word and type `C-u 1 C-c C-c c`. This makes it easy to edit existing plain text. The value of the prefix argument tells Emacs how many words following point to include between braces—1 for one word, 2 for two words, and so on. Use a negative argument to enclose the previous word or words. If you do not specify a prefix argument, Emacs inserts the `@`-command string and positions the cursor between the braces. This feature works only for those `@`-commands that operate on a word or words within one line, such as `@kbd` and `@var`.

This set of insert commands was created after analyzing the frequency with which different `@`-commands are used in the *GNU Emacs Manual* and the *GDB Manual*. If you wish to add your own insert commands, you can bind a keyboard macro to a key, use abbreviations, or extend the code in `texinfo.el`.

`C-c C-c C-d` (`texinfo-start-menu-description`) is an insert command that works differently from the other insert commands. It inserts a node's section or chapter title in the space for the description in a menu entry line. (A menu entry has three parts, the entry name, the node name, and the description. Only the node name is required, but a description helps explain what the node is about. See Section 7.2 [The Parts of a Menu], page 68.)

To use `texinfo-start-menu-description`, position point in a menu entry line and type `C-c C-c C-d`. The command looks for and copies the title that goes with the node name, and inserts the title as a description; it positions point at beginning of the inserted text so you can edit it. The function does not insert the title if the menu entry line already contains a description.

This command is only an aid to writing descriptions; it does not do the whole job. You must edit the inserted text since a title tends to use the same words as a node name but a useful description uses different words.

2.3 Showing the Section Structure of a File

You can show the section structure of a Texinfo file by using the `C-c C-s` command (`texinfo-show-structure`). This command shows the section structure of a Texinfo file by listing the lines that begin with the @-commands for `@chapter`, `@section`, and the like. It constructs what amounts to a table of contents. These lines are displayed in another buffer called the '`*Occur*`' buffer. In that buffer, you can position the cursor over one of the lines and use the `C-c C-c` command (`occur-mode-goto-occurrence`), to jump to the corresponding spot in the Texinfo file.

`C-c C-s`
`M-x texinfo-show-structure`
        Show the `@chapter`, `@section`, and such lines of a Texinfo file.

`C-c C-c`
`M-x occur-mode-goto-occurrence`
        Go to the line in the Texinfo file corresponding to the line under the cursor in the '`*Occur*`' buffer.

If you call `texinfo-show-structure` with a prefix argument by typing `C-u C-c C-s`, it will list not only those lines with the @-commands for `@chapter`, `@section`, and the like, but also the `@node` lines. (This is how the `texinfo-show-structure` command worked without an argument in the first version of Texinfo. It was changed because `@node` lines clutter up the '`*Occur*`' buffer and are usually not needed.) You can use `texinfo-show-structure` with a prefix argument to check whether the 'Next', 'Previous', and 'Up' pointers of an `@node` line are correct.

Often, when you are working on a manual, you will be interested only in the structure of the current chapter. In this case, you can mark off the region of the buffer that you are interested in by using the `C-x n n` (`narrow-to-region`) command and `texinfo-show-structure` will work on only that region. To see the whole buffer again, use `C-x n w` (`widen`). (See section "Narrowing" in *The GNU Emacs Manual*, for more information about the narrowing commands.)

In addition to providing the `texinfo-show-structure` command, Texinfo mode sets the value of the page delimiter variable to match the chapter-level @-commands. This enables you to use the `C-x ]` (`forward-page`) and `C-x [` (`backward-page`) commands to move forward and backward by chapter, and to use the `C-x p` (`narrow-to-page`) command to narrow to a chapter. See section "Pages" in *The GNU Emacs Manual*, for more information about the page commands.

2.4 Updating Nodes and Menus

Texinfo mode provides commands for automatically creating or updating menus and node pointers. The commands are called "update" commands because their most frequent use is for updating a Texinfo file after you have worked on it; but you can use them to insert the 'Next', 'Previous', and 'Up' pointers into an `@node` line that has none and to create menus in a file that has none.

If you do not use the updating commands, you need to write menus and node pointers by hand, which is a tedious task.

You can use the updating commands

- to insert or update the 'Next', 'Previous', and 'Up' pointers of a node,
- to insert or update the menu for a section, and
- to create a master menu for a Texinfo source file.

You can also use the commands to update all the nodes and menus in a region or in a whole Texinfo file.

The updating commands work only with conventional Texinfo files, which are structured hierarchically like books. In such files, a structuring command line must follow closely after each `@node` line, except for the 'Top' `@node` line. (A *structuring command line* is a line beginning with `@chapter`, `@section`, or other similar command.)

You can write the structuring command line on the line that follows immediately after an `@node` line or else on the line that follows after a single `@comment` line or a single `@ifinfo` line. You cannot interpose more than one line between the `@node` line and the structuring command line; and you may interpose only an `@comment` line or an `@ifinfo` line.

Commands which work on a whole buffer require that the 'Top' node be followed by a node with an `@chapter` or equivalent-level command. Note that the menu updating commands will not create a main or master menu for a Texinfo file that has only `@chapter`-level nodes! The menu updating commands only create menus *within* nodes for lower level nodes. To create a menu of chapters, you must provide a 'Top' node.

The menu updating commands remove menu entries that refer to other Info files since they do not refer to nodes within the current buffer. This is a deficiency. Rather than use menu entries, you can use cross references to refer to other Info files. None of the updating commands affect cross references.

Texinfo mode has five updating commands that are used most often: two are for updating the node pointers or menu of a single node (or a region); two are for updating every node pointer and menu in a file; and one, the `texinfo-master-menu` command, is for creating a master menu for a complete file, and optionally, for updating every node and menu in the whole Texinfo file.

The `texinfo-master-menu` command is the primary command:

`C-c C-u m`
`M-x texinfo-master-menu`
> Create or update a master menu that includes all the other menus (incorporating the descriptions from pre-existing menus, if any).
>
> With an argument (prefix argument, `C-u,` if interactive), first create or update all the nodes and all the regular menus in the buffer before constructing the master menu. (See Section 3.5 [The Top Node and Master Menu], page 43, for more about a master menu.)
>
> For `texinfo-master-menu` to work, the Texinfo file must have a 'Top' node and at least one subsequent node.
>
> After extensively editing a Texinfo file, you can type the following:
>
>> `C-u M-x texinfo-master-menu`
>
> or
>
>> `C-u C-c C-u m`
>
> This updates all the nodes and menus completely and all at once.

The other major updating commands do smaller jobs and are designed for the person who updates nodes and menus as he or she writes a Texinfo file.

The commands are:

`C-c C-u C-n`
`M-x texinfo-update-node`
> Insert the 'Next', 'Previous', and 'Up' pointers for the node that point is within (i.e., for the `@node` line preceding point). If the `@node` line has pre-existing 'Next', 'Previous', or 'Up' pointers in

Chapter 2: Using Texinfo Mode

it, the old pointers are removed and new ones inserted. With an argument (prefix argument, C-u, if interactive), this command updates all @node lines in the region (which is the text between point and mark).

`C-c C-u C-m`
`M-x texinfo-make-menu`

Create or update the menu in the node that point is within. With an argument (C-u as prefix argument, if interactive), the command makes or updates menus for the nodes which are either within or a part of the region.

Whenever `texinfo-make-menu` updates an existing menu, the descriptions from that menu are incorporated into the new menu. This is done by copying descriptions from the existing menu to the entries in the new menu that have the same node names. If the node names are different, the descriptions are not copied to the new menu.

`C-c C-u C-e`
`M-x texinfo-every-node-update`

Insert or update the 'Next', 'Previous', and 'Up' pointers for every node in the buffer.

`C-c C-u C-a`
`M-x texinfo-all-menus-update`

Create or update all the menus in the buffer. With an argument (C-u as prefix argument, if interactive), first insert or update all the node pointers before working on the menus.

If a master menu exists, the `texinfo-all-menus-update` command updates it; but the command does not create a new master menu if none already exists. (Use the `texinfo-master-menu` command for that.)

When working on a document that does not merit a master menu, you can type the following:

   `C-u C-c C-u C-a`

or

   `C-u M-x texinfo-all-menus-update`

This updates all the nodes and menus.

The `texinfo-column-for-description` variable specifies the column to which menu descriptions are indented. By default, the value is 32 although it is often useful to reduce it to as low as 24. You can set the variable with the `M-x edit-options` command (see section "Editing Variable Values" in *The GNU Emacs Manual*) or with the `M-x set-variable` command (see section "Examining and Setting Variables" in *The GNU Emacs Manual*).

Also, the `texinfo-indent-menu-description` command may be used to indent existing menu descriptions to a specified column. Finally, if you wish, you can use the `texinfo-insert-node-lines` command to insert missing `@node` lines into a file. (See Section 2.4.2 [Other Updating Commands], page 23, for more information.)

2.4.1 Updating Requirements

To use the updating commands, you must organize the Texinfo file hierarchically with chapters, sections, subsections, and the like. When you construct the hierarchy of the manual, do not 'jump down' more than one level at a time: you can follow the 'Top' node with a chapter, but not with a section; you can follow a chapter with a section, but not with a subsection. However, you may 'jump up' any number of levels at one time—for example, from a subsection to a chapter.

Each `@node` line, with the exception of the line for the 'Top' node, must be followed by a line with a structuring command such as `@chapter`, `@section`, or `@unnumberedsubsec`.

Each `@node` line/structuring-command line combination must look either like this:

```
@node     Comments, Minimum, Conventions, Overview
@comment  node-name, next,    previous,    up
@section Comments
```

or like this (without the `@comment` line):

```
@node Comments, Minimum, Conventions, Overview
@section Comments
```

In this example, 'Comments' is the name of both the node and the section. The next node is called 'Minimum' and the previous node is called 'Conventions'. The 'Comments' section is within the 'Overview' node, which is specified by the 'Up' pointer. (Instead of an `@comment` line, you can write an `@ifinfo` line.)

If a file has a 'Top' node, it must be called 'top' or 'Top' and be the first node in the file.

The menu updating commands create a menu of sections within a chapter, a menu of subsections within a section, and so on. This means that you must have a 'Top' node if you want a menu of chapters.

Incidentally, the `makeinfo` command will create an Info file for a hierarchically organized Texinfo file that lacks 'Next', 'Previous' and 'Up' pointers. Thus, if you can be sure that your Texinfo file will be formatted with `makeinfo`, you have no need for the 'update node' commands. (See Chapter 20 [Creating an Info File], page 159, for more information about

Chapter 2: Using Texinfo Mode   23

`makeinfo`.) However, both `makeinfo` and the `texinfo-format-`... commands require that you insert menus in the file.

2.4.2 Other Updating Commands

In addition to the five major updating commands, Texinfo mode possesses several less frequently used updating commands:

`M-x texinfo-insert-node-lines`

Insert `@node` lines before the `@chapter`, `@section`, and other sectioning commands wherever they are missing throughout a region in a Texinfo file.

With an argument (`C-u` as prefix argument, if interactive), the `texinfo-insert-node-lines` command not only inserts `@node` lines but also inserts the chapter or section titles as the names of the corresponding nodes. In addition, it inserts the titles as node names in pre-existing `@node` lines that lack names. Since node names should be more concise than section or chapter titles, you must manually edit node names so inserted.

For example, the following marks a whole buffer as a region and inserts `@node` lines and titles throughout:

`C-x h C-u M-x texinfo-insert-node-lines`

(Note that this command inserts titles as node names in `@node` lines; the `texinfo-start-menu-description` command (see Section 2.2 [Inserting], page 16) inserts titles as descriptions in menu entries, a different action. However, in both cases, you need to edit the inserted text.)

`M-x texinfo-multiple-files-update`

Update nodes and menus in a document built from several separate files. With `C-u` as a prefix argument, create and insert a master menu in the outer file. With a numeric prefix argument, such as `C-u 2`, first update all the menus and all the 'Next', 'Previous', and 'Up' pointers of all the included files before creating and inserting a master menu in the outer file. The `texinfo-multiple-files-update` command is described in the appendix on `@include` files. See Section E.2 [texinfo-multiple-files-update], page 201.

`M-x texinfo-indent-menu-description`

Indent every description in the menu following point to the specified column. You can use this command to give yourself more space for descriptions. With an argument (`C-u` as prefix argument, if interactive), the `texinfo-indent-menu-description` command indents every description in every menu in the region.

However, this command does not indent the second and subsequent lines of a multi-line description.

M-x texinfo-sequential-node-update

Insert the names of the nodes immediately following and preceding the current node as the 'Next' or 'Previous' pointers regardless of those nodes' hierarchical level. This means that the 'Next' node of a subsection may well be the next chapter. Sequentially ordered nodes are useful for novels and other documents that you read through sequentially. (However, in Info, the `g* RET` command lets you look through the file sequentially, so sequentially ordered nodes are not strictly necessary.) With an argument (prefix argument, if interactive), the `texinfo-sequential-node-update` command sequentially updates all the nodes in the region.

2.5 Formatting for Info

Texinfo mode provides several commands for formatting part or all of a Texinfo file for Info. Often, when you are writing a document, you want to format only part of a file—that is, a region.

You can use either the `texinfo-format-region` or the `makeinfo-region` command to format a region:

```
C-c C-e C-r
M-x texinfo-format-region
C-c C-m C-r
M-x makeinfo-region
```
        Format the current region for Info.

You can use either the `texinfo-format-buffer` or the `makeinfo-buffer` command to format a whole buffer:

```
C-c C-e C-b
M-x texinfo-format-buffer
C-c C-m C-b
M-x makeinfo-buffer
```
        Format the current buffer for Info.

For example, after writing a Texinfo file, you can type the following:

    `C-u C-c C-u m`

or

    `C-u M-x texinfo-master-menu`

This updates all the nodes and menus. Then type the following to create an Info file:

```
     C-c C-m C-b
```
or
```
     M-x makeinfo-buffer
```

For the Info formatting commands to work, the file *must* include a line that has `@setfilename` in its header.

Not all systems support the `makeinfo`-based formatting commands.

See Chapter 20 [Create an Info File], page 159, for details about Info formatting.

2.6 Formatting and Printing

Typesetting and printing a Texinfo file is a multi-step process in which you first create a file for printing (called a DVI file), and then print the file. Optionally, you may also create indices. To do this, you must run the `texindex` command after first running the `tex` typesetting command; and then you must run the `tex` command again. Or else run the `texi2dvi` command which automatically creates indices as needed.

Often, when you are writing a document, you want to typeset and print only part of a file to see what it will look like. You can use the `texinfo-tex-region` and related commands for this purpose. Use the `texinfo-tex-buffer` command to format all of a buffer.

`C-c C-t C-b`
`M-x texinfo-tex-buffer`
> Run `texi2dvi` on the buffer. In addition to running TeX on the buffer, this command automatically creates or updates indices as needed.

`C-c C-t C-r`
`M-x texinfo-tex-region`
> Run TeX on the region.

`C-c C-t C-i`
`M-x texinfo-texindex`
> Run `texindex` to sort the indices of a Texinfo file formatted with `texinfo-tex-region`. The `texinfo-tex-region` command does not run `texindex` automatically; it only runs the `tex` typesetting command. You must run the `texinfo-tex-region` command a second time after sorting the raw index files with the `texindex` command. (Usually, you do not format an index when you format a region, only when you format a buffer. Now that the `texi2dvi` command exists, there is no little need for this command.)

```
C-c C-t C-p
M-x texinfo-tex-print
```
> Print the file (or the part of the file) previously formatted with `texinfo-tex-buffer` or `texinfo-tex-region`.

For `texinfo-tex-region` or `texinfo-tex-buffer` to work, the file *must* start with a '`\input texinfo`' line and must include an `@settitle` line. The file must end with `@bye` on a line by itself. (When you use `texinfo-tex-region`, you must surround the `@settitle` line with start-of-header and end-of-header lines.)

See Chapter 19 [Format/Print Hardcopy], page 149, for a description of the other TeX related commands, such as `tex-show-print-queue`.

2.7 Texinfo Mode Summary

In Texinfo mode, each set of commands has default keybindings that begin with the same keys. All the commands that are custom-created for Texinfo mode begin with `C-c`. The keys are somewhat mnemonic.

Insert Commands

The insert commands are invoked by typing `C-c` twice and then the first letter of the `@`-command to be inserted. (It might make more sense mnemonically to use `C-c C-i`, for 'custom insert', but `C-c C-c` is quick to type.)

`C-c C-c c`	Insert '`@code`'.
`C-c C-c d`	Insert '`@dfn`'.
`C-c C-c e`	Insert '`@end`'.
`C-c C-c i`	Insert '`@item`'.
`C-c C-c n`	Insert '`@node`'.
`C-c C-c s`	Insert '`@samp`'.
`C-c C-c v`	Insert '`@var`'.
`C-c C-c {`	Insert braces.
`C-c C-c ]`	
`C-c C-c }`	Move out of enclosing braces.
`C-c C-c C-d`	Insert a node's section title in the space for the description in a menu entry line.

Show Structure

The `texinfo-show-structure` command is often used within a narrowed region.

`C-c C-s`	List all the headings.

The Master Update Command

The `texinfo-master-menu` command creates a master menu; and can be used to update every node and menu in a file as well.

`C-c C-u m`
`M-x texinfo-master-menu`
>Create or update a master menu.

`C-u C-c C-u m`   With `C-u` as a prefix argument, first create or update all nodes and regular menus, and then create a master menu.

Update Pointers

The update pointer commands are invoked by typing `C-c C-u` and then either `C-n` for `texinfo-update-node` or `C-e` for `texinfo-every-node-update`.

`C-c C-u C-n`   Update a node.
`C-c C-u C-e`   Update every node in the buffer.

Update Menus

Invoke the update menu commands by typing `C-c C-u` and then either `C-m` for `texinfo-make-menu` or `C-a` for `texinfo-all-menus-update`. To update both nodes and menus at the same time, precede `C-c C-u C-a` with `C-u`.

`C-c C-u C-m`   Make or update a menu.

`C-c C-u C-a`   Make or update all menus in a buffer.

`C-u C-c C-u C-a`   With `C-u` as a prefix argument, first create or update all nodes and then create or update all menus.

Format for Info

The Info formatting commands that are written in Emacs Lisp are invoked by typing `C-c C-e` and then either `C-r` for a region or `C-b` for the whole buffer.

The Info formatting commands that are written in C and based on the `makeinfo` program are invoked by typing `C-c C-m` and then either `C-r` for a region or `C-b` for the whole buffer.

Use the `texinfo-format...` commands:

`C-c C-e C-r`	Format the region.
`C-c C-e C-b`	Format the buffer.

Use `makeinfo`:

`C-c C-m C-r`	Format the region.
`C-c C-m C-b`	Format the buffer.
`C-c C-m C-l`	Recenter the `makeinfo` output buffer.
`C-c C-m C-k`	Kill the `makeinfo` formatting job.

Typeset and Print

The TeX typesetting and printing commands are invoked by typing `C-c C-t` and then another control command: `C-r` for `texinfo-tex-region`, `C-b` for `texinfo-tex-buffer`, and so on.

`C-c C-t C-r`	Run TeX on the region.
`C-c C-t C-b`	Run `texi2dvi` on the buffer.
`C-c C-t C-i`	Run `texindex`.
`C-c C-t C-p`	Print the DVI file.
`C-c C-t C-q`	Show the print queue.
`C-c C-t C-d`	Delete a job from the print queue.
`C-c C-t C-k`	Kill the current TeX formatting job.
`C-c C-t C-x`	Quit a currently stopped TeX formatting job.
`C-c C-t C-l`	Recenter the output buffer.

Other Updating Commands

The 'other updating commands' do not have standard keybindings because they are rarely used.

`M-x texinfo-insert-node-lines`
    Insert missing `@node` lines in region.
    With `C-u` as a prefix argument,
    use section titles as node names.

`M-x texinfo-multiple-files-update`
    Update a multi-file document.
    With `C-u 2` as a prefix argument,
    create or update all nodes and menus
    in all included files first.

`M-x texinfo-indent-menu-description`
    Indent descriptions.

`M-x texinfo-sequential-node-update`
: Insert node pointers in strict sequence.

3 Beginning a Texinfo File

Certain pieces of information must be provided at the beginning of a Texinfo file, such as the name of the file and the title of the document.

Generally, the beginning of a Texinfo file has four parts:

1. The header, delimited by special comment lines, that includes the commands for naming the Texinfo file and telling TeX what definitions' file to use when processing the Texinfo file.
2. A short statement of what the file is about, with a copyright notice and copying permissions. This is enclosed in @ifinfo and @end ifinfo commands so that the formatters place it only in the Info file.
3. A title page and copyright page, with a copyright notice and copying permissions. This is enclosed between @titlepage and @end titlepage commands. The title and copyright page appear only in the printed manual.
4. The 'Top' node that contains a menu for the whole Info file. The contents of this node appear only in the Info file.

Also, optionally, you may include the copying conditions for a program and a warranty disclaimer. The copying section will be followed by an introduction or else by the first chapter of the manual.

Since the copyright notice and copying permissions for the Texinfo document (in contrast to the copying permissions for a program) are in parts that appear only in the Info file or only in the printed manual, this information must be given twice.

3.1 Sample Texinfo File Beginning

The following sample shows what is needed.

```
\input texinfo    @c -*-texinfo-*-
@c %**start of header
@setfilename name-of-info-file
@settitle name-of-manual
@setchapternewpage odd
@c %**end of header

@ifinfo
This file documents ...

Copyright year copyright-owner

Permission is granted to ...
@end ifinfo
```

```
@c  This title page illustrates only one of the
@c  two methods of forming a title page.
```
@titlepage
@title *name-of-manual-when-printed*
@subtitle *subtitle-if-any*
@subtitle *second-subtitle*
@author *author*

```
@c  The following two commands
@c  start the copyright page.
```
@page
@vskip 0pt plus 1filll
Copyright @copyright{} *year copyright-owner*

Published by ...

Permission is granted to ...
@end titlepage

@node Top, Overview, (dir), (dir)

@ifinfo
This document describes ...

This document applies to version ...
of the program named ...
@end ifinfo

@menu
* Copying::   Your rights and freedoms.
* First Chapter::   Getting started ...
* Second Chapter::   ...
   ...
   ...
@end menu

@node   First Chapter, Second Chapter, top,   top
@comment node-name,   next,   previous, up
@chapter First Chapter
@cindex Index entry for First Chapter

Chapter 3: Beginning a Texinfo File   33

3.2 The Texinfo File Header

Texinfo files start with at least three lines that provide Info and TeX with necessary information. These are the \input texinfo line, the @settitle line, and the @setfilename line. If you want to run TeX on just a part of the Texinfo File, you must write the @settitle and @setfilename lines between start-of-header and end-of-header lines.

Thus, the beginning of a Texinfo file looks like this:

```
\input texinfo    @c -*-texinfo-*-
@setfilename sample.info
@settitle Sample Document
```

or else like this:

```
\input texinfo    @c -*-texinfo-*-
@c %**start of header
@setfilename sample.info
@settitle Sample Document
@c %**end of header
```

3.2.1 The First Line of a Texinfo File

Every Texinfo file that is to be the top-level input to TeX must begin with a line that looks like this:

```
\input texinfo    @c -*-texinfo-*-
```

This line serves two functions:

1. When the file is processed by TeX, the \input texinfo command tells TeX to load the macros needed for processing a Texinfo file. These are in a file called 'texinfo.tex', which is usually located in the '/usr/lib/tex/macros' directory. TeX uses the backslash, '\', to mark the beginning of a command, just as Texinfo uses @. The 'texinfo.tex' file causes the switch from '\' to '@'; before the switch occurs, TeX requires '\', which is why it appears at the beginning of the file.

2. When the file is edited in GNU Emacs, the '-*-texinfo-*-' mode specification tells Emacs to use Texinfo mode.

3.2.2 Start of Header

Write a start-of-header line on the second line of a Texinfo file. Follow the start-of-header line with @setfilename and @settitle lines and, optionally, with other command lines, such as @smallbook or @footnotestyle; and then by an end-of-header line (see Section 3.2.7 [End of Header], page 37).

With these lines, you can format part of a Texinfo file for Info or typeset part for printing.

A start-of-header line looks like this:

`@c %**start of header`

The odd string of characters, '`%**`', is to ensure that no other comment is accidentally taken for a start-of-header line.

3.2.3 `@setfilename`

In order to be made into an Info file, a Texinfo file must contain a line that looks like this:

`@setfilename` *info-file-name*

Write the `@setfilename` command at the beginning of a line and follow it on the same line by the Info file name. Do not write anything else on the line; anything on the line after the command is considered part of the file name, including a comment.

The `@setfilename` line specifies the name of the Info file to be generated. This name should be different from the name of the Texinfo file. The convention is to write a name with a '`.info`' extension, to produce an Info file name such as '`texinfo.info`'.

Some operating systems cannot handle long file names. You can run into a problem even when the file name you specify is itself short enough. This occurs because the Info formatters split a long Info file into short indirect subfiles, and name them by appending '-1', '-2', ..., '-10', '-11', and so on, to the original file name. (See Section 20.7 [Tag Files and Split Files], page 164.) The subfile name '`texinfo.info-10`', for example, is too long for some systems; so the Info file name for this document is actually '`texinfo`' rather than '`texinfo.info`'.

The Info formatting commands ignore everything written before the `@setfilename` line, which is why the very first line of the file (the `\input` line) does not need to be commented out. The `@setfilename` line is ignored when you typeset a printed manual.

3.2.4 `@settitle`

In order to be made into a printed manual, a Texinfo file must contain a line that looks like this:

`@settitle` *title*

Write the `@settitle` command at the beginning of a line and follow it on the same line by the title. This tells TeX the title to use in a header or footer. Do not write anything else on the line; anything on the line after the command is considered part of the title, including a comment.

Conventionally, when TeX formats a Texinfo file for double-sided output, the title is printed in the left-hand (even-numbered) page headings and the current chapter title is printed in the right-hand (odd-numbered) page headings. (TeX learns the title of each chapter from each @chapter command.) Page footers are not printed.

Even if you are printing in a single-sided style, TeX looks for an @settitle command line, in case you include the manual title in the heading.

The @settitle command should precede everything that generates actual output in TeX.

Although the title in the @settitle command is usually the same as the title on the title page, it does not affect the title as it appears on the title page. Thus, the two do not need not match exactly; and the title in the @settitle command can be a shortened or expanded version of the title as it appears on the title page. (See Section 3.4.1 [@titlepage], page 38.)

TeX prints page headings only for that text that comes after the @end titlepage command in the Texinfo file, or that comes after an @headings command that turns on headings. (See Section 3.4.6 [The @headings Command], page 42, for more information.)

You may, if you wish, create your own, customized headings and footings. See Appendix F [Page Headings], page 207, for a detailed discussion of this process.

3.2.5 @setchapternewpage

In a book or a manual, text is usually printed on both sides of the paper, chapters start on right-hand pages, and right-hand pages have odd numbers. But in short reports, text often is printed only on one side of the paper. Also in short reports, chapters sometimes do not start on new pages, but are printed on the same page as the end of the preceding chapter, after a small amount of vertical whitespace.

You can use the @setchapternewpage command with various arguments to specify how TeX should start chapters and whether it should typeset pages for printing on one or both sides of the paper (single-sided or double-sided printing).

Write the @setchapternewpage command at the beginning of a line followed by its argument.

For example, you would write the following to cause each chapter to start on a fresh odd-numbered page:

    @setchapternewpage odd

You can specify one of three alternatives with the @setchapternewpage command:

@setchapternewpage off
: Cause TeX to typeset a new chapter on the same page as the last chapter, after skipping some vertical whitespace. Also, cause TeX to format page headers for single-sided printing. (You can override the headers format with the **@headings double** command; see Section 3.4.6 [The **@headings** Command], page 42.)

@setchapternewpage on
: Cause TeX to start new chapters on new pages and to typeset page headers for single-sided printing. This is the form most often used for short reports.

    This alternative is the default.

@setchapternewpage odd
: Cause TeX to start new chapters on new, odd-numbered pages (right-handed pages) and to typeset for double-sided printing. This is the form most often used for books and manuals.

Texinfo does not have an **@setchapternewpage even** command.

(You can countermand or modify an **@setchapternewpage** command with an **@headings** command. See Section 3.4.6 [The **@headings** Command], page 42.)

At the beginning of a manual or book, pages are not numbered—for example, the title and copyright pages of a book are not numbered. By convention, table of contents pages are numbered with roman numerals and not in sequence with the rest of the document.

Since an Info file does not have pages, the **@setchapternewpage** command has no effect on it.

Usually, you do not write an **@setchapternewpage** command for single-sided printing, but accept the default which is to typeset for single-sided printing and to start new chapters on new pages. Usually, you write an **@setchapternewpage odd** command for double-sided printing.

3.2.6 Paragraph Indenting

The Info formatting commands may insert spaces at the beginning of the first line of each paragraph, thereby indenting that paragraph. You can use the **@paragraphindent** command to specify the indentation. Write an **@paragraphindent** command at the beginning of a line followed by either 'asis' or a number. The template is:

  @paragraphindent *indent*

The Info formatting commands indent according to the value of *indent*:

- If the value of *indent* is '**asis**', the Info formatting commands do not change the existing indentation.

Chapter 3: Beginning a Texinfo File

- If the value of *indent* is 0, the Info formatting commands delete existing indentation.

- If the value of *indent* is greater than 0, the Info formatting commands indent the paragraph by that number of spaces.

The default value of *indent* is 'asis'.

Write the `@paragraphindent` command before or shortly after the end-of-header line at the beginning of a Texinfo file. (If you write the command between the start-of-header and end-of-header lines, the region formatting commands indent paragraphs as specified.)

A peculiarity of the `texinfo-format-buffer` and `texinfo-format-region` commands is that they do not indent (nor fill) paragraphs that contain `@w` or `@*` commands. See Appendix H [Refilling Paragraphs], page 223, for a detailed description of what goes on.

3.2.7 End of Header

Follow the header lines with an end-of-header line. An end-of-header line looks like this:

    @c %**end of header

If you include the `@setchapternewpage` command between the start-of-header and end-of-header lines, TeX will typeset a region as that command specifies. Similarly, if you include an `@smallbook` command between the start-of-header and end-of-header lines, TeX will typeset a region in the "small" book format.

See Section 3.2.2 [Start of Header], page 33.

3.3 Summary and Copying Permissions for Info

The title page and the copyright page appear only in the printed copy of the manual; therefore, the same information must be inserted in a section that appears only in the Info file. This section usually contains a brief description of the contents of the Info file, a copyright notice, and copying permissions.

The copyright notice should read:

    Copyright *year copyright-owner*

and be put on a line by itself.

Standard text for the copyright permissions is contained in an appendix to this manual; see Section D.1 ['ifinfo' Copying Permissions], page 198, for the complete text.

The permissions text appears in an Info file *before* the first node. This mean that a reader does *not* see this text when reading the file using Info, except when using the advanced Info command g *.

3.4 The Title and Copyright Pages

A manual's name and author are usually printed on a title page. Sometimes copyright information is printed on the title page as well; more often, copyright information is printed on the back of the title page.

The title and copyright pages appear in the printed manual, but not in the Info file. Because of this, it is possible to use several slightly obscure TeX typesetting commands that cannot be used in an Info file. In addition, this part of the beginning of a Texinfo file contains the text of the copying permissions that will appear in the printed manual.

See Section D.2 [Titlepage Copying Permissions], page 198, for the standard text for the copyright permissions.

3.4.1 @titlepage

Start the material for the title page and following copyright page with `@titlepage` on a line by itself and end it with `@end titlepage` on a line by itself.

The `@end titlepage` command starts a new page and turns on page numbering. (See Appendix F [Page Headings], page 207, for details about how to generate of page headings.) All the material that you want to appear on unnumbered pages should be put between the `@titlepage` and `@end titlepage` commands. By using the `@page` command you can force a page break within the region delineated by the `@titlepage` and `@end titlepage` commands and thereby create more than one unnumbered page. This is how the copyright page is produced. (The `@titlepage` command might perhaps have been better named the `@titleandadditionalpages` command, but that would have been rather long!)

When you write a manual about a computer program, you should write the version of the program to which the manual applies on the title page. If the manual changes more frequently than the program or is independent of it, you should also include an edition number[1] for the manual. This helps readers keep track of which manual is for which version of the program. (The 'Top' node should also contain this information; see Section 5.3 [@top], page 53.)

---

[1] We have found that it is helpful to refer to versions of manuals as 'editions' and versions of programs as 'versions'; otherwise, we find we are liable to confuse each other in conversation by referring to both the documentation and the software with the same words.

Texinfo provides two methods for creating a title page. One method uses the `@titlefont`, `@sp`, and `@center` commands to generate a title page in which the words on the page are centered.

The second method uses the `@title`, `@subtitle`, and `@author` commands to create a title page with black rules under the title and author lines and the subtitle text set flush to the right hand side of the page. With this method, you do not specify any of the actual formatting of the title page. You specify the text you want, and Texinfo does the formatting. You may use either method.

3.4.2 `@titlefont`, `@center`, and `@sp`

You can use the `@titlefont`, `@sp`, and `@center` commands to create a title page for a printed document. (This is the first of the two methods for creating a title page in Texinfo.)

Use the `@titlefont` command to select a large font suitable for the title itself.

For example:

`@titlefont{Texinfo}`

Use the `@center` command at the beginning of a line to center the remaining text on that line. Thus,

`@center @titlefont{Texinfo}`

centers the title, which in this example is "Texinfo" printed in the title font.

Use the `@sp` command to insert vertical space. For example:

`@sp 2`

This inserts two blank lines on the printed page. (See Section 15.3 [`@sp`], page 124, for more information about the `@sp` command.)

A template for this method looks like this:

```
@titlepage
@sp 10
@center @titlefont{name-of-manual-when-printed}
@sp 2
@center subtitle-if-any
@sp 2
@center author
...
@end titlepage
```

The spacing of the example fits an 8 1/2 by 11 inch manual.

3.4.3 @title, @subtitle, and @author

You can use the `@title`, `@subtitle`, and `@author` commands to create a title page in which the vertical and horizontal spacing is done for you automatically. This contrasts with the method described in the previous section, in which the `@sp` command is needed to adjust vertical spacing.

Write the `@title`, `@subtitle`, or `@author` commands at the beginning of a line followed by the title, subtitle, or author.

The `@title` command produces a line in which the title is set flush to the left-hand side of the page in a larger than normal font. The title is underlined with a black rule.

The `@subtitle` command sets subtitles in a normal-sized font flush to the right-hand side of the page.

The `@author` command sets the names of the author or authors in a middle-sized font flush to the left-hand side of the page on a line near the bottom of the title page. The names are underlined with a black rule that is thinner than the rule that underlines the title. (The black rule only occurs if the `@author` command line is followed by an `@page` command line.)

There are two ways to use the `@author` command: you can write the name or names on the remaining part of the line that starts with an `@author` command:

```
@author by Jane Smith and John Doe
```

or you can write the names one above each other by using two (or more) `@author` commands:

```
@author Jane Smith
@author John Doe
```

(Only the bottom name is underlined with a black rule.)

A template for this method looks like this:

```
@titlepage
@title name-of-manual-when-printed
@subtitle subtitle-if-any
@subtitle second-subtitle
@author author
@page
...
@end titlepage
```

3.4.4 Copyright Page and Permissions

By international treaty, the copyright notice for a book should be either on the title page or on the back of the title page. The copyright notice should include the year followed by the name of the organization or person who owns the copyright.

When the copyright notice is on the back of the title page, that page is customarily not numbered. Therefore, in Texinfo, the information on the copyright page should be within `@titlepage` and `@end titlepage` commands.

Use the `@page` command to cause a page break. To push the copyright notice and the other text on the copyright page towards the bottom of the page, you can write a somewhat mysterious line after the `@page` command that reads like this:

```
@vskip 0pt plus 1filll
```

This is a TeX command that is not supported by the Info formatting commands. The `@vskip` command inserts whitespace. The '`0pt plus 1filll`' means to put in zero points of mandatory whitespace, and as much optional whitespace as needed to push the following text to the bottom of the page. Note the use of three '`l`'s in the word '`filll`'; this is the correct usage in TeX.

In a printed manual, the `@copyright{}` command generates a 'c' inside a circle. (In Info, it generates '(C)'.) The copyright notice itself has the following legally defined sequence:

Copyright © *year copyright-owner*

It is customary to put information on how to get a manual after the copyright notice, followed by the copying permissions for the manual.

Note that permissions must be given here as well as in the summary segment within `@ifinfo` and `@end ifinfo` that immediately follows the header since this text appears only in the printed manual and the '`ifinfo`' text appears only in the Info file.

See Appendix D [Sample Permissions], page 197, for the standard text.

3.4.5 Heading Generation

An `@end titlepage` command on a line by itself not only marks the end of the title and copyright pages, but also causes TeX to start generating page headings and page numbers.

To repeat what is said elsewhere, Texinfo has two standard page heading formats, one for documents which are printed on one side of each sheet of paper (single-sided printing), and the other for documents which are printed on both sides of each sheet (double-sided printing). (See Section 3.2.5 [@setchapternewpage], page 35.) You can specify these formats in different ways:

- The conventional way is to write an `@setchapternewpage` command before the title page commands, and then have the `@end titlepage` command start generating page headings in the manner desired. (See Section 3.2.5 [@setchapternewpage], page 35.)

- Alternatively, you can use the @headings command to prevent page headings from being generated or to start them for either single or double-sided printing. (Write an @headings command immediately after the @end titlepage command. See Section 3.4.6 [The @headings Command], page 42, for more information.)
- Or, you may specify your own page heading and footing format. See Appendix F [Page Headings], page 207, for detailed information about page headings and footings.

Most documents are formatted with the standard single-sided or double-sided format, using @setchapternewpage odd for double-sided printing and no @setchapternewpage command for single-sided printing.

3.4.6 The @headings Command

The @headings command is rarely used. It specifies what kind of page headings and footings to print on each page. Usually, this is controlled by the @setchapternewpage command. You need the @headings command only if the @setchapternewpage command does not do what you want, or if you want to turn off pre-defined page headings prior to defining your own. Write an @headings command immediately after the @end titlepage command.

There are four ways to use the @headings command:

@headings off
: Turn off printing of page headings.

@headings single
: Turn on page headings appropriate for single-sided printing.

@headings double
@headings on
: Turn on page headings appropriate for double-sided printing. The two commands, @headings on and @headings double, are synonymous.

For example, suppose you write @setchapternewpage off before the @titlepage command to tell TeX to start a new chapter on the same page as the end of the last chapter. This command also causes TeX to typeset page headers for single-sided printing. To cause TeX to typeset for double sided printing, write @headings double after the @end titlepage command.

You can stop TeX from generating any page headings at all by writing @headings off on a line of its own immediately after the line containing the @end titlepage command, like this:

    @end titlepage

```
@headings off
```

The `@headings off` command overrides the `@end titlepage` command, which would otherwise cause TeX to print page headings.

You can also specify your own style of page heading and footing. See Appendix F [Page Headings], page 207, for more information.

3.5 The 'Top' Node and Master Menu

The 'Top' node is the node from which you enter an Info file.

A 'Top' node should contain a brief description of the Info file and an extensive, master menu for the whole Info file. This helps the reader understand what the Info file is about. Also, you should write the version number of the program to which the Info file applies; or, at least, the edition number.

The contents of the 'Top' node should appear only in the Info file; none of it should appear in printed output, so enclose it between `@ifinfo` and `@end ifinfo` commands. (TeX does not print either an `@node` line or a menu; they appear only in Info; strictly speaking, you are not required to enclose these parts between `@ifinfo` and `@end ifinfo`, but it is simplest to do so. See Chapter 18 [Conditionally Visible Text], page 143.)

Sometimes, you will want to place an `@top` sectioning command line containing the title of the document immediately after the `@node Top` line (see Section 6.2.5 [The `@top` Sectioning Command], page 64, for more information).

For example, the beginning of the Top node of this manual contains an `@top` sectioning command, a short description, and edition and version information. It looks like this:

```
...
@end titlepage

@ifinfo
@node Top, Copying, (dir), (dir)
@top Texinfo

Texinfo is a documentation system...

This is edition...
...
@end ifinfo
```

```
@menu
* Copying::             Texinfo is freely
                            redistributable.
* Overview::            What is Texinfo?
  ...
@end menu
```

In a 'Top' node, the 'Previous', and 'Up' nodes usually refer to the top level directory of the whole Info system, which is called '(dir)'. The 'Next' node refers to the first node that follows the main or master menu, which is usually the copying permissions, introduction, or first chapter.

3.5.1 Parts of a Master Menu

A *master menu* is a detailed main menu listing all the nodes in a file.

A master menu is enclosed in @menu and @end menu commands and does not appear in the printed document.

Generally, a master menu is divided into parts.

- The first part contains the major nodes in the Texinfo file: the nodes for the chapters, chapter-like sections, and the appendices.
- The second part contains nodes for the indices.
- The third and subsequent parts contain a listing of the other, lower level nodes, often ordered by chapter. This way, rather than go through an intermediary menu, an inquirer can go directly to a particular node when searching for specific information. These menu items are not required; add them if you think they are a convenience.

Each section in the menu can be introduced by a descriptive line. So long as the line does not begin with an asterisk, it will not be treated as a menu entry. (See Section 7.1 [Writing a Menu], page 68, for more information.)

For example, the master menu for this manual looks like the following (but has many more entries):

```
@menu
* Copying::             Texinfo is freely
                            redistributable.
* Overview::            What is Texinfo?
* Texinfo Mode::        Special features in GNU Emacs.
  ...
  ...
* Command and Variable Index::
                        An entry for each @-command.
* Concept Index::       An entry for each concept.
```

```
             --- The Detailed Node Listing ---

         Overview of Texinfo

             * Info Files::          What is an Info file?
             * Printed Manuals::     Characteristics of
                                       a printed manual.
             ...
             ...

         Using Texinfo Mode

             * Info on a Region::    Formatting part of a file
                                       for Info.
             ...
             ...
         @end menu
```

3.6 Software Copying Permissions

If the Texinfo file has a section containing the "General Public License" and the distribution information and a warranty disclaimer for the software that is documented, this section usually follows the 'Top' node. The General Public License is very important to Project GNU software. It ensures that you and others will continue to have a right to use and share the software.

The copying and distribution information and the disclaimer are followed by an introduction or else by the first chapter of the manual.

Although an introduction is not a required part of a Texinfo file, it is very helpful. Ideally, it should state clearly and concisely what the file is about and who would be interested in reading it. In general, an introduction would follow the licensing and distribution information, although sometimes people put it earlier in the document. Usually, an introduction is put in an @unnumbered section. (See Section 5.5 [The @unnumbered and @appendix Commands], page 53.)

4 Ending a Texinfo File

The end of a Texinfo file should include the commands that create indices and generate detailed and summary tables of contents. And it must include the `@bye` command that marks the last line processed by TeX.

For example:

```
@node     Concept Index,    , Variables Index, Top
@c        node-name,     next, previous,       up
@unnumbered Concept Index

@printindex cp

@contents
@bye
```

4.1 Index Menus and Printing an Index

To print an index means to include it as part of a manual or Info file. This does not happen automatically just because you use `@cindex` or other index-entry generating commands in the Texinfo file; those just cause the raw data for the index to be accumulated. To generate an index, you must include the `@printindex` command at the place in the document where you want the index to appear. Also, as part of the process of creating a printed manual, you must run a program called `texindex` (see Chapter 19 [Format/Print Hardcopy], page 149) to sort the raw data to produce a sorted index file. The sorted index file is what is actually used to print the index.

Texinfo offers six different types of predefined index: the concept index, the function index, the variables index, the keystroke index, the program index, and the data type index (see Section 12.2 [Predefined Indices], page 107). Each index type has a two-letter name: 'cp', 'fn', 'vr', 'ky', 'pg', and 'tp'. You may merge indices, or put them into separate sections (see Section 12.4 [Combining Indices], page 110); or you may define your own indices (see Section 12.5 [Defining New Indices], page 111).

The `@printindex` command takes a two-letter index name, reads the corresponding sorted index file and formats it appropriately into an index.

The `@printindex` command does not generate a chapter heading for the index. Consequently, you should precede the `@printindex` command with a suitable section or chapter command (usually `@unnumbered`) to supply the chapter heading and put the index into the table of contents. Precede the `@unnumbered` command with an `@node` line.

For example:

```
@node Variable Index, Concept Index, Function Index, Top
@comment     node-name,         next,       previous, up
@unnumbered Variable Index

@printindex vr

@node     Concept Index,     , Variable Index, Top
@comment        node-name, next,    previous, up
@unnumbered Concept Index

@printindex cp
@summarycontents
@contents
@bye
```

(Readers often prefer that the concept index come last in a book, since that makes it easiest to find.)

4.2 Generating a Table of Contents

The @chapter, @section, and other structuring commands supply the information to make up a table of contents, but they do not cause an actual table to appear in the manual. To do this, you must use the @contents and @summarycontents commands:

@contents
: Generate a table of contents in a printed manual, including all chapters, sections, subsections, etc., as well as appendices and unnumbered chapters. (Headings generated by the @heading series of commands do not appear in the table of contents.) The @contents command should be written on a line by itself.

@shortcontents
@summarycontents
: (@summarycontents is a synonym for @shortcontents; the two commands are exactly the same.)

  Generate a short or summary table of contents that lists only the chapters (and appendices and unnumbered chapters). Omit sections, subsections and subsubsections. Only a long manual needs a short table of contents in addition to the full table of contents.

  Write the @shortcontents command on a line by itself right *before* the @contents command.

The table of contents commands automatically generate a chapter-like heading at the top of the first table of contents page. Write the table of contents commands at the very end of a Texinfo file, just before the @bye command, following any index sections—anything in the Texinfo file after the table of contents commands will be omitted from the table of contents.

When you print a manual with a table of contents, the table of contents are printed last and numbered with roman numerals. You need to place those pages in their proper place, after the title page, yourself. (This is the only collating you need to do for a printed manual. The table of contents is printed last because it is generated after the rest of the manual is typeset.)

Here is an example of where to write table of contents commands:

indices...
`@shortcontents`
`@contents`
`@bye`

Since an Info file uses menus instead of tables of contents, the Info formatting commands ignore the `@contents` and `@shortcontents` commands.

4.3 `@bye` File Ending

An `@bye` command terminates TeX or Info formatting. None of the formatting commands see any of the file following `@bye`. The `@bye` command should be on a line by itself.

If you wish, you may follow the `@bye` line with notes. These notes will not be formatted and will not appear in either Info or a printed manual; it is as if text after `@bye` were within `@ignore`...`@end ignore`. Also, you may follow the `@bye` line with a local variables list. See Section 19.6 [Using Local Variables and the Compile Command], page 153, for more information.

5 Chapter Structuring

The *chapter structuring* commands divide a document into a hierarchy of chapters, sections, subsections, and subsubsections. These commands generate large headings; they also provide information for the table of contents of a printed manual (see Section 4.2 [Generating a Table of Contents], page 48).

The chapter structuring commands do not create an Info node structure, so normally you should put an `@node` command immediately before each chapter structuring command (see Chapter 6 [Nodes], page 59). The only time you are likely to use the chapter structuring commands without using the node structuring commands is if you are writing a document that contains no cross references and will never be transformed into Info format.

It is unlikely that you will ever write a Texinfo file that is intended only as an Info file and not as a printable document. If you do, you might still use chapter structuring commands to create a heading at the top of each node—but you don't need to.

5.1 Tree Structure of Sections

A Texinfo file is usually structured like a book with chapters, sections, subsections, and the like. This structure can be visualized as a tree (or rather as an upside-down tree) with the root at the top and the levels corresponding to chapters, sections, subsection, and subsubsections.

Here is a diagram that shows a Texinfo file with three chapters, each of which has two sections.

```
                            Top
                             |
         -------------------------------------------
         |                   |                     |
         |                   |                     |
      Chapter 1           Chapter 2            Chapter 3
         |                   |                     |
     ---------           ---------             ---------
     |       |           |       |             |       |
     |       |           |       |             |       |
   Section Section    Section Section       Section Section
    1.1     1.2        2.1     2.2           3.1     3.2
```

In a Texinfo file that has this structure, the beginning of Chapter 2 looks like this:

```
@node     Chapter 2,  Chapter 3, Chapter 1, top
@chapter Chapter 2
```

The chapter structuring commands are described in the sections that follow; the `@node` and `@menu` commands are described in following chapters. (See Chapter 6 [Nodes], page 59, and see Chapter 7 [Menus], page 67.)

5.2 Types of Structuring Command

The chapter structuring commands fall into four groups or series, each of which contains structuring commands corresponding to the hierarchical levels of chapters, sections, subsections, and subsubsections.

The four groups are the `@chapter` series, the `@unnumbered` series, the `@appendix` series, and the `@heading` series.

Each command produces titles that have a different appearance on the printed page or Info file; only some of the commands produce titles that are listed in the table of contents of a printed book or manual.

- The `@chapter` and `@appendix` series of commands produce numbered or lettered entries both in the body of a printed work and in its table of contents.

- The `@unnumbered` series of commands produce unnumbered entries both in the body of a printed work and in its table of contents. The `@top` command, which has a special use, is a member of this series (see Section 5.3 [`@top`], page 53).

- The `@heading` series of commands produce unnumbered headings that do not appear in a table of contents. The heading commands never start a new page.

- The `@majorheading` command produces results similar to using the `@chapheading` command but generates a larger vertical whitespace before the heading.

- When an `@setchapternewpage` command says to do so, the `@chapter`, `@unnumbered`, and `@appendix` commands start new pages in the printed manual; the `@heading` commands do not.

Here are the four groups of chapter structuring commands:

Numbered	Unnumbered	Lettered and numbered	No new pages Unnumbered
In contents	In contents	In contents	Not in contents
	`@top`		`@majorheading`
`@chapter`	`@unnumbered`	`@appendix`	`@chapheading`
`@section`	`@unnumberedsec`	`@appendixsec`	`@heading`
`@subsection`	`@unnumberedsubsec`	`@appendixsubsec`	`@subheading`
`@subsubsection`	`@unnumberedsubsubsec`	`@appendixsubsubsec`	`@subsubheading`

5.3 @top

The `@top` command is a special sectioning command that you use only after an `@node Top` line at the beginning of a Texinfo file. The `@top` command tells the `makeinfo` formatter which node is the 'Top' node. It has the same typesetting effect as `@unnumbered` (see Section 5.5 [@unnumbered], page 53). For detailed information, see Section 6.2.5 [The @top Command], page 64.

5.4 @chapter

`@chapter` identifies a chapter in the document. Write the command at the beginning of a line and follow it on the same line by the title of the chapter.

For example, this chapter in this manual is entitled "Chapter Structuring"; the `@chapter` line looks like this:

```
@chapter Chapter Structuring
```

In TeX, the `@chapter` command creates a chapter in the document, specifying the chapter title. The chapter is numbered automatically.

In Info, the `@chapter` command causes the title to appear on a line by itself, with a line of asterisks inserted underneath. Thus, in Info, the above example produces the following output:

```
Chapter Structuring
*******************
```

5.5 @unnumbered, @appendix

Use the `@unnumbered` command to create a chapter that appears in a printed manual without chapter numbers of any kind. Use the `@appendix` command to create an appendix in a printed manual that is labelled by letter instead of by number.

For Info file output, the `@unnumbered` and `@appendix` commands are equivalent to `@chapter`: the title is printed on a line by itself with a line of asterisks underneath. (See Section 5.4 [@chapter], page 53.)

To create an appendix or an unnumbered chapter, write an `@appendix` or `@unnumbered` command at the beginning of a line and follow it on the same line by the title, as you would if you were creating a chapter.

5.6 @majorheading, @chapheading

The `@majorheading` and `@chapheading` commands put chapter-like headings in the body of a document.

However, neither command causes TeX to produce a numbered heading or an entry in the table of contents; and neither command causes TeX to start a new page in a printed manual.

In TeX, an `@majorheading` command generates a larger vertical whitespace before the heading than an `@chapheading` command but is otherwise the same.

In Info, the `@majorheading` and `@chapheading` commands are equivalent to `@chapter`: the title is printed on a line by itself with a line of asterisks underneath. (See Section 5.4 [`@chapter`], page 53.)

5.7 @section

In a printed manual, an `@section` command identifies a numbered section within a chapter. The section title appears in the table of contents. In Info, an `@section` command provides a title for a segment of text, underlined with '='.

This section is headed with an `@section` command and looks like this in the Texinfo file:

    @section @code{@@section}

To create a section, write the `@section` command at the beginning of a line and follow it on the same line by the section title.

Thus,

    @section This is a section

produces

    This is a section
    =================

in Info.

5.8 @unnumberedsec, @appendixsec, @heading

The `@unnumberedsec`, `@appendixsec`, and `@heading` commands are, respectively, the unnumbered, appendix-like, and heading-like equivalents of the `@section` command. (See Section 5.7 [`@section`], page 54.)

`@unnumberedsec`
> The `@unnumberedsec` command may be used within an unnumbered chapter or within a regular chapter or appendix to provide an unnumbered section.

`@appendixsec`
`@appendixsection`
> `@appendixsection` is a longer spelling of the `@appendixsec` command; the two are synonymous.

Chapter 5: Chapter Structuring   55

@heading   Conventionally, the @appendixsec or @appendixsection command is used only within appendices.

@heading   You may use the @heading command anywhere you wish for a section-style heading that will not appear in the table of contents.

5.9 The @subsection Command

Subsections are to sections as sections are to chapters. (See Section 5.7 [@section], page 54.) In Info, subsection titles are underlined with '-'. For example,

    @subsection This is a subsection

produces

    This is a subsection

In a printed manual, subsections are listed in the table of contents and are numbered three levels deep.

5.10 The @subsection-like Commands

The @unnumberedsubsec, @appendixsubsec, and @subheading commands are, respectively, the unnumbered, appendix-like, and heading-like equivalents of the @subsection command. (See Section 5.9 [@subsection], page 55.)

In Info, the @subsection-like commands generate a title underlined with hyphens. In a printed manual, an @subheading command produces a heading like that of a subsection except that it is not numbered and does not appear in the table of contents. Similarly, an @unnumberedsubsec command produces an unnumbered heading like that of a subsection and an @appendixsubsec command produces a subsection-like heading labelled with a letter and numbers; both of these commands produce headings that appear in the table of contents.

5.11 The 'subsub' Commands

The fourth and lowest level sectioning commands in Texinfo are the 'subsub' commands. They are:

@subsubsection
           Subsubsections are to subsections as subsections are to sections. (See Section 5.9 [@subsection], page 55.) In a printed manual, subsubsection titles appear in the table of contents and are numbered four levels deep.

`@unnumberedsubsubsec`
> Unnumbered subsubsection titles appear in the table of contents of a printed manual, but lack numbers. Otherwise, unnumbered subsubsections are the same as subsubsections. In Info, unnumbered subsubsections look exactly like ordinary subsubsections.

`@appendixsubsubsec`
> Conventionally, appendix commands are used only for appendices and are lettered and numbered appropriately in a printed manual. They also appear in the table of contents. In Info, appendix subsubsections look exactly like ordinary subsubsections.

`@subsubheading`
> The `@subsubheading` command may be used anywhere that you need a small heading that will not appear in the table of contents. In Info, subsubheadings look exactly like ordinary subsubsection headings.

In Info, 'subsub' titles are underlined with periods. For example,

```
@subsubsection This is a subsubsection
```

produces

```
This is a subsubsection
.......................
```

5.12 `@raisesections` and `@lowersections`

The `@raisesections` and `@lowersections` commands raise and lower the hierarchical level of chapters, sections, subsections and the like. The `@raisesections` command changes sections to chapters, subsections to sections, and so on. The `@lowersections` command changes chapters to sections, sections to subsections, and so on.

An `@lowersections` command is useful if you wish to include text that is written as an outer or standalone Texinfo file in another Texinfo file as an inner, included file. If you write the command at the beginning of the file, all your `@chapter` commands are formatted as if they were `@section` commands, all your `@section` command are formatted as if they were `@subsection` commands, and so on.

`@raisesections` raises a command one level in the chapter structuring hierarchy:

Change	To
@subsection	@section,
@section	@chapter,
@heading	@chapheading,
	etc.

@lowersections lowers a command one level in the chapter structuring hierarchy:

Change	To
@chapter	@section,
@subsection	@subsubsection,
@heading	@subheading,
	etc.

An @raisesections or @lowersections command changes only those structuring commands that follow the command in the Texinfo file. Write an @raisesections or @lowersections command on a line of its own.

An @lowersections command cancels an @raisesections command, and vice versa.

Repeated use of the commands continue to raise or lower the hierarchical level a step at a time.

An attempt to raise above 'chapters' reproduces chapter commands; an attempt to lower below 'subsubsections' reproduces subsubsection commands.

6 Nodes

Nodes are the primary segments of a Texinfo file. They do not themselves impose a hierarchic or any other kind of structure on a file. Nodes contain *node pointers* that name other nodes, and can contain *menus* which are lists of nodes. In Info, the movement commands can carry you to a pointed-to node or to a node listed in a menu. Node pointers and menus provide structure for Info files just as chapters, sections, subsections, and the like, provide structure for printed books.

The node and menu commands and the chapter structuring commands are independent of each other:

- In Info, node and menu commands provide structure. The chapter structuring commands generate headings with different kinds of underlining—asterisks for chapters, hyphens for sections, and so on; they do nothing else.

- In TeX, the chapter structuring commands generate chapter and section numbers and tables of contents. The node and menu commands provide information for cross references; they do nothing else.

You can use node pointers and menus to structure an Info file any way you want; and you can write a Texinfo file so that its Info output has a different structure than its printed output. However, most Texinfo files are written such that the structure for the Info output corresponds to the structure for the printed output. It is not convenient to do otherwise.

Generally, printed output is structured in a tree-like hierarchy in which the chapters are the major limbs from which the sections branch out. Similarly, node pointers and menus are organized to create a matching structure in the Info output.

6.1 Node and Menu Illustration

Here is a copy of the diagram shown earlier that illustrates a Texinfo file with three chapters, each of which contains two sections.

Note that the "root" is at the top of the diagram and the "leaves" are at the bottom. This is how such a diagram is drawn conventionally; it illustrates an upside-down tree. For this reason, the root node is called the 'Top' node, and 'Up' node pointers carry you closer to the root.

```
                                    Top
                                     |
          ---------------------------------------------------
          |                          |                      |
      Chapter 1                  Chapter 2              Chapter 3
          |                          |                      |
      ---------                  ---------              ---------
      |       |                  |       |              |       |
   Section Section            Section Section        Section Section
    1.1     1.2                 2.1     2.2            3.1     3.2
```

Write the beginning of the node for Chapter 2 like this:

```
@node      Chapter 2,   Chapter 3,  Chapter 1,  top
@comment   node-name,   next,       previous,   up
```

This **@node** line says that the name of this node is "Chapter 2", the name of the 'Next' node is "Chapter 3", the name of the 'Previous' node is "Chapter 1", and the name of the 'Up' node is "Top".

Please Note: 'Next' refers to the next node at the same hierarchical level in the manual, not necessarily to the next node within the Texinfo file. In the Texinfo file, the subsequent node may be at a lower level—a section-level node may follow a chapter-level node, and a subsection-level node may follow a section-level node. 'Next' and 'Previous' refer to nodes at the *same* hierarchical level. (The 'Top' node contains the exception to this rule. Since the 'Top' node is the only node at that level, 'Next' refers to the first following node, which is almost always a chapter or chapter-level node.)

To go to Sections 2.1 and 2.2 using Info, you need a menu inside Chapter 2. (See Chapter 7 [Menus], page 67.) You would write the menu just before the beginning of Section 2.1, like this:

```
@menu
* Sect. 2.1::     Description of this section.
* Sect. 2.2::
@end menu
```

Write the node for Sect. 2.1 like this:

```
@node      Sect. 2.1, Sect. 2.2, Chapter 2, Chapter 2
@comment   node-name, next,      previous,  up
```

In Info format, the 'Next' and 'Previous' pointers of a node usually lead to other nodes at the same level—from chapter to chapter or from section to section (sometimes, as shown, the 'Previous' pointer points up); an 'Up' pointer usually leads to a node at the level above (closer to the 'Top' node); and a 'Menu' leads to nodes at a level below (closer to 'leaves'). (A cross

Chapter 6: Nodes 61

reference can point to a node at any level; see Chapter 8 [Cross References], page 71.)

Usually, an @node command and a chapter structuring command are used in sequence, along with indexing commands. (You may follow the @node line with a comment line that reminds you which pointer is which.)

Here is the beginning of the chapter in this manual called "Ending a Texinfo File". This shows an @node line followed by a comment line, an @chapter line, and then by indexing lines.

```
@node     Ending a File, Structuring, Beginning a File, Top
@comment node-name,    next,         previous,          up
@chapter Ending a Texinfo File
@cindex Ending a Texinfo file
@cindex Texinfo file ending
@cindex File ending
```

6.2 The @node Command

A *node* is a segment of text that begins at an @node command and continues until the next @node command. The definition of node is different from that for chapter or section. A chapter may contain sections and a section may contain subsections; but a node cannot contain subnodes; the text of a node continues only until the next @node command in the file. A node usually contains only one chapter structuring command, the one that follows the @node line. On the other hand, in printed output nodes are used only for cross references, so a chapter or section may contain any number of nodes. Indeed, a chapter usually contains several nodes, one for each section, subsection, and subsubsection.

To create a node, write an @node command at the beginning of a line, and follow it with four arguments, separated by commas, on the rest of the same line. These arguments are the name of the node, and the names of the 'Next', 'Previous', and 'Up' pointers, in that order. You may insert spaces before each pointer if you wish; the spaces are ignored. You must write the name of the node, and the names of the 'Next', 'Previous', and 'Up' pointers, all on the same line. Otherwise, the formatters fail. (See Info file '`info`', node '`Top`', for more information about nodes in Info.)

Usually, you write one of the chapter-structuring command lines immediately after an @node line—for example, an @section or @subsection line. (See Section 5.2 [Types of Structuring Command], page 52.)

> **Please note:** The GNU Emacs Texinfo mode updating commands work only with Texinfo files in which @node lines are followed by chapter structuring lines. See Section 2.4.1 [Updating Requirements], page 22.

TeX uses @node lines to identify the names to use for cross references. For this reason, you must write @node lines in a Texinfo file that you intend to format for printing, even if you do not intend to format it for Info. (Cross references, such as the one at the end of this sentence, are made with @xref and its related commands; see Chapter 8 [Cross References], page 71.)

The name of a node identifies the node. The pointers enable you to reach other nodes and consist of the names of those nodes.

Normally, a node's 'Up' pointer contains the name of the node whose menu mentions that node. The node's 'Next' pointer contains the name of the node that follows that node in that menu and its 'Previous' pointer contains the name of the node that precedes it in that menu. When a node's 'Previous' node is the same as its 'Up' node, both node pointers name the same node.

Usually, the first node of a Texinfo file is the 'Top' node, and its 'Up' and 'Previous' pointers point to the 'dir' file, which contains the main menu for all of Info.

The 'Top' node itself contains the main or master menu for the manual. Also, it is helpful to include a brief description of the manual in the 'Top' node. See Section 6.2.4 [First Node], page 64, for information on how to write the first node of a Texinfo file.

6.2.1 How to Write an @node Line

The easiest way to write an @node line is to write @node at the beginning of a line and then the name of the node, like this:

   @node *node-name*

If you are using GNU Emacs, you can use the update node commands provided by Texinfo mode to insert the names of the pointers; or you can leave the pointers out of the Texinfo file and let `makeinfo` insert node pointers into the Info file it creates. (See Chapter 2 [Texinfo Mode], page 15, and Section 6.3 [makeinfo Pointer Creation], page 65.)

Alternatively, you can insert the 'Next', 'Previous', and 'Up' pointers yourself. If you do this, you may find it helpful to use the Texinfo mode keyboard command C-c C-c n. This command inserts '@node' and a comment line listing the names of the pointers in their proper order. The comment line helps you keep track of which arguments are for which pointers. This comment line is especially useful if you are not familiar with Texinfo.

The template for a node line with 'Next', 'Previous', and 'Up' pointers looks like this:

   @node *node-name, next, previous, up*

If you wish, you can ignore @node lines altogether in your first draft and then use the `texinfo-insert-node-lines` command to create @node lines

Chapter 6: Nodes

for you. However, we do not recommend this practice. It is better to name the node itself at the same time that you write a segment so you can easily make cross references. A large number of cross references are an especially important feature of a good Info file.

After you have inserted an `@node` line, you should immediately write an `@`-command for the chapter or section and insert its name. Next (and this is important!), put in several index entries. Usually, you will find at least two and often as many as four or five ways of referring to the node in the index. Use them all. This will make it much easier for people to find the node.

6.2.2 @node Line Tips

Here are three suggestions:

- Try to pick node names that are informative but short.

  In the Info file, the file name, node name, and pointer names are all inserted on one line, which may run into the right edge of the window. (This does not cause a problem with Info, but is ugly.)

- Try to pick node names that differ from each other near the beginnings of their names. This way, it is easy to use automatic name completion in Info.

- By convention, node names are capitalized just as they would be for section or chapter titles—initial and significant words are capitalized; others are not.

6.2.3 @node Line Requirements

Here are several requirements for `@node` lines:

- All the node names for a single Info file must be unique.

  Duplicates confuse the Info movement commands. This means, for example, that if you end every chapter with a summary, you must name each summary node differently. You cannot just call each one "Summary". You may, however, duplicate the titles of chapters, sections, and the like. Thus you can end each chapter in a book with a section called "Summary", so long as the node names for those sections are all different.

- A pointer name must be the name of a node.

  The node to which a pointer points may come before or after the node containing the pointer.

- You cannot use any of the Texinfo `@`-commands in a node name; `@`-commands confuse Info.

Thus, the beginning of the section called `@chapter` looks like this:

```
@node chapter, unnumbered & appendix, makeinfo top, Structuring
@comment node-name, next, previous, up
@section @code{@@chapter}
@findex chapter
```

- You cannot use commas, colons, or apostrophes within a node name; these confuse TeX or the Info formatters.

  For example, the following is a section title:

  `@code{@@unnumberedsec}, @code{@@appendixsec}, @code{@@heading}`

  The corresponding node name is:

  `unnumberedsec appendixsec heading`

- Case is significant.

6.2.4 The First Node

The first node of a Texinfo file is the 'Top' node, except in an included file (see Appendix E [Include Files], page 201).

The 'Top' node (which must be named 'top' or 'Top') should have as its 'Up' and 'Previous' nodes the name of a node in another file, where there is a menu that leads to this file. Specify the file name in parentheses. If the file is to be installed directly in the Info directory file, use '(dir)' as the parent of the 'Top' node; this is short for '(dir)top', and specifies the 'Top' node in the 'dir' file, which contains the main menu for Info. For example, the `@node Top` line of this manual looks like this:

`@node Top, Overview, (dir), (dir)`

(You may use the Texinfo updating commands or the `makeinfo` utility to insert these 'Next' and '(dir)' pointers automatically.)

See Chapter 21 [Install an Info File], page 167, for more information about installing an Info file in the 'info' directory.

The 'Top' node contains the main or master menu for the document.

6.2.5 The `@top` Sectioning Command

A special sectioning command, `@top`, has been created for use with the `@node Top` line. The `@top` sectioning command tells `makeinfo` that it marks the 'Top' node in the file. It provides the information that `makeinfo` needs to insert node pointers automatically. Write the `@top` command at the beginning of the line immediately following the `@node Top` line. Write the title on the remaining part of the same line as the `@top` command.

In Info, the `@top` sectioning command causes the title to appear on a line by itself, with a line of asterisks inserted underneath.

In TeX and `texinfo-format-buffer`, the `@top` sectioning command is merely a synonym for `@unnumbered`. Neither of these formatters require an `@top` command, and do nothing special with it. You can use `@chapter` or `@unnumbered` after the `@node Top` line when you use these formatters. Also, you can use `@chapter` or `@unnumbered` when you use the Texinfo updating commands to create or update pointers and menus.

6.2.6 The 'Top' Node Summary

You can help readers by writing a summary in the 'Top' node, after the `@top` line, before the main or master menu. The summary should briefly describe the document. In Info, this summary will appear just before the master menu. In a printed manual, this summary will appear on a page of its own.

If you do not want the summary to appear on a page of its own in a printed manual, you can enclose the whole of the 'Top' node, including the `@node Top` line and the `@top` sectioning command line or other sectioning command line between `@ifinfo` and `@end ifinfo`. This prevents any of the text from appearing in the printed output. (see Chapter 18 [Conditionally Visible Text], page 143). You can repeat the brief description from the 'Top' node within `@iftex ... @end iftex` at the beginning of the first chapter, for those who read the printed manual. This saves paper and may look neater.

You should write the version number of the program to which the manual applies in the summary. This helps the reader keep track of which manual is for which version of the program. If the manual changes more frequently than the program or is independent of it, you should also include an edition number for the manual. (The title page should also contain this information: see Section 3.4.1 [`@titlepage`], page 38.)

6.3 Creating Pointers with `makeinfo`

The `makeinfo` program has a feature for automatically creating node pointers for a hierarchically organized file that lacks them.

When you take advantage of this feature, you do not need to write the 'Next', 'Previous', and 'Up' pointers after the name of a node. However, you must write a sectioning command, such as `@chapter` or `@section`, on the line immediately following each truncated `@node` line. You cannot write a comment line after a node line; the section line must follow it immediately.

In addition, you must follow the 'Top' `@node` line with a line beginning with `@top` to mark the 'Top' node in the file. See Section 5.3 [`@top`], page 53.

Finally, you must write the name of each node (except for the 'Top' node) in a menu that is one or more hierarchical levels above the node's hierarchical level.

This node pointer insertion feature in `makeinfo` is an alternative to the menu and pointer creation and update commands in Texinfo mode. (See Section 2.4 [Updating Nodes and Menus], page 19.) It is especially helpful to people who do not use GNU Emacs for writing Texinfo documents.

7 Menus

Menus contain pointers to subordinate nodes.[1] In Info, you use menus to go to such nodes. Menus have no effect in printed manuals and do not appear in them.

By convention, a menu is put at the end of a node since a reader who uses the menu may not see text that follows it.

A node that has a menu should not contain much text. If you have a lot of text and a menu, move most of the text into a new subnode—all but a few lines. Otherwise, a reader with a terminal that displays only a few lines may miss the menu and its associated text. As a practical matter, you should locate a menu within 20 lines of the beginning of the node.

The short text before a menu may look awkward in a printed manual. To avoid this, you can write a menu near the beginning of its node and follow the menu by an `@node` line, and then an `@heading` line located within `@ifinfo` and `@end ifinfo`. This way, the menu, `@node` line, and title appear only in the Info file, not the printed document.

For example, the preceding two paragraphs follow an Info-only menu, `@node` line, and heading, and look like this:

```
@menu
* Menu Location::              Put a menu in a short node.
* Writing a Menu::             What is a menu?
* Menu Parts::                 A menu entry has three parts.
* Less Cluttered Menu Entry::  Two part menu entry.
* Menu Example::               Two and three part entries.
* Other Info Files::           How to refer to a different
                               Info file.
@end menu

@node Menu Location, Writing a Menu,  , Menus
@ifinfo
@heading Menus Need Short Nodes
@end ifinfo
```

The Texinfo file for this document contains more than a dozen examples of this procedure. One is at the beginning of this chapter; another is at the beginning of the "Cross References" chapter.

---

[1] Menus can carry you to any node, regardless of the hierarchical structure; even to nodes in a different Info file. However, the GNU Emacs Texinfo mode updating commands work only to create menus of subordinate nodes. Conventionally, cross references are used to refer to other nodes.

7.1 Writing a Menu

A menu consists of an `@menu` command on a line by itself followed by menu entry lines or menu comment lines and then by an `@end menu` command on a line by itself.

A menu looks like this:

```
@menu
Larger Units of Text

* Files::                       All about handling files.
* Multiples: Buffers.           Multiple buffers; editing
                                  several files at once.
@end menu
```

In a menu, every line that begins with an '`*` ' is a *menu entry*. (Note the space after the asterisk.) A line that does not start with an '`*` ' may also appear in a menu. Such a line is not a menu entry but is a menu comment line that appears in the Info file. In the example above, the line '`Larger Units of Text`' is a menu comment line; the two lines starting with '`*` ' are menu entries.

7.2 The Parts of a Menu

A menu entry has three parts, only the second of which is required:

1. The menu entry name.
2. The name of the node (required).
3. A description of the item.

The template for a menu entry looks like this:

```
* menu-entry-name: node-name.    description
```

Follow the menu entry name with a single colon and follow the node name with tab, comma, period, or newline.

In Info, a user selects a node with the `m` (`Info-menu`) command. The menu entry name is what the user types after the `m` command.

The third part of a menu entry is a descriptive phrase or sentence. Menu entry names and node names are often short; the description explains to the reader what the node is about. The description, which is optional, can spread over two or more lines. A useful description complements the node name rather than repeats it.

Chapter 7: Menus

7.3 Less Cluttered Menu Entry

When the menu entry name and node name are the same, you can write the name immediately after the asterisk and space at the beginning of the line and follow the name with two colons.

For example, write

    `* Name::`   *description*

instead of

    `* Name: Name.`   *description*

You should use the node name for the menu entry name whenever possible, since it reduces visual clutter in the menu.

7.4 A Menu Example

A menu looks like this in Texinfo:

```
@menu
* menu entry name: Node name.    A short description.
* Node name::                    This form is preferred.
@end menu
```

This produces:

```
* menu:

* menu entry name: Node name.    A short description.
* Node name::                    This form is preferred.
```

Here is an example as you might see it in a Texinfo file:

```
@menu
Larger Units of Text

* Files::                        All about handling files.
* Multiples: Buffers.            Multiple buffers; editing
                                    several files at once.

@end menu
```

This produces:

```
* menu:
Larger Units of Text

* Files::                        All about handling files.
* Multiples: Buffers.            Multiple buffers; editing
                                    several files at once.
```

In this example, the menu has two entries. 'Files' is both a menu entry name and the name of the node referred to by that name. 'Multiples' is the menu entry name; it refers to the node named 'Buffers'. The line 'Larger Units of Text' is a comment; it appears in the menu, but is not an entry.

Since no file name is specified with either 'Files' or 'Buffers', they must be the names of nodes in the same Info file (see Section 7.5 [Referring to Other Info Files], page 70).

7.5 Referring to Other Info Files

You can create a menu entry that enables a reader in Info to go to a node in another Info file by writing the file name in parentheses just before the node name. In this case, you should use the three-part menu entry format, which saves the reader from having to type the file name.

The format looks like this:

```
@menu
* first-entry-name: (filename)nodename.       description
* second-entry-name: (filename)second-node.   description
@end menu
```

For example, to refer directly to the 'Outlining' and 'Rebinding' nodes in the *Emacs Manual*, you would write a menu like this:

```
@menu
* Outlining: (emacs)Outline Mode.  The major mode for
                                   editing outlines.
* Rebinding: (emacs)Rebinding.     How to redefine the
                                   meaning of a key.
@end menu
```

If you do not list the node name, but only name the file, then Info presumes that you are referring to the 'Top' node.

The 'dir' file that contains the main menu for Info has menu entries that list only file names. These take you directly to the 'Top' nodes of each Info document. (See Chapter 21 [Install an Info File], page 167.)

For example:

```
* Info: (info).      Documentation browsing system.
* Emacs: (emacs).    The extensible, self-documenting
                     text editor.
```

(The 'dir' top level directory for the Info system is an Info file, not a Texinfo file, but a menu entry looks the same in both types of file.)

Note that the GNU Emacs Texinfo mode menu updating commands only work with nodes within the current buffer, so you cannot use them to create menus that refer to other files. You must write such menus by hand.

8 Cross References

Cross references are used to refer the reader to other parts of the same or different Texinfo files. In Texinfo, nodes are the places to which cross references can refer.

Often, but not always, a printed document should be designed so that it can be read sequentially. People tire of flipping back and forth to find information that should be presented to them as they need it.

However, in any document, some information will be too detailed for the current context, or incidental to it; use cross references to provide access to such information. Also, an on-line help system or a reference manual is not like a novel; few read such documents in sequence from beginning to end. Instead, people look up what they need. For this reason, such creations should contain many cross references to help readers find other information that they may not have read.

In a printed manual, a cross reference results in a page reference, unless it is to another manual altogether, in which case the cross reference names that manual.

In Info, a cross reference results in an entry that you can follow using the Info 'f' command. (See Info file 'info', node 'Help-Adv'.)

The various cross reference commands use nodes to define cross reference locations. This is evident in Info, in which a cross reference takes you to the specified node. TeX also uses nodes to define cross reference locations, but the action is less obvious. When TeX generates a DVI file, it records nodes' page numbers and uses the page numbers in making references. Thus, if you are writing a manual that will only be printed, and will not be used on-line, you must nonetheless write @node lines to name the places to which you make cross references.

8.1 Different Cross Reference Commands

There are four different cross reference commands:

@xref   Used to start a sentence in the printed manual saying 'See ...' or an Info cross-reference saying '*Note *name*: *node*.'.

@ref   Used within or, more often, at the end of a sentence; same as @xref for Info; produces just the reference in the printed manual without a preceding 'See'.

@pxref   Used within parentheses to make a reference that suits both an Info file and a printed book. Starts with a lower case 'see' within the printed manual. ('p' is for 'parenthesis'.)

@inforef Used to make a reference to an Info file for which there is no printed manual.

(The `@cite` command is used to make references to books and manuals for which there is no corresponding Info file and, therefore, no node to which to point. See Section 9.1.8 [`@cite`], page 87.)

8.2 Parts of a Cross Reference

A cross reference command requires only one argument, which is the name of the node to which it refers. But a cross reference command may contain up to four additional arguments. By using these arguments, you can provide a cross reference name for Info, a topic description or section title for the printed output, the name of a different Info file, and the name of a different printed manual.

Here is a simple cross reference example:

`@xref{Node name}.`

which produces

`*Note Node name::.`

and

See Section *nnn* [Node name], page *ppp*.

Here is an example of a full five-part cross reference:

`@xref{Node name, Cross Reference Name, Particular Topic, info-file-name, A Printed Manual}, for details.`

which produces

`*Note Cross Reference Name: (info-file-name)Node name, for details.`

in Info and

See section "Particular Topic" in *A Printed Manual*, for details.

in a printed book.

The five possible arguments for a cross reference are:

1. The node name (required). This is the node to which the cross reference takes you. In a printed document, the location of the node provides the page reference only for references within the same document.

2. The cross reference name for the Info reference, if it is to be different from the node name. If you include this argument, it argument becomes the first part of the cross reference. It is usually omitted.

3. A topic description or section name. Often, this is the title of the section. This is used as the name of the reference in the printed manual. If omitted, the node name is used.

4. The name of the Info file in which the reference is located, if it is different from the current file.

Chapter 8: Cross References   73

5. The name of a printed manual from a different Texinfo file.

The template for a full five argument cross reference looks like this:

@xref{node-name, cross-reference-name, title-or-topic,
info-file-name, printed-manual-title}.

Cross references with one, two, three, four, and five arguments are described separately following the description of @xref.

Write a node name in a cross reference in exactly the same way as in the @node line, including the same capitalization; otherwise, the formatters may not find the reference.

You can write cross reference commands within a paragraph, but note how Info and TeX format the output of each of the various commands: write @xref at the beginning of a sentence; write @pxref only within parentheses, and so on.

8.3 @xref

The @xref command generates a cross reference for the beginning of a sentence. The Info formatting commands convert it into an Info cross reference, which the Info 'f' command can use to bring you directly to another node. The TeX typesetting commands convert it into a page reference, or a reference to another book or manual.

Most often, an Info cross reference looks like this:

*Note node-name::.

or like this

*Note cross-reference-name: node-name.

In TeX, a cross reference looks like this:

See Section section-number [node-name], page page.

or like this

See Section section-number [title-or-topic], page page.

The @xref command does not generate a period or comma to end the cross reference in either the Info file or the printed output. You must write that period or comma yourself; otherwise, Info will not recognize the end of the reference. (The @pxref command works differently. See Section 8.6 [@pxref], page 79.)

> **Please note:** A period or comma **must** follow the closing brace of an @xref. It is required to terminate the cross reference. This period or comma will appear in the output, both in the Info file and in the printed manual.

@xref must refer to an Info node by name. Use @node to define the node (see Section 6.2.1 [Writing a Node], page 62).

`@xref` is followed by several arguments inside braces, separated by commas. Whitespace before and after these commas is ignored.

A cross reference requires only the name of a node; but it may contain up to four additional arguments. Each of these variations produces a cross reference that looks somewhat different.

Please note: Commas separate arguments in a cross reference; avoid including them in the title or other part lest the formatters mistake them for separators.

8.3.1 @xref with One Argument

The simplest form of `@xref` takes one argument, the name of another node in the same Info file. The Info formatters produce output that the Info readers can use to jump to the reference; TeX produces output that specifies the page and section number for you.

For example,

    @xref{Tropical Storms}.

produces

    *Note Tropical Storms::.

and

    See Section 3.1 [Tropical Storms], page 24.

(Note that in the preceding example the closing brace is followed by a period.)

You can write a clause after the cross reference, like this:

    @xref{Tropical Storms}, for more info.

which produces

    *Note Tropical Storms::, for more info.

    See Section 3.1 [Tropical Storms], page 24, for more info.

(Note that in the preceding example the closing brace is followed by a comma, and then by the clause, which is followed by a period.)

8.3.2 @xref with Two Arguments

With two arguments, the second is used as the name of the Info cross reference, while the first is still the name of the node to which the cross reference points.

The template is like this:

    @xref{*node-name*, *cross-reference-name*}.

For example,

    @xref{Electrical Effects, Lightning}.

produces:

    *Note Lightning: Electrical Effects.

and

    See Section 5.2 [Electrical Effects], page 57.

(Note that in the preceding example the closing brace is followed by a period; and that the node name is printed, not the cross reference name.)

You can write a clause after the cross reference, like this:

    @xref{Electrical Effects, Lightning}, for more info.

which produces

    *Note Lightning: Electrical Effects, for more info.

and

    See Section 5.2 [Electrical Effects], page 57, for more info.

(Note that in the preceding example the closing brace is followed by a comma, and then by the clause, which is followed by a period.)

8.3.3 @xref with Three Arguments

A third argument replaces the node name in the TeX output. The third argument should be the name of the section in the printed output, or else state the topic discussed by that section. Often, you will want to use initial upper case letters so it will be easier to read when the reference is printed. Use a third argument when the node name is unsuitable because of syntax or meaning.

Remember to avoid placing a comma within the title or topic section of a cross reference, or within any other section. The formatters divide cross references into arguments according to the commas; a comma within a title or other section will divide it into two arguments. In a reference, you need to write a title such as "Clouds, Mist, and Fog" without the commas.

Also, remember to write a comma or period after the closing brace of a @xref to terminate the cross reference. In the following examples, a clause follows a terminating comma.

The template is like this:

    @xref{*node-name*, *cross-reference-name*, *title-or-topic*}.

For example,

    @xref{Electrical Effects, Lightning, Thunder and Lightning},
    for details.

produces

>   *Note Lightning: Electrical Effects, for details.

and

>   See Section 5.2 [Thunder and Lightning], page 57, for details.

If a third argument is given and the second one is empty, then the third argument serves both. (Note how two commas, side by side, mark the empty second argument.)

```
@xref{Electrical Effects, , Thunder and Lightning},
for details.
```

produces

>   *Note Thunder and Lightning: Electrical Effects, for details.

and

>   See Section 5.2 [Thunder and Lightning], page 57, for details.

As a practical matter, it is often best to write cross references with just the first argument if the node name and the section title are the same, and with the first and third arguments if the node name and title are different.

Here are several examples from *The GAWK Manual*:

```
@xref{Sample Program}.
@xref{Glossary}.
@xref{Case-sensitivity, ,Case-sensitivity in Matching}.
@xref{Close Output, , Closing Output Files and Pipes},
    for more information.
@xref{Regexp, , Regular Expressions as Patterns}.
```

8.3.4 @xref with Four and Five Arguments

In a cross reference, a fourth argument specifies the name of another Info file, different from the file in which the reference appears, and a fifth argument specifies its title as a printed manual.

Remember that a comma or period must follow the closing brace of an @xref command to terminate the cross reference. In the following examples, a clause follows a terminating comma.

The template is:

>   @xref{*node-name*, *cross-reference-name*, *title-or-topic*,
>   *info-file-name*, *printed-manual-title*}.

For example,

```
@xref{Electrical Effects, Lightning, Thunder and Lightning,
weather, An Introduction to Meteorology}, for details.
```

produces

>   *Note Lightning: (weather)Electrical Effects, for details.

The name of the Info file is enclosed in parentheses and precedes the name of the node.

In a printed manual, the reference looks like this:

> See section "Thunder and Lightning" in *An Introduction to Meteorology*, for details.

The title of the printed manual is typeset in italics; and the reference lacks a page number since TEX cannot know to which page a reference refers when that reference is to another manual.

Often, you will leave out the second argument when you use the long version of `@xref`. In this case, the third argument, the topic description, will be used as the cross reference name in Info.

The template looks like this:

> `@xref{`*node-name*`, ,` *title-or-topic*`,` *info-file-name*`,`
> *printed-manual-title*`}, for details.`

which produces

> `*Note` *title-or-topic*`:` (*info-file-name*)*node-name*`, for details.`

and

> See section *title-or-topic* in *printed-manual-title*, for details.

For example,

> `@xref{Electrical Effects, , Thunder and Lightning,`
> `weather, An Introduction to Meteorology}, for details.`

produces

> `*Note Thunder and Lightning: (weather)Electrical Effects,`
> `for details.`

and

> See section "Thunder and Lightning" in *An Introduction to Meteorology*, for details.

On rare occasions, you may want to refer to another Info file that is within a single printed manual—when multiple Texinfo files are incorporated into the same TEX run but make separate Info files. In this case, you need to specify only the fourth argument, and not the fifth.

8.4 Naming a 'Top' Node

In a cross reference, you must always name a node. This means that in order to refer to a whole manual, you must identify the 'Top' node by writing it as the first argument to the `@xref` command. (This is different from the way you write a menu entry; see Section 7.5 [Referring to Other Info Files], page 70.) At the same time, to provide a meaningful section topic or title in the printed cross reference (instead of the word 'Top'), you must write an appropriate entry for the third argument to the **@xref** command.

Thus, to make a cross reference to *The GNU Make Manual*, write:

    `@xref{Top, , Overview, make, The GNU Make Manual}`.

which produces

    `*Note Overview: (make)Top.`

and

    See section "Overview" in *The GNU Make Manual*.

In this example, 'Top' is the name of the first node, and '`Overview`' is the name of the first section of the manual.

8.5 @ref

@ref is nearly the same as **@xref** except that it does not generate a 'See' in the printed output, just the reference itself. This makes it useful as the last part of a sentence.

For example,

    `For more information, see @ref{Hurricanes}`.

produces

    `For more information, see *Note Hurricanes.`

and

    For more information, see Section 8.2 [Hurricanes], page 123.

The **@ref** command sometimes leads writers to express themselves in a manner that is suitable for a printed manual but looks awkward in the Info format. Bear in mind that your audience will be using both the printed and the Info format.

For example,

    `Sea surges are described in @ref{Hurricanes}`.

produces

    Sea surges are described in Section 6.7 [Hurricanes], page 72.

in a printed document, and the following in Info:

    `Sea surges are described in *Note Hurricanes::.`

Caution: You *must* write a period or comma immediately after an **@ref** command with two or more arguments. Otherwise, Info will not find the end of the cross reference entry and its attempt to follow the cross reference will fail. As a general rule, you should write a period or comma after every **@ref** command. This looks best in both the printed and the Info output.

Chapter 8: Cross References   79

8.6 @pxref

The parenthetical reference command, `@pxref`, is nearly the same as `@xref`, but you use it *only* inside parentheses and you do *not* type a comma or period after the command's closing brace. The command differs from `@xref` in two ways:

1. TeX typesets the reference for the printed manual with a lower case 'see' rather than an upper case 'See'.
2. The Info formatting commands automatically end the reference with a closing colon or period.

Because one type of formatting automatically inserts closing punctuation and the other does not, you should use `@pxref` *only* inside parentheses as part of another sentence. Also, you yourself should not insert punctuation after the reference, as you do with `@xref`.

`@pxref` is designed so that the output looks right and works right between parentheses both in printed output and in an Info file. In a printed manual, a closing comma or period should not follow a cross reference within parentheses; such punctuation is wrong. But in an Info file, suitable closing punctuation must follow the cross reference so Info can recognize its end. `@pxref` spares you the need to use complicated methods to put a terminator into one form of the output and not the other.

With one argument, a parenthetical cross reference looks like this:

 `... storms cause flooding (@pxref{Hurricanes}) ...`

which produces

 `... storms cause flooding (*Note Hurricanes::) ...`

and

 ... storms cause flooding (see Section 6.7 [Hurricanes], page 72) ...

With two arguments, a parenthetical cross reference has this template:

 `... (@pxref{`*node-name, cross-reference-name*`}) ...`

which produces

 `... (*Note` *cross-reference-name*: *node-name*.`) ...`

and

 ... (see Section *nnn* [*node-name*], page *ppp*) ...

`@pxref` can be used with up to five arguments just like `@xref` (see Section 8.3 [@xref], page 73).

> **Please note:** Use `@pxref` only as a parenthetical reference. Do not try to use `@pxref` as a clause in a sentence. It will look bad in either the Info file, the printed output, or both.

Also, parenthetical cross references look best at the ends of sentences. Although you may write them in the middle of a sentence, that location breaks up the flow of text.

8.7 @inforef

@inforef is used for cross references to Info files for which there are no printed manuals. Even in a printed manual, **@inforef** generates a reference directing the user to look in an Info file.

The command takes either two or three arguments, in the following order:
1. The node name.
2. The cross reference name (optional).
3. The Info file name.

Separate the arguments with commas, as with **@xref**. Also, you must terminate the reference with a comma or period after the '}', as you do with **@xref**.

The template is:

    @inforef{*node-name*, *cross-reference-name*, *info-file-name***}**,

Thus,

    `@inforef{Expert, Advanced Info commands, info},`
    `for more information.`

produces

    `*Note Advanced Info commands: (info)Expert,`
    `for more information.`

and

    See Info file 'info', node 'Expert', for more information.

Similarly,

    `@inforef{Expert, , info}, for more information.`

produces

    `*Note (info)Expert::, for more information.`

and

    See Info file 'info', node 'Expert', for more information.

The converse of **@inforef** is **@cite**, which is used to refer to printed works for which no Info form exists. See Section 9.1.8 [@cite], page 87.

9 Marking Words and Phrases

In Texinfo, you can mark words and phrases in a variety of ways. The Texinfo formatters use this information to determine how to highlight the text. You can specify, for example, whether a word or phrase is a defining occurrence, a metasyntactic variable, or a symbol used in a program. Also, you can emphasize text.

9.1 Indicating Definitions, Commands, etc.

Texinfo has commands for indicating just what kind of object a piece of text refers to. For example, metasyntactic variables are marked by `@var`, and code by `@code`. Since the pieces of text are labelled by commands that tell what kind of object they are, it is easy to change the way the Texinfo formatters prepare such text. (Texinfo is an *intentional* formatting language rather than a *typesetting* formatting language.)

For example, in a printed manual, code is usually illustrated in a typewriter font; `@code` tells TeX to typeset this text in this font. But it would be easy to change the way TeX highlights code to use another font, and this change would not effect how keystroke examples are highlighted. If straight typesetting commands were used in the body of the file and you wanted to make a change, you would need to check every single occurrence to make sure that you were changing code and not something else that should not be changed.

The highlighting commands can be used to generate useful information from the file, such as lists of functions or file names. It is possible, for example, to write a program in Emacs Lisp (or a keyboard macro) to insert an index entry after every paragraph that contains words or phrases marked by a specified command. You could do this to construct an index of functions if you had not already made the entries.

The commands serve a variety of purposes:

`@code{`*sample-code*`}`
: Indicate text that is a literal example of a piece of a program.

`@kbd{`*keyboard-characters*`}`
: Indicate keyboard input.

`@key{`*key-name*`}`
: Indicate the conventional name for a key on a keyboard.

`@samp{`*text*`}`
: Indicate text that is a literal example of a sequence of characters.

`@var{`*metasyntactic-variable*`}`
: Indicate a metasyntactic variable.

`@file{`*file-name*`}`
: Indicate the name of a file.

`@dfn{`*term*`}`
: Indicate the introductory or defining use of a term.

`@cite{`*reference*`}`
: Indicate the name of a book.

9.1.1 `@code{`*sample-code*`}`

Use the `@code` command to indicate text that is a piece of a program and which consists of entire syntactic tokens. Enclose the text in braces.

Thus, you should use `@code` for an expression in a program, for the name of a variable or function used in a program, or for a keyword. Also, you should use `@code` for the name of a program, such as `diff`, that is a name used in the machine. (You should write the name of a program in the ordinary text font if you regard it as a new English word, such as 'Emacs' or 'Bison'.)

Use `@code` for environment variables such as `TEXINPUTS`, and other variables.

Use `@code` for command names in command languages that resemble programming languages, such as Texinfo or the shell. For example, `@code` and `@samp` are produced by writing '`@code{@@code}`' and '`@code{@@samp}`' in the Texinfo source, respectively.

Note, however, that you should not use `@code` for shell options such as '-c' when such options stand alone. (Use `@samp`.) Also, an entire shell command often looks better if written using `@samp` rather than `@code`. In this case, the rule is to choose the more pleasing format.

It is incorrect to alter the case of a word inside an `@code` command when it appears at the beginning of a sentence. Most computer languages are case sensitive. In C, for example, `Printf` is different from the identifier `printf`, and most likely is a misspelling of it. Even in languages which are not case sensitive, it is confusing to a human reader to see identifiers spelled in different ways. Pick one spelling and always use that. If you do not want to start a sentence with a command written all in lower case, you should rearrange the sentence.

Do not use the `@code` command for a string of characters shorter than a syntactic token. If you are writing about '`TEXINPU`', which is just a part of the name for the `TEXINPUTS` environment variable, you should use `@samp`.

In particular, you should not use the `@code` command when writing about the characters used in a token; do not, for example, use `@code` when you are explaining what letters or printable symbols can be used in the names of functions. (Use `@samp`.) Also, you should not use `@code` to mark text that is

Chapter 9: Marking Words and Phrases

considered input to programs unless the input is written in a language that is like a programming language. For example, you should not use `@code` for the keystroke commands of GNU Emacs (use `@kbd` instead) although you may use `@code` for the names of the Emacs Lisp functions that the keystroke commands invoke.

In the printed manual, `@code` causes TeX to typeset the argument in a typewriter face. In the Info file, it causes the Info formatting commands to use single quotation marks around the text.

For example,

```
Use @code{diff} to compare two files.
```

produces this in the printed manual:

Use `diff` to compare two files.

and this in the Info file:

```
Use 'diff' to compare two files.
```

9.1.2 `@kbd{`*keyboard-characters*`}`

Use the `@kbd` command for characters of input to be typed by users. For example, to refer to the characters `M-a`, write

```
@kbd{M-a}
```

and to refer to the characters `M-x shell`, write

```
@kbd{M-x shell}
```

The `@kbd` command has the same effect as `@code` in Info, but may produce a different font in a printed manual.

You can embed another @-command inside the braces of an `@kbd` command. Here, for example, is the way to describe a command that would be described more verbosely as "press an 'r' and then press the RET key":

```
@kbd{r @key{RET}}
```

This produces: `r RET`

You also use the `@kbd` command if you are spelling out the letters you type; for example:

```
To give the @code{logout} command,
type the characters @kbd{l o g o u t @key{RET}}.
```

This produces:

To give the `logout` command, type the characters `l o g o u t RET`.

(Also, this example shows that you can add spaces for clarity. If you really want to mention a space character as one of the characters of input, write `@key{SPC}` for it.)

9.1.3 @key{*key-name*}

Use the `@key` command for the conventional name for a key on a keyboard, as in:

`@key{RET}`

You can use the `@key` command within the argument of an `@kbd` command when the sequence of characters to be typed includes one or more keys that are described by name.

For example, to produce `C-x ESC` you would type:

`@kbd{C-x @key{ESC}}`

Here is a list of the recommended names for keys; they are all in upper case:

SPC	Space
RET	Return
LFD	Linefeed
TAB	Tab
BS	Backspace
ESC	Escape
DEL	Delete
SFT	Shift
CTL	Control
META	Meta

There are subtleties to handling words like 'meta' or 'ctl' that are names of shift keys. When mentioning a character in which the shift key is used, such as `Meta-a`, use the `@kbd` command alone; do not use the `@key` command; but when you are referring to the shift key in isolation, use the `@key` command. For example, write '`@kbd{Meta-a}`' to produce `Meta-a` and '`@key{META}`' to produce `META`. This is because `Meta-a` refers to keys that you press on a keyboard, but `META` refers to a key without implying that you press it. In short, use `@kbd` for what you do, and use `@key` for what you talk about: "Press `@kbd{M-a}` to move point to the beginning of the sentence. The `@key{META}` key is often in the lower left of the keyboard."

9.1.4 @samp{*text*}

Use the `@samp` command to indicate text that is a literal example or 'sample' of a sequence of characters in a file, string, pattern, etc. Enclose the text in braces. The argument appears within single quotation marks in both the Info file and the printed manual; in addition, it is printed in a fixed-width font.

```
To match @samp{foo} at the end of the line,
use the regexp @samp{foo$}.
```

produces

To match 'foo' at the end of the line, use the regexp 'foo$'.

Any time you are referring to single characters, you should use **@samp** unless **@kbd** is more appropriate. Use **@samp** for the names of command-line options. Also, you may use **@samp** for entire statements in C and for entire shell commands—in this case, **@samp** often looks better than **@code**. Basically, **@samp** is a catchall for whatever is not covered by **@code**, **@kbd**, or **@key**.

Only include punctuation marks within braces if they are part of the string you are specifying. Write punctuation marks outside the braces if those punctuation marks are part of the English text that surrounds the string. In the following sentence, for example, the commas and period are outside of the braces:

```
In English, the vowels are @samp{a}, @samp{e},
@samp{i}, @samp{o}, @samp{u}, and sometimes
@samp{y}.
```

This produces:

In English, the vowels are 'a', 'e', 'i', 'o', 'u', and sometimes 'y'.

9.1.5 @var{metasyntactic-variable}

Use the **@var** command to indicate metasyntactic variables. A *metasyntactic variable* is something that stands for another piece of text. For example, you should use a metasyntactic variable in the documentation of a function to describe the arguments that are passed to that function.

Do not use **@var** for the names of particular variables in programming languages. These are specific names from a program, so **@code** is correct for them. For example, the Lisp variable `texinfo-tex-command` is not a metasyntactic variable; it is properly formatted using **@code**.

The effect of **@var** in the Info file is to change the case of the argument to all upper case; in the printed manual, to italicize it.

For example,

```
To delete file @var{filename},
type @code{rm @var{filename}}.
```

produces

To delete file *filename*, type **rm** *filename*.

(Note that **@var** may appear inside **@code**, **@samp**, **@file**, etc.)

Write a metasyntactic variable all in lower case without spaces, and use hyphens to make it more readable. Thus, the Texinfo source for the illustration of how to begin a Texinfo manual looks like this:

```
\input texinfo
@@setfilename @var{info-file-name}
@@settitle @var{name-of-manual}
```

This produces:

```
\input texinfo
@setfilename info-file-name
@settitle name-of-manual
```

In some documentation styles, metasyntactic variables are shown with angle brackets, for example:

```
..., type rm <filename>
```

However, that is not the style that Texinfo uses. (You can, of course, modify the sources to TeX and the Info formatting commands to output the `<...>` format if you wish.)

9.1.6 @file{file-name}

Use the `@file` command to indicate text that is the name of a file, buffer, or directory, or is the name of a node in Info. You can also use the command for file name suffixes. Do not use `@file` for symbols in a programming language; use `@code`.

Currently, `@file` is equivalent to `@samp` in its effects. For example,

```
The @file{.el} files are in
the @file{/usr/local/emacs/lisp} directory.
```

produces

The '.el' files are in the '/usr/local/emacs/lisp' directory.

9.1.7 @dfn{term}

Use the `@dfn` command to identify the introductory or defining use of a technical term. Use the command only in passages whose purpose is to introduce a term which will be used again or which the reader ought to know. Mere passing mention of a term for the first time does not deserve `@dfn`. The command generates italics in the printed manual, and double quotation marks in the Info file. For example:

```
Getting rid of a file is called @dfn{deleting} it.
```

produces

Getting rid of a file is called *deleting* it.

As a general rule, a sentence containing the defining occurrence of a term should be a definition of the term. The sentence does not need to say explicitly that it is a definition, but it should contain the information of a definition—it should make the meaning clear.

9.1.8 `@cite{`*reference*`}`

Use the `@cite` command for the name of a book that lacks a companion Info file. The command produces italics in the printed manual, and quotation marks in the Info file.

(If a book is written in Texinfo, it is better to use a cross reference command since a reader can easily follow such a reference in Info. See Section 8.3 [`@xref`], page 73.)

9.2 Emphasizing Text

Usually, Texinfo changes the font to mark words in the text according to what category the words belong to; an example is the `@code` command. Most often, this is the best way to mark words. However, sometimes you will want to emphasize text without indicating a category. Texinfo has two commands to do this. Also, Texinfo has several commands that specify the font in which TeX will typeset text. These commands have no affect on Info and only one of them, the `@r` command, has any regular use.

9.2.1 `@emph{`*text*`}` and `@strong{`*text*`}`

The `@emph` and `@strong` commands are for emphasis; `@strong` is stronger. In printed output, `@emph` produces *italics* and `@strong` produces **bold**.

For example,

```
@quotation
@strong{Caution:} @code{rm * .[^.]*} removes @emph{all}
files in the directory.
@end quotation
```

produces the following in printed output:

Caution: `rm * .[^.]*` removes *all* files in the directory.

and the following in Info:

```
*Caution*: `rm * .[^.]*' removes *all*
files in the directory.
```

The `@strong` command is seldom used except to mark what is, in effect, a typographical element, such as the word 'Caution' in the preceding example.

In the Info file, both `@emph` and `@strong` put asterisks around the text.

Caution: Do not use `@emph` or `@strong` with the word 'Note'; Info will mistake the combination for a cross reference. Use a phrase such as **Please note** or **Caution** instead.

9.2.2 `@sc{`*text*`}`: The Small Caps Font

Use the '`@sc`' command to set text in the printed output in A SMALL CAPS FONT and set text in the Info file in upper case letters.

Write the text between braces in lower case, like this:

```
The @sc{acm} and @sc{ieee} are technical societies.
```

This produces:

The ACM and IEEE are technical societies.

TeX typesets the small caps font in a manner that prevents the letters from 'jumping out at you on the page'. This makes small caps text easier to read than text in all upper case. The Info formatting commands set all small caps text in upper case.

If the text between the braces of an `@sc` command is upper case, TeX typesets in FULL-SIZE CAPITALS. Use full-size capitals sparingly.

You may also use the small caps font for a jargon word such as ATO (a NASA word meaning 'abort to orbit').

There are subtleties to using the small caps font with a jargon word such as CDR, a word used in Lisp programming. In this case, you should use the small caps font when the word refers to the second and subsequent elements of a list (the CDR of the list), but you should use '`@code`' when the word refers to the Lisp function of the same spelling.

9.2.3 Fonts for Printing, Not Info

Texinfo provides four font commands that specify font changes in the printed manual but have no effect in the Info file. `@i` requests *italic* font (in some versions of TeX, a slanted font is used), `@b` requests **bold** face, `@t` requests the `fixed-width`, typewriter-style font used by `@code`, and `@r` requests a roman font, which is the usual font in which text is printed. All four commands apply to an argument that follows, surrounded by braces.

Only the `@r` command has much use: in example programs, you can use the `@r` command to convert code comments from the fixed-width font to a roman font. This looks better in printed output.

For example,

```
@lisp
(+ 2 2)    ; @r{Add two plus two.}
@end lisp
```

produces

```
(+ 2 2)        ; Add two plus two.
```

If possible, you should avoid using the other three font commands. If you need to use one, it probably indicates a gap in the Texinfo language.

9.2.4 Customized Highlighting

You can use regular TeX commands inside of `@iftex` ... `@end iftex` to create your own customized highlighting commands for Texinfo. The easiest way to do this is to equate your customized commands with pre-existing commands, such as those for italics. Such new commands work only with TeX.

You can use the `@definfoenclose` command inside of `@ifinfo` ... `@end ifinfo` to define commands for Info with the sames names as new commands for TeX. `@definfoenclose` creates new commands for Info that mark text by enclosing it in strings that precede and follow the text.[1]

Here is how to create a new `@`-command called `@phoo` that causes TeX to typeset its argument in italics and causes Info to display the argument between '`//`' and '`\\`'.

For TeX, write the following to equate the `@phoo` command with the existing `@i` italics command:

```
@iftex
@global@let@phoo=@i
@end iftex
```

This defines `@phoo` as a command that causes TeX to typeset the argument to `@phoo` in italics. `@global@let` tells TeX to equate the next argument with the argument that follows the equals sign.

For Info, write the following to tell the Info formatters to enclose the argument between '`//`' and '`\\`':

```
@ifinfo
@definfoenclose phoo, //, \\
@end ifinfo
```

Write the `@definfoenclose` command on a line and follow it with three arguments separated by commas (commas are used as separators in an `@node` line in the same way).

- The first argument to `@definfoenclose` is the `@`-command name **without** the '`@`';
- the second argument is the Info start delimiter string; and,
- the third argument is the Info end delimiter string.

---

[1] Currently, `@definfoenclose` works only with `texinfo-format-buffer` and `texinfo-format-region`, not with `makeinfo`.

The latter two arguments enclose the highlighted text in the Info file. A delimiter string may contain spaces. Neither the start nor end delimiter is required. However, if you do not provide a start delimiter, you must follow the command name with two commas in a row; otherwise, the Info formatting commands will misinterpret the end delimiter string as a start delimiter string.

After you have defined **@phoo** both for TeX and for Info, you can then write **@phoo{bar}** to see '//bar\\' in Info and see *bar* in italics in printed output.

Note that each definition applies to its own formatter: one for TeX, the other for Info.

Here is another example:

```
@ifinfo
@definfoenclose headword, , :
@end ifinfo
@iftex
@global@let@headword=@b
@end iftex
```

This defines **@headword** as an Info formatting command that inserts nothing before and a colon after the argument and as a TeX formatting command to typeset its argument in bold.

10 Quotations and Examples

Quotations and examples are blocks of text consisting of one or more whole paragraphs that are set off from the bulk of the text and treated differently. They are usually indented.

In Texinfo, you always begin a quotation or example by writing an @-command at the beginning of a line by itself, and end it by writing an @end command that is also at the beginning of a line by itself. For instance, you begin an example by writing @example by itself at the beginning of a line and end the example by writing @end example on a line by itself, at the beginning of that line.

10.1 The Block Enclosing Commands

Here are commands for quotations and examples:

@quotation
: Indicate text that is quoted. The text is filled, indented, and printed in a roman font by default.

@example
: Illustrate code, commands, and the like. The text is printed in a fixed-width font, and indented but not filled.

@lisp
: Illustrate Lisp code. The text is printed in a fixed-width font, and indented but not filled.

@smallexample
: Illustrate code, commands, and the like. Similar to @example, except that in TeX this command typesets text in a smaller font for the smaller @smallbook format than for the 8.5 by 11 inch format.

@smalllisp
: Illustrate Lisp code. Similar to @lisp, except that in TeX this command typesets text in a smaller font for the smaller @smallbook format than for the 8.5 by 11 inch format.

@display
: Display illustrative text. The text is indented but not filled, and no font is specified (so, by default, the font is roman).

@format
: Print illustrative text. The text is not indented and not filled and no font is specified (so, by default, the font is roman).

The @exdent command is used within the above constructs to undo the indentation of a line.

The @flushleft and @flushright commands are used to line up the left or right margins of unfilled text.

The `@noindent` command may be used after one of the above constructs to prevent the following text from being indented as a new paragraph.

You can use the `@cartouche` command within one of the above constructs to highlight the example or quotation by drawing a box with rounded corners around it. (The `@cartouche` command affects only the printed manual; it has no effect in the Info file; see Section 10.11 [Drawing Cartouches Around Examples], page 97.)

10.2 `@quotation`

The text of a quotation is processed normally except that:
- the margins are closer to the center of the page, so the whole of the quotation is indented;
- the first lines of paragraphs are indented no more than other lines;
- in the printed output, interparagraph spacing is reduced.

This is an example of text written between an `@quotation` command and an `@end quotation` command. An `@quotation` command is most often used to indicate text that is excerpted from another (real or hypothetical) printed work.

Write an `@quotation` command as text on a line by itself. This line will disappear from the output. Mark the end of the quotation with a line beginning with and containing only `@end quotation`. The `@end quotation` line will likewise disappear from the output. Thus, the following,

```
@quotation
This is
a foo.
@end quotation
```

produces

This is a foo.

10.3 `@example`

The `@example` command is used to indicate an example that is not part of the running text, such as computer input or output.

```
This is an example of text written between an
@example command
and an @end example command.
The text is indented but not filled.
```

Chapter 10: Quotations and Examples   93

> In the printed manual, the text is typeset in a
> fixed-width font, and extra spaces and blank lines are
> significant. In the Info file, an analogous result is
> obtained by indenting each line with five spaces.

Write an `@example` command at the beginning of a line by itself. This line will disappear from the output. Mark the end of the example with an `@end example` command, also written at the beginning of a line by itself. The `@end example` will disappear from the output.

For example,

```
@example
mv foo bar
@end example
```

produces

```
mv foo bar
```

Since the lines containing `@example` and `@end example` will disappear, you should put a blank line before the `@example` and another blank line after the `@end example`. (Remember that blank lines between the beginning `@example` and the ending `@end example` will appear in the output.)

> **Caution:** Do not use tabs in the lines of an example (or anywhere else in Texinfo, for that matter)! TeX treats tabs as single spaces, and that is not what they look like. This is a problem with TeX. (If necessary, in Emacs, you can use `M-x untabify` to convert tabs in a region to multiple spaces.)

Examples are often, logically speaking, "in the middle" of a paragraph, and the text continues after an example should not be indented. The `@noindent` command prevents a piece of text from being indented as if it were a new paragraph.

(The `@code` command is used for examples of code that are embedded within sentences, not set off from preceding and following text. See Section 9.1.1 [@code], page 82.)

10.4 @noindent

An example or other inclusion can break a paragraph into segments. Ordinarily, the formatters indent text that follows an example as a new paragraph. However, you can prevent this by writing `@noindent` at the beginning of a line by itself preceding the continuation text.

For example:

```
@example
This is an example
@end example

@noindent
This line is not indented.  As you can see, the
beginning of the line is fully flush left with the line
that follows after it.  (This whole example is between
@code{@@display} and @code{@@end display}.)
```

produces

> This is an example

This line is not indented. As you can see, the beginning of the line is fully flush left with the line that follows after it. (This whole example is between `@display` and `@end display`.)

To adjust the number of blank lines properly in the Info file output, remember that the line containing `@noindent` does not generate a blank line, and neither does the `@end example` line.

In the Texinfo source file for this manual, each line that says 'produces' is preceded by a line containing `@noindent`.

Do not put braces after an `@noindent` command; they are not necessary, since `@noindent` is a command used outside of paragraphs (see Appendix I [Command Syntax], page 225).

10.5 `@lisp`

The `@lisp` command is used for Lisp code. It is synonymous with the `@example` command.

> This is an example of text written between an
> `@lisp` command and an `@end lisp` command.

Use `@lisp` instead of `@example` so as to preserve information regarding the nature of the example. This is useful, for example, if you write a function that evaluates only and all the Lisp code in a Texinfo file. Then you can use the Texinfo file as a Lisp library.[1]

Mark the end of `@lisp` with `@end lisp` on a line by itself.

---

[1] It would be straightforward to extend Texinfo to work in a similar fashion for C, FORTRAN, or other languages.

Chapter 10: Quotations and Examples   95

10.6 `@smallexample` and `@smalllisp`

In addition to the regular `@example` and `@lisp` commands, Texinfo has two other "example-style" commands. These are the `@smallexample` and `@smalllisp` commands. Both these commands are designed for use with the `@smallbook` command that causes TeX to produce a printed manual in a 7 by 9.25 inch format rather than the regular 8.5 by 11 inch format.

In TeX, the `@smallexample` and `@smalllisp` commands typeset text in a smaller font for the smaller `@smallbook` format than for the 8.5 by 11 inch format. Consequently, many examples containing long lines fit in a narrower, `@smallbook` page without needing to be shortened. Both commands typeset in the normal font size when you format for the 8.5 by 11 inch size; indeed, in this situation, the `@smallexample` and `@smalllisp` commands are defined to be the `@example` and `@lisp` commands.

In Info, the `@smallexample` and `@smalllisp` commands are equivalent to the `@example` and `@lisp` commands, and work exactly the same.

Mark the end of `@smallexample` or `@smalllisp` with `@end smallexample` or `@end smalllisp`, respectively.

Here is an example written in the small font used by the `@smallexample` and `@smalllisp` commands:

```
This is an example of text written between @smallexample and
@end smallexample.  In Info and in an 8.5 by 11 inch manual,
this text appears in its normal size; but in a 7 by 9.25 inch manual,
this text appears in a smaller font.
```

The `@smallexample` and `@smalllisp` commands make it easier to prepare smaller format manuals without forcing you to edit examples by hand to fit them onto narrower pages.

As a general rule, a printed document looks better if you write all the examples in a chapter consistently in `@example` or in `@smallexample`. Only occasionally should you mix the two formats.

See Section 19.10 [Printing "Small" Books], page 156, for more information about the `@smallbook` command.

10.7 `@display`

The `@display` command begins a kind of example. It is like the `@example` command except that, in a printed manual, `@display` does not select the fixed-width font. In fact, it does not specify the font at all, so that the text appears in the same font it would have appeared in without the `@display` command.

```
This is an example of text written between an @display command
and an @end display command.  The @display command
indents the text, but does not fill it.
```

10.8 @format

The `@format` command is similar to `@example` except that, in the printed manual, `@format` does not select the fixed-width font and does not narrow the margins.

This is an example of text written between an `@format` command
and an `@end format` command. As you can see
from this example,
the `@format` command does not fill the text.

10.9 @exdent: Undoing a Line's Indentation

The `@exdent` command removes any indentation a line might have. The command is written at the beginning of a line and applies only to the text that follows the command that is on the same line. Do not use braces around the text. In a printed manual, the text on an `@exdent` line is printed in the roman font.

`@exdent` is usually used within examples. Thus,

```
@example
This line follows an @@example command.
@exdent This line is exdented.
This line follows the exdented line.
The @@end example comes on the next line.
@end group
```

produces

```
    This line follows an @example command.
This line is exdented.
    This line follows the exdented line.
    The @end example comes on the next line.
```

In practice, the `@exdent` command is rarely used. Usually, you un-indent text by ending the example and returning the page to its normal width.

10.10 @flushleft and @flushright

The `@flushleft` and `@flushright` commands line up the ends of lines on the left and right margins of a page, but do not fill the text. The commands are written on lines of their own, without braces. The `@flushleft` and `@flushright` commands are ended by `@end flushleft` and `@end flushright` commands on lines of their own.

Chapter 10: Quotations and Examples 97

For example,

```
@flushleft
This text is
written flushleft.
@end flushleft
```

produces

This text is
written flushleft.

Flushright produces the type of indentation often used in the return address of letters.
For example,

```
@flushright
Here is an example of text written
flushright.  The @code{@flushright} command
right justifies every line but leaves the
left end ragged.
@end flushright
```

produces

> Here is an example of text written
> flushright. The `@flushright` command
> right justifies every line but leaves the
> left end ragged.

10.11 Drawing Cartouches Around Examples

In a printed manual, the `@cartouche` command draws a box with rounded corners around its contents. You can use this command to further highlight an example or quotation. For instance, you could write a manual in which one type of example is surrounded by a cartouche for emphasis.

The `@cartouche` command affects only the printed manual; it has no effect in the Info file.
For example,

```
@example
@cartouche
% pwd
/usr/local/lib/emacs/info
@end cartouche
@end example
```

surrounds the two-line example with a box with rounded corners, in the printed manual.

In a printed manual, the example looks like this:

```
% pwd
/usr/local/lib/emacs/info
```

11 Making Lists and Tables

Texinfo has several ways of making lists and two-column tables. Lists can be bulleted or numbered, while two-column tables can highlight the items in the first column.

Texinfo automatically indents the text in lists or tables, and numbers an enumerated list. This last feature is useful if you modify the list, since you do not need to renumber it yourself.

Numbered lists and tables begin with the appropriate `@`-command at the beginning of a line, and end with the corresponding `@end` command on a line by itself. The table and itemized-list commands also require that you write formatting information on the same line as the beginning `@`-command.

Begin an enumerated list, for example, with an `@enumerate` command and end the list with an `@end enumerate` command. Begin an itemized list with an `@itemize` command, followed on the same line by a formatting command such as `@bullet`, and end the list with an `@end itemize` command.

Precede each element of a list with an `@item` or `@itemx` command.

Here is an itemized list of the different kinds of table and lists:

- Itemized lists with and without bullets.
- Enumerated lists, using numbers or letters.
- Two-column tables with highlighting.

Here is an enumerated list with the same items:

1. Itemized lists with and without bullets.
2. Enumerated lists, using numbers or letters.
3. Two-column tables with highlighting.

And here is a two-column table with the same items and their `@`-commands:

`@itemize`   Itemized lists with and without bullets.

`@enumerate`
        Enumerated lists, using numbers or letters.

`@table`
`@ftable`
`@vtable`   Two-column tables with highlighting.

11.1 Making an Itemized List

The `@itemize` command produces sequences of indented paragraphs, with a bullet or other mark inside the left margin at the beginning of each paragraph for which such a mark is desired.

Begin an itemized list by writing `@itemize` at the beginning of a line. Follow the command, on the same line, with a character or a Texinfo command that generates a mark. Usually, you will write `@bullet` after `@itemize`, but you can use `@minus`, or any character or any special symbol that results in a single character in the Info file. (When you write `@bullet` or `@minus` after an `@itemize` command, you may omit the '{}'.)

Write the text of the indented paragraphs themselves after the `@itemize`, up to another line that says `@end itemize`.

Before each paragraph for which a mark in the margin is desired, write a line that says just `@item`. Do not write any other text on this line.

Usually, you should put a blank line before an `@item`. This puts a blank line in the Info file. (TeX inserts the proper interline whitespace in either case.) Except when the entries are very brief, these blank lines make the list look better.

Here is an example of the use of `@itemize`, followed by the output it produces. Note that `@bullet` produces an '*' in Info and a round dot in TeX.

```
@itemize @bullet
@item
Some text for foo.

@item
Some text
for bar.
@end itemize
```

This produces:

- Some text for foo.

- Some text for bar.

Itemized lists may be embedded within other itemized lists. Here is a list marked with dashes embedded in a list marked with bullets:

```
@itemize @bullet
@item
First item.

@itemize @minus
@item
Inner item.

@item
Second inner item.
@end itemize

@item
Second outer item.
@end itemize
```

This produces:

- First item.
  - Inner item.
  - Second inner item.
- Second outer item.

11.2 Making a Numbered or Lettered List

@enumerate is like **@itemize** except that the marks in the left margin contain successive integers or letters. (See Section 11.1 [**@itemize**], page 100.)

Write the **@enumerate** command at the beginning of a line. The command does not require an argument, but accepts either a number or a letter as an option. Without an argument, **@enumerate** starts the list with the number 1. With a numeric argument, such as 3, the command starts the list with that number. With an upper or lower case letter, such as **a** or **A**, the command starts the list with that letter.

Write the text of the enumerated list in the same way you write an itemized list: put **@item** on a line of its own before the start of each paragraph that you want enumerated. Do not write any other text on the line beginning with **@item**.

You should put a blank line between entries in the list. This generally makes it easier to read the Info file.

Here is an example of **@enumerate** without an argument:

```
@enumerate
@item
Underlying causes.

@item
Proximate causes.
@end enumerate
```

This produces:
1. Underlying causes.
2. Proximate causes.

Here is an example with an argument of 3:

```
@enumerate 3
@item
Predisposing causes.

@item
Precipitating causes.

@item
Perpetuating causes.
@end enumerate
```

This produces:

3. Predisposing causes.
4. Precipitating causes.
5. Perpetuating causes.

Here is a brief summary of the alternatives. The summary is constructed using **@enumerate** with an argument of a.

a. **@enumerate**

   Without an argument, produce a numbered list, starting with the number 1.

b. **@enumerate** *positive-integer*

   With a (positive) numeric argument, start a numbered list with that number. You can use this to continue a list that you interrupted with other text.

c. `@enumerate` *upper-case-letter*

   With an upper case letter as argument, start a list in which each item is marked by a letter, beginning with that upper case letter.

d. `@enumerate` *lower-case-letter*

   With a lower case letter as argument, start a list in which each item is marked by a letter, beginning with that lower case letter.

You can also nest enumerated lists, as in an outline.

11.3 Making a Two-column Table

`@table` is similar to `@itemize`, but the command allows you to specify a name or heading line for each item. (See Section 11.1 [`@itemize`], page 100.) The `@table` command is used to produce two-column tables, and is especially useful for glossaries and explanatory exhibits.

Write the `@table` command at the beginning of a line and follow it on the same line with an argument that is a Texinfo command such as `@code`, `@samp`, `@var`, or `@kbd`. Although these commands are usually followed by arguments in braces, in this case you use the command name without an argument because `@item` will supply the argument. This command will be applied to the text that goes into the first column of each item and determines how it will be highlighted. For example, `@samp` will cause the text in the first column to be highlighted with an `@samp` command.

You may also choose to use the `@asis` command as an argument to `@table`. `@asis` is a command that does nothing; if you use this command after `@table`, TeX and the Info formatting commands output the first column entries without added highlighting ('as is').

(The `@table` command may work with other commands besides those listed here. However, you can only use commands that normally take arguments in braces.)

Begin each table entry with an `@item` command at the beginning of a line. Write the first column text on the same line as the `@item` command. Write the second column text on the line following the `@item` line and on subsequent lines. (You do not need to type anything for an empty second column entry.) You may write as many lines of supporting text as you wish, even several paragraphs. But only text on the same line as the `@item` will be placed in the first column.

Normally, you should put a blank line before an `@item` line. This puts a blank like in the Info file. Except when the entries are very brief, a blank line looks better.

The following table, for example, highlights the text in the first column with an `@samp` command:

```
@table @samp
@item foo
This is the text for
@samp{foo}.

@item bar
Text for @samp{bar}.
@end table
```

This produces:

'`foo`'   This is the text for '`foo`'.

'`bar`'   Text for '`bar`'.

If you want to list two or more named items with a single block of text, use the `@itemx` command. (See Section 11.3.2 [`@itemx`], page 104.)

11.3.1 `@ftable` and `@vtable`

The `@ftable` and `@vtable` commands are the same as the `@table` command except that `@ftable` automatically enters each of the items in the first column of the table into the index of functions and `@vtable` automatically enters each of the items in the first column of the table into the index of variables. This simplifies the task of creating indices. Only the items on the same line as the `@item` commands are indexed, and they are indexed in exactly the form that they appear on that line. See Chapter 12 [Creating Indices], page 107, for more information about indices.

Begin a two-column table using `@ftable` or `@vtable` by writing the `@`-command at the beginning of a line, followed on the same line by an argument that is a Texinfo command such as `@code`, exactly as you would for an `@table` command; and end the table with an `@end ftable` or `@end vtable` command on a line by itself.

11.3.2 `@itemx`

Use the `@itemx` command inside a table when you have two or more first column entries for the same item, each of which should appear on a line of its own. Use `@itemx` for all but the first entry. The `@itemx` command works exactly like `@item` except that it does not generate extra vertical space above the first column text.

Chapter 11: Making Lists and Tables

For example,

```
@table @code
@item upcase
@itemx downcase
These two functions accept a character or a string as
argument, and return the corresponding upper case (lower
case) character or string.
@end table
```

This produces:

upcase
downcase   These two functions accept a character or a string as argument, and return the corresponding upper case (lower case) character or string.

(Note also that this example illustrates multi-line supporting text in a two-column table.)

12 Creating Indices

Using Texinfo, you can generate indices without having to sort and collate entries manually. In an index, the entries are listed in alphabetical order, together with information on how to find the discussion of each entry. In a printed manual, this information consists of page numbers. In an Info file, this information is a menu entry leading to the first node referenced.

Texinfo provides several predefined kinds of index: an index for functions, an index for variables, an index for concepts, and so on. You can combine indices or use them for other than their canonical purpose. If you wish, you can define your own indices.

12.1 Making Index Entries

When you are making index entries, it is good practice to think of the different ways people may look for something. Different people *do not* think of the same words when they look something up. A helpful index will have items indexed under all the different words that people may use. For example, one reader may think it obvious that the two-letter names for indices should be listed under "Indices, two-letter names", since the word "Index" is the general concept. But another reader may remember the specific concept of two-letter names and search for the entry listed as "Two letter names for indices". A good index will have both entries and will help both readers.

Like typesetting, the construction of an index is a highly skilled, professional art, the subtleties of which are not appreciated until you need to do it yourself.

See Section 4.1 [Printing Indices & Menus], page 47, for information about printing an index at the end of a book or creating an index menu in an Info file.

12.2 Predefined Indices

Texinfo provides six predefined indices:

- A *concept index* listing concepts that are discussed.
- A *function index* listing functions (such as entry points of libraries).
- A *variables index* listing variables (such as global variables of libraries).
- A *keystroke index* listing keyboard commands.
- A *program index* listing names of programs.
- A *data type index* listing data types (such as structures defined in header files).

Not every manual needs all of these, and most manuals use two or three of them. This manual has two indices: a concept index and an @-command index (that is actually the function index but is called a command index in the chapter heading). Two or more indices can be combined into one using the `@synindex` or `@syncodeindex` commands. See Section 12.4 [Combining Indices], page 110.

12.3 Defining the Entries of an Index

The data to make an index come from many individual indexing commands scattered throughout the Texinfo source file. Each command says to add one entry to a particular index; after formatting, the index will give the current page number or node name as the reference.

An index entry consists of an indexing command at the beginning of a line followed, on the rest of the line, by the entry.

For example, this section begins with the following five entries for the concept index:

```
@cindex Defining indexing entries
@cindex Index entries
@cindex Entries for an index
@cindex Specifying index entries
@cindex Creating index entries
```

Each predefined index has its own indexing command—`@cindex` for the concept index, `@findex` for the function index, and so on.

Concept index entries consist of text. The best way to write an index is to choose entries that are terse yet clear. If you can do this, the index often looks better if the entries are not capitalized, but written just as they would appear in the middle of a sentence. (Capitalize proper names and acronyms that always call for upper case letters.) This is the case convention we use in most GNU manuals' indices.

If you don't see how to make an entry terse yet clear, make it longer and clear—not terse and confusing. If many of the entries are several words long, the index may look better if you use a different convention: to capitalize the first word of each entry. But do not capitalize a case-sensitive name such as a C or Lisp function name or a shell command; that would be a spelling error.

Whichever case convention you use, please use it consistently!

Entries in indices other than the concept index are symbol names in programming languages, or program names; these names are usually case-sensitive, so use upper and lower case as required for them.

By default, entries for a concept index are printed in a small roman font and entries for the other indices are printed in a small `@code` font. You may change the way part of an entry is printed with the usual Texinfo commands,

Chapter 12: Creating Indices

such as `@file` for file names and `@emph` for emphasis (see Chapter 9 [Marking Text], page 81).

The six indexing commands for predefined indices are:

`@cindex` *concept*
:   Make an entry in the concept index for *concept*.

`@findex` *function*
:   Make an entry in the function index for *function*.

`@vindex` *variable*
:   Make an entry in the variable index for *variable*.

`@kindex` *keystroke*
:   Make an entry in the key index for *keystroke*.

`@pindex` *program*
:   Make an entry in the program index for *program*.

`@tindex` *data type*
:   Make an entry in the data type index for *data type*.

> **Caution:** Do not use a colon in an index entry. In Info, a colon separates the menu entry name from the node name. An extra colon confuses Info. See Section 7.2 [The Parts of a Menu], page 68, for more information about the structure of a menu entry.

If you write several identical index entries in different places in a Texinfo file, the index in the printed manual will list all the pages to which those entries refer. However, the index in the Info file will list **only** the node that references the **first** of those index entries. Therefore, it is best to write indices in which each entry refers to only one place in the Texinfo file. Fortunately, this constraint is a feature rather than a loss since it means that the index will be easy to use. Otherwise, you could create an index that lists several pages for one entry and your reader would not know to which page to turn. If you have two identical entries for one topic, change the topics slightly, or qualify them to indicate the difference.

You are not actually required to use the predefined indices for their canonical purposes. For example, suppose you wish to index some C preprocessor macros. You could put them in the function index along with actual functions, just by writing `@findex` commands for them; then, when you print the "Function Index" as an unnumbered chapter, you could give it the title 'Function and Macro Index' and all will be consistent for the reader. Or you could put the macros in with the data types by writing `@tindex` commands for them, and give that index a suitable title so the reader will understand. (See Section 4.1 [Printing Indices & Menus], page 47.)

12.4 Combining Indices

Sometimes you will want to combine two disparate indices such as functions and concepts, perhaps because you have few enough of one of them that a separate index for them would look silly.

You could put functions into the concept index by writing **@cindex** commands for them instead of **@findex** commands, and produce a consistent manual by printing the concept index with the title 'Function and Concept Index' and not printing the 'Function Index' at all; but this is not a robust procedure. It works only if your document is never included as part of another document that is designed to have a separate function index; if your document were to be included with such a document, the functions from your document and those from the other would not end up together. Also, to make your function names appear in the right font in the concept index, you would need to enclose every one of them between the braces of **@code**.

12.4.1 @syncodeindex

When you want to combine functions and concepts into one index, you should index the functions with **@findex** and index the concepts with **@cindex**, and use the **@syncodeindex** command to redirect the function index entries into the concept index.

The **@syncodeindex** command takes two arguments; they are the name of the index to redirect, and the name of the index to redirect it to. The template looks like this:

> **@syncodeindex** *from to*

For this purpose, the indices are given two-letter names:

'cp'	concept index
'fn'	function index
'vr'	variable index
'ky'	key index
'pg'	program index
'tp'	data type index

Write an **@syncodeindex** command before or shortly after the end-of-header line at the beginning of a Texinfo file. For example, to merge a function index with a concept index, write the following:

> **@syncodeindex fn cp**

This will cause all entries designated for the function index to merge in with the concept index instead.

To merge both a variables index and a function index into a concept index, write the following:

```
@syncodeindex vr cp
@syncodeindex fn cp
```

The `@syncodeindex` command puts all the entries from the 'from' index (the redirected index) into the `@code` font, overriding whatever default font is used by the index to which the entries are now directed. This way, if you direct function names from a function index into a concept index, all the function names are printed in the `@code` font as you would expect.

12.4.2 @synindex

The `@synindex` command is nearly the same as the `@syncodeindex` command, except that it does not put the 'from' index entries into the `@code` font; rather it puts them in the roman font. Thus, you use `@synindex` when you merge a concept index into a function index.

See Section 4.1 [Printing Indices & Menus], page 47, for information about printing an index at the end of a book or creating an index menu in an Info file.

12.5 Defining New Indices

In addition to the predefined indices, you may use the `@defindex` and `@defcodeindex` commands to define new indices. These commands create new indexing `@`-commands with which you mark index entries. The `@defindex` command is used like this:

```
@defindex name
```

The name of an index should be a two letter word, such as 'au'. For example:

```
@defindex au
```

This defines a new index, called the 'au' index. At the same time, it creates a new indexing command, `@auindex`, that you can use to make index entries. Use the new indexing command just as you would use a predefined indexing command.

For example, here is a section heading followed by a concept index entry and two 'au' index entries.

```
@section Cognitive Semantics
@cindex kinesthetic image schemas
@auindex Johnson, Mark
@auindex Lakoff, George
```

(Evidently, 'au' serves here as an abbreviation for "author".) Texinfo constructs the new indexing command by concatenating the name of the index with 'index'; thus, defining an 'au' index leads to the automatic creation of an @auindex command.

Use the @printindex command to print the index, as you do with the predefined indices. For example:

```
@node Author Index, Subject Index, , Top
@unnumbered Author Index

@printindex au
```

The @defcodeindex is like the @defindex command, except that, in the printed output, it prints entries in an @code font instead of a roman font. Thus, it parallels the @findex command rather than the @cindex command.

You should define new indices within or right after the end-of-header line of a Texinfo file, before any @synindex or @syncodeindex commands (see Section 3.2 [Header], page 33).

13 Special Insertions

Texinfo provides several commands for formatting dimensions, for inserting single characters that have special meaning in Texinfo, such as braces, and for inserting special graphic symbols that do not correspond to characters, such as dots and bullets.

These are:

- Braces, '@' and periods.
- Format a dimension, such as '12 pt'.
- Dots and bullets.
- The TEX logo and the copyright symbol.
- A minus sign.

13.1 Inserting '@', Braces, and Periods

'@' and curly braces are special characters in Texinfo. To insert these characters so they appear in text, you must put an '@' in front of these characters to prevent Texinfo from misinterpreting them.

Periods are also special. Depending on whether the period is inside or at the end of a sentence, less or more space is inserted after a period in a typeset manual. Since it is not always possible for Texinfo to determine when a period ends a sentence and when it is used in an abbreviation, special commands are needed in some circumstances. (Usually, Texinfo can guess how to handle periods, so you do not need to use the special commands; you just enter a period as you would if you were using a typewriter, which means you put two spaces after the period, question mark, or exclamation mark that ends a sentence.)

Do not put braces after any of these commands; they are not necessary.

13.1.1 Inserting '@' with @@

@@ stands for a single '@' in either printed or Info output.

Do not put braces after an @@ command.

13.1.2 Inserting '{' and '}'with @{ and @}

@{ stands for a single '{' in either printed or Info output.

@} stands for a single '}' in either printed or Info output.

Do not put braces after either an @{ or an @} command.

13.1.3 Spacing After Colons and Periods

Use the `@:` command after a period, question mark, exclamation mark, or colon that should not be followed by extra space. For example, use `@:` after periods that end abbreviations which are not at the ends of sentences. `@:` has no effect on the Info file output.

For example,

```
The s.o.p.@: has three parts ...
The s.o.p. has three parts ...
```

produces the following. If you look carefully at this printed output, you will see a little more whitespace after 's.o.p.' in the second line.

> The s.o.p. has three parts ...
> The s.o.p. has three parts ...

`@:` has no effect on the Info output. ('`s.o.p`' is an acronym for "Standard Operating Procedure".)

Use `@.` instead of a period at the end of a sentence that ends with a single capital letter. Otherwise, TeX will think the letter is an abbreviation and will not insert the correct end-of-sentence spacing. Here is an example:

```
Give it to M.I.B. and to M.E.W@.  Also, give it to R.J.C@.
Give it to M.I.B. and to M.E.W.  Also, give it to R.J.C.
```

produces the following. If you look carefully at this printed output, you will see a little more whitespace after the '`W`' in the first line.

> Give it to M.I.B. and to M.E.W. Also, give it to R.J.C.
> Give it to M.I.B. and to M.E.W. Also, give it to R.J.C.

In the Info file output, `@.` is equivalent to a simple '.'.

The meanings of `@:` and `@.` in Texinfo are designed to work well with the Emacs sentence motion commands. This made it necessary for them to be incompatible with some other formatting systems that use `@`-commands.

Do not put braces after either an `@:` or an `@.` command.

13.2 `@dmn{`*dimension*`}`: Format a Dimension

At times, you may want to write '`12pt`' or '`8.5in`' with little or no space between the number and the abbreviation for the dimension. You can use the `@dmn` command to do this. On seeing the command, TeX inserts just enough space for proper typesetting; the Info formatting commands insert no space at all, since the Info file does not require it.

To use the `@dmn` command, write the number and then follow it immediately, with no intervening space, by `@dmn`, and then by the dimension within braces.

For example,

```
A4 paper is 8.27@dmn{in} wide.
```

produces

A4 paper is 8.27 in wide.

Not everyone uses this style. Instead of writing '8.27@dmn{in}' in the Texinfo file, you may write '8.27 in.' or '8.27 inches'. (In these cases, the formatters may insert a line break between the number and the dimension. Also, if you write a period after an abbreviation within a sentence, you should write '@:' after the period to prevent TeX from inserting extra whitespace. See Section 13.1.3 [Spacing After Colons and Periods], page 114.)

13.3 Inserting Ellipsis, Dots, and Bullets

An *ellipsis* (a line of dots) is not typeset as a string of periods, so a special command is used for ellipsis in Texinfo. The @bullet command is special, too. Each of these commands is followed by a pair of braces, '{}', without any whitespace between the name of the command and the braces. (You need to use braces with these commands because you can use them next to other text; without the braces, the formatters would be confused. See Appendix I [@-Command Syntax], page 225, for further information.)

13.3.1 @dots{}

Use the @dots{} command to generate an ellipsis, which is three dots in a row, appropriately spaced, like this: '...'. Do not simply write three periods in the input file; that would work for the Info file output, but would produce the wrong amount of space between the periods in the printed manual.

Similarly, the @enddots{} command helps you correctly set an end-of-sentence ellipsis (four dots).

Here is an ellipsis: ...

Here are three periods in a row: ...

In printed output, the three periods in a row are closer together than the dots in the ellipsis.

13.3.2 @bullet{}

Use the @bullet{} command to generate a large round dot, or the closest possible thing to one. In Info, an asterisk is used.

Here is a bullet: •

When you use @bullet in @itemize, you do not need to type the braces, because @itemize supplies them. (See Section 11.1 [@itemize], page 100.)

13.4 Inserting TeX and the Copyright Symbol

The logo 'TeX' is typeset in a special fashion and it needs an @-command. The copyright symbol, '©', is also special. Each of these commands is followed by a pair of braces, '{}', without any whitespace between the name of the command and the braces.

13.4.1 @TeX{}

Use the `@TeX{}` command to generate 'TeX'. In a printed manual, this is a special logo that is different from three ordinary letters. In Info, it just looks like 'TeX'. The `@TeX{}` command is unique among Texinfo commands in that the T and the X are in upper case.

13.4.2 @copyright{}

Use the `@copyright{}` command to generate '©'. In a printed manual, this is a 'c' inside a circle, and in Info, this is '(C)'.

13.5 @minus{}: Inserting a Minus Sign

Use the `@minus{}` command to generate a minus sign. In a fixed-width font, this is a single hyphen, but in a proportional font, the symbol is the customary length for a minus sign—a little longer than a hyphen.

You can compare the two forms:

'−' is a minus sign generated with '`@minus{}`',

'-' is a hyphen generated with the character '-'.

In the fixed-width font used by Info, `@minus{}` is the same as a hyphen.

You should not use `@minus{}` inside `@code` or `@example` because the width distinction is not made in the fixed-width font they use.

When you use `@minus` to specify the mark beginning each entry in an itemized list, you do not need to type the braces (see Section 11.1 [`@itemize`], page 100.)

13.6 @math: Inserting Mathematical Expressions

You can write a short mathematical expression with the `@math` command. Write the mathematical expression between braces, like this:

`@math{(a + b)(a + b) = a^2 + 2ab + b^2}`

Chapter 13: Special Insertions

This produces the following in TeX:

$(a + b)(a + b) = a^2 + 2ab + b^2$

and the following in Info:

```
(a + b)(a + b) = a^2 + 2ab + b^2
```

The @math command has no effect on the Info output. Currently, it has limited effect on typeset output. However, this may change since TeX itself is designed for mathematical typesetting and does a splendid job.

Certainly, for complex mathematical expressions, you could use TeX directly. See Section 18.1 [Using Ordinary TeX Commands], page 143. When you use TeX directly, remember to write the mathematical expression between one or two '$' (dollar-signs) as appropriate.

14 Glyphs for Examples

In Texinfo, code is often illustrated in examples that are delimited by `@example` and `@end example`, or by `@lisp` and `@end lisp`. In such examples, you can indicate the results of evaluation or an expansion using '⇒' or '↦'. Likewise, there are commands to insert glyphs to indicate printed output, error messages, equivalence of expressions, and the location of point.

The glyph-insertion commands do not need to be used within an example, but most often they are. Every glyph-insertion command is followed by a pair of left- and right-hand braces.

⇒	`@result{}` points to the result of an expression.
↦	`@expansion{}` shows the results of a macro expansion.
⊣	`@print{}` indicates printed output.
error	`@error{}` indicates that the following text is an error message.
≡	`@equiv{}` indicates the exact equivalence of two forms.
★	`@point{}` shows the location of point.

14.1 ⇒: Indicating Evaluation

Use the `@result{}` command to indicate the result of evaluating an expression.

The `@result{}` command is displayed as '=>' in Info and as '⇒' in the printed output.

Thus, the following,

```
(cdr '(1 2 3))
     ⇒ (2 3)
```

may be read as "`(cdr '(1 2 3))` evaluates to `(2 3)`".

14.2 ↦: Indicating an Expansion

When an expression is a macro call, it expands into a new expression. You can indicate the result of the expansion with the `@expansion{}` command.

The `@expansion{}` command is displayed as '==>' in Info and as '↦' in the printed output.

For example, the following

```
@lisp
(third '(a b c))
     @expansion{} (car (cdr (cdr '(a b c))))
     @result{} c
@end lisp
```

produces

```
(third '(a b c))
    ↦ (car (cdr (cdr '(a b c))))
    ⇒ c
```

which may be read as:

(third '(a b c)) expands to (car (cdr (cdr '(a b c)))); the result of evaluating the expression is c.

Often, as in this case, an example looks better if the @expansion{} and @result{} commands are indented five spaces.

14.3 ⊣: Indicating Printed Output

Sometimes an expression will print output during its execution. You can indicate the printed output with the @print{} command.

The @print{} command is displayed as '-|' in Info and as '⊣' in the printed output.

In the following example, the printed text is indicated with '⊣', and the value of the expression follows on the last line.

```
(progn (print 'foo) (print 'bar))
    ⊣ foo
    ⊣ bar
    ⇒ bar
```

In a Texinfo source file, this example is written as follows:

```
@lisp
(progn (print 'foo) (print 'bar))
     @print{} foo
     @print{} bar
     @result{} bar
@end lisp
```

14.4 error : Indicating an Error Message

A piece of code may cause an error when you evaluate it. You can designate the error message with the @error{} command.

The @error{} command is displayed as 'error-->' in Info and as ' error ' in the printed output.

Thus,

```
@lisp
(+ 23 'x)
@error{} Wrong type argument: integer-or-marker-p, x
```

Chapter 14: Glyphs for Examples   121

    @end lisp
produces
    (+ 23 'x)
    `error` Wrong type argument: integer-or-marker-p, x
This indicates that the following error message is printed when you evaluate
the expression:
    Wrong type argument: integer-or-marker-p, x
    Note that '`error`' itself is not part of the error message.

14.5 ≡ : Indicating Equivalence

Sometimes two expressions produce identical results. You can indicate
the exact equivalence of two forms with the @equiv{} command.

The @equiv{} command is displayed as '==' in Info and as '≡' in the
printed output.

Thus,
    @lisp
    (make-sparse-keymap) @equiv{} (list 'keymap)
    @end lisp
produces
    (make-sparse-keymap) ≡ (list 'keymap)
This indicates that evaluating (make-sparse-keymap) produces identical
results to evaluating (list 'keymap).

14.6 Indicating Point in a Buffer

Sometimes you need to show an example of text in an Emacs buffer. In
such examples, the convention is to include the entire contents of the buffer
in question between two lines of dashes containing the buffer name.

You can use the '@point{}' command to show the location of point in
the text in the buffer. (The symbol for point, of course, is not part of the
text in the buffer; it indicates the place *between* two characters where point
is located.)

The @point{} command is displayed as '-!-' in Info and as '⋆' in the
printed output.

The following example shows the contents of buffer 'foo' before and after
evaluating a Lisp command to insert the word changed.

```
---------- Buffer: foo ----------
This is the ⋆contents of foo.
---------- Buffer: foo ----------

(insert "changed ")
     ⇒ nil
---------- Buffer: foo ----------
This is the changed ⋆contents of foo.
---------- Buffer: foo ----------
```

In a Texinfo source file, the example is written like this:

```
@example
---------- Buffer: foo ----------
This is the @point{}contents of foo.
---------- Buffer: foo ----------

(insert "changed ")
     @result{} nil
---------- Buffer: foo ----------
This is the changed @point{}contents of foo.
---------- Buffer: foo ----------
@end example
```

15 Making and Preventing Breaks

Usually, a Texinfo file is processed both by TeX and by one of the Info formatting commands. Line, paragraph, or page breaks sometimes occur in the 'wrong' place in one or other form of output. You must ensure that text looks right both in the printed manual and in the Info file.

For example, in a printed manual, page breaks may occur awkwardly in the middle of an example; to prevent this, you can hold text together using a grouping command that keeps the text from being split across two pages. Conversely, you may want to force a page break where none would occur normally. Fortunately, problems like these do not often arise. When they do, use the break, break prevention, or pagination commands.

The break commands create line and paragraph breaks:

@*   Force a line break.

@sp *n*   Skip *n* blank lines.

The line-break-prevention command holds text together all on one line:

@w{*text*} Prevent *text* from being split and hyphenated across two lines.

The pagination commands apply only to printed output, since Info files do not have pages.

@page   Start a new page in the printed manual.

@group   Hold text together that must appear on one printed page.

@need *mils*
            Start a new printed page if not enough space on this one.

15.1 @*: Generate Line Breaks

The @* command forces a line break in both the printed manual and in Info.

For example,

    This line @* is broken @*in two places.

produces

    This line
     is broken
    in two places.

(Note that the space after the first @* command is faithfully carried down to the next line.)

The @* command is often used in a file's copyright page:

```
This is edition 2.0 of the Texinfo documentation,@*
and is for ...
```

In this case, the @* command keeps TeX from stretching the line across the whole page in an ugly manner.

Please note: Do not write braces after an @* command; they are not needed.

Do not write an @refill command at the end of a paragraph containing an @* command; it will cause the paragraph to be refilled after the line break occurs, negating the effect of the line break.

15.2 @w{text}: Prevent Line Breaks

@w{text} outputs text and prohibits line breaks within text.

You can use the @w command to prevent TeX from automatically hyphenating a long name or phrase that accidentally falls near the end of a line.

```
You can copy GNU software from @w{@file{prep.ai.mit.edu}}.
```

produces

You can copy GNU software from 'prep.ai.mit.edu'.

In the Texinfo file, you must write the @w command and its argument (all the affected text) all on one line.

Caution: Do not write an @refill command at the end of a paragraph containing an @w command; it will cause the paragraph to be refilled and may thereby negate the effect of the @w command.

15.3 @sp n: Insert Blank Lines

A line beginning with and containing only @sp n generates n blank lines of space in both the printed manual and the Info file. @sp also forces a paragraph break. For example,

```
@sp 2
```

generates two blank lines.

The @sp command is most often used in the title page.

15.4 @page: Start a New Page

A line containing only @page starts a new page in a printed manual. The command has no effect on Info files since they are not paginated. An @page

Chapter 15: Making and Preventing Breaks   125

command is often used in the `@titlepage` section of a Texinfo file to start the copyright page.

15.5 @group: Prevent Page Breaks

The `@group` command (on a line by itself) is used inside an `@example` or similar construct to begin an unsplittable vertical group, which will appear entirely on one page in the printed output. The group is terminated by a line containing only `@end group`. These two lines produce no output of their own, and in the Info file output they have no effect at all.

Although `@group` would make sense conceptually in a wide variety of contexts, its current implementation works reliably only within `@example` and variants, and within `@display`, `@format`, `@flushleft` and `@flushright`. See Chapter 10 [Quotations and Examples], page 91. (What all these commands have in common is that each line of input produces a line of output.) In other contexts, `@group` can cause anomalous vertical spacing.

This formatting requirement means that you should write:

```
@example
@group
...
@end group
@end example
```

with the `@group` and `@end group` commands inside the `@example` and `@end example` commands.

The `@group` command is most often used to hold an example together on one page. In this Texinfo manual, more than 100 examples contain text that is enclosed between `@group` and `@end group`.

If you forget to end a group, you may get strange and unfathomable error messages when you run TeX. This is because TeX keeps trying to put the rest of the Texinfo file onto the one page and does not start to generate error messages until it has processed considerable text. It is a good rule of thumb to look for a missing `@end group` if you get incomprehensible error messages in TeX.

15.6 @need *mils*: Prevent Page Breaks

A line containing only `@need` *n* starts a new page in a printed manual if fewer than *n* mils (thousandths of an inch) remain on the current page. Do not use braces around the argument *n*. The `@need` command has no effect on Info files since they are not paginated.

This paragraph is preceded by an **@need** command that tells TeX to start a new page if fewer than 800 mils (eight-tenths inch) remain on the page. It looks like this:

```
@need 800
This paragraph is preceded by ...
```

The **@need** command is useful for preventing orphans (single lines at the bottoms of printed pages).

16 Definition Commands

The `@deffn` command and the other *definition commands* enable you to describe functions, variables, macros, commands, user options, special forms and other such artifacts in a uniform format.

In the Info file, a definition causes the entity category—'Function', 'Variable', or whatever—to appear at the beginning of the first line of the definition, followed by the entity's name and arguments. In the printed manual, the command causes TeX to print the entity's name and its arguments on the left margin and print the category next to the right margin. In both output formats, the body of the definition is indented. Also, the name of the entity is entered into the appropriate index: `@deffn` enters the name into the index of functions, `@defvr` enters it into the index of variables, and so on.

A manual need not and should not contain more than one definition for a given name. An appendix containing a summary should use `@table` rather than the definition commands.

16.1 The Template for a Definition

The `@deffn` command is used for definitions of entities that resemble functions. To write a definition using the `@deffn` command, write the `@deffn` command at the beginning of a line and follow it on the same line by the category of the entity, the name of the entity itself, and its arguments (if any). Then write the body of the definition on succeeding lines. (You may embed examples in the body.) Finally, end the definition with an `@end deffn` command written on a line of its own. (The other definition commands follow the same format.)

The template for a definition looks like this:

> `@deffn` *category name arguments...*
> *body-of-definition*
> `@end deffn`

For example,

> `@deffn Command forward-word count`
> `This command moves point forward @var{count} words`
> `(or backward if @var{count} is negative). ...`
> `@end deffn`

produces

> **forward-word** *count*   Command
>   This function moves point forward *count* words (or backward if *count* is negative). ...

Capitalize the category name like a title. If the name of the category contains spaces, as in the phrase 'Interactive Command', write braces around it. For example:

```
@deffn {Interactive Command} isearch-forward
 ...
@end deffn
```

Otherwise, the second word will be mistaken for the name of the entity.

Some of the definition commands are more general than others. The `@deffn` command, for example, is the general definition command for functions and the like—for entities that may take arguments. When you use this command, you specify the category to which the entity belongs. The `@deffn` command possesses three predefined, specialized variations, `@defun`, `@defmac`, and `@defspec`, that specify the category for you: "Function", "Macro", and "Special Form" respectively. The `@defvr` command also is accompanied by several predefined, specialized variations for describing particular kinds of variables.

The template for a specialized definition, such as `@defun`, is similar to the template for a generalized definition, except that you do not need to specify the category:

```
@defun name arguments...
body-of-definition
@end defun
```

Thus,

```
@defun buffer-end flag
This function returns @code{(point-min)} if @var{flag}
is less than 1, @code{(point-max)} otherwise.
 ...
@end defun
```

produces

> **buffer-end** *flag*   *Function*
>   This function returns `(point-min)` if *flag* is less than 1, `(point-max)` otherwise. ...

See Section 16.6 [A Sample Function Definition], page 139, for a more detailed example of a function definition, including the use of `@example` inside the definition.

The other specialized commands work like `@defun`.

16.2 Optional and Repeated Arguments

Some entities take optional or repeated arguments, which may be specified by a distinctive glyph that uses square brackets and ellipses. For example, a special form often breaks its argument list into separate arguments in more complicated ways than a straightforward function.

An argument enclosed within square brackets is optional. Thus, the phrase '[*optional-arg*]' means that *optional-arg* is optional. An argument followed by an ellipsis is optional and may be repeated more than once. Thus, '*repeated-args*...' stands for zero or more arguments. Parentheses are used when several arguments are grouped into additional levels of list structure in Lisp.

Here is the `@defspec` line of an example of an imaginary special form:

> **foobar** (*var* [*from to* [*inc*]]) *body*...   Special Form

In this example, the arguments *from* and *to* are optional, but must both be present or both absent. If they are present, *inc* may optionally be specified as well. These arguments are grouped with the argument *var* into a list, to distinguish them from *body*, which includes all remaining elements of the form.

In a Texinfo source file, this `@defspec` line is written like this (except it would not be split over two lines, as it is in this example).

```
@defspec foobar (@var{var} [@var{from} @var{to}
    [@var{inc}]]) @var{body}@dots{}
```

The function is listed in the Command and Variable Index under '`foobar`'.

16.3 Two or More 'First' Lines

To create two or more 'first' or header lines for a definition, follow the first `@deffn` line by a line beginning with `@deffnx`. The `@deffnx` command works exactly like `@deffn` except that it does not generate extra vertical white space between it and the preceding line.

For example,

```
@deffn {Interactive Command} isearch-forward
@deffnx {Interactive Command} isearch-backward
These two search commands are similar except ...
@end deffn
```

produces

> **isearch-forward**   Interactive Command
> **isearch-backward**   Interactive Command
> These two search commands are similar except ...

Each of the other definition commands has an 'x' form: `@defunx`, `@defvrx`, `@deftypefunx`, etc.

The 'x' forms work just like `@itemx`; see Section 11.3.2 [`@itemx`], page 104.

16.4 The Definition Commands

Texinfo provides more than a dozen definition commands, all of which are described in this section.

The definition commands automatically enter the name of the entity in the appropriate index: for example, `@deffn`, `@defun`, and `@defmac` enter function names in the index of functions; `@defvr` and `@defvar` enter variable names in the index of variables.

Although the examples that follow mostly illustrate Lisp, the commands can be used for other programming languages.

16.4.1 Functions and Similar Entities

This section describes the commands for describing functions and similar entities:

`@deffn` *category name arguments...*
> The `@deffn` command is the general definition command for functions, interactive commands, and similar entities that may take arguments. You must choose a term to describe the category of entity being defined; for example, "Function" could be used if the entity is a function. The `@deffn` command is written at the beginning of a line and is followed on the same line by the category of entity being described, the name of this particular entity, and its arguments, if any. Terminate the definition with `@end deffn` on a line of its own.
>
> For example, here is a definition:
>
> ```
> @deffn Command forward-char nchars
> Move point forward @var{nchars} characters.
> @end deffn
> ```
>
> This shows a rather terse definition for a "command" named `forward-char` with one argument, *nchars*.
>
> `@deffn` prints argument names such as *nchars* in italics or upper case, as if `@var` had been used, because we think of these names as metasyntactic variables—they stand for the actual argument values. Within the text of the description, write an argument name explicitly with `@var` to refer to the value of the argument. In the example above, we used '`@var{nchars}`' in this way.
>
> The template for `@deffn` is:

Chapter 16: Definition Commands

>   @deffn category name arguments...
>   body-of-definition
>   @end deffn

@defun name arguments...
: The @defun command is the definition command for functions. @defun is equivalent to '@deffn Function ...'.

    For example,

    >   @defun set symbol new-value
    >   Change the value of the symbol @var{symbol}
    >   to @var{new-value}.
    >   @end defun

    shows a rather terse definition for a function set whose arguments are *symbol* and *new-value*. The argument names on the @defun line automatically appear in italics or upper case as if they were enclosed in @var. Terminate the definition with @end defun on a line of its own.

    The template is:

    >   @defun function-name arguments...
    >   body-of-definition
    >   @end defun

    @defun creates an entry in the index of functions.

@defmac name arguments...
: The @defmac command is the definition command for macros. @defmac is equivalent to '@deffn Macro ...' and works like @defun.

@defspec name arguments...
: The @defspec command is the definition command for special forms. (In Lisp, a special form is an entity much like a function.) @defspec is equivalent to '@deffn {Special Form} ...' and works like @defun.

16.4.2 Variables and Similar Entities

Here are the commands for defining variables and similar entities:

@defvr category name
: The @defvr command is a general definition command for something like a variable—an entity that records a value. You must choose a term to describe the category of entity being defined; for example, "Variable" could be used if the entity is a variable. Write the @defvr command at the beginning of a line and followed it on the same line by the category of the entity and the name of the entity.

Capitalize the category name like a title. If the name of the
category contains spaces, as in the name 'User Option', write
braces around it. Otherwise, the second word will be mistaken
for the name of the entity, for example:

```
@defvr {User Option} fill-column
This buffer-local variable specifies
the maximum width of filled lines.
...
@end defvr
```

Terminate the definition with `@end defvr` on a line of its own.
The template is:

```
@defvr category name
body-of-definition
@end defvr
```

`@defvr` creates an entry in the index of variables for *name*.

`@defvar` *name*

The `@defvar` command is the definition command for variables.
`@defvar` is equivalent to '`@defvr Variable ...`'.
For example:

```
@defvar kill-ring
...
@end defvar
```

The template is:

```
@defvar name
body-of-definition
@end defvar
```

`@defvar` creates an entry in the index of variables for *name*.

`@defopt` *name*

The `@defopt` command is the definition command for user options. `@defopt` is equivalent to '`@defvr {User Option} ...`' and works like `@defvar`.

16.4.3 Functions in Typed Languages

The `@deftypefn` command and its variations are for describing functions in C or any other language in which you must declare types of variables and functions.

`@deftypefn` *category data-type name arguments...*

The `@deftypefn` command is the general definition command
for functions and similar entities that may take arguments and

Chapter 16: Definition Commands

that are typed. The `@deftypefn` command is written at the beginning of a line and is followed on the same line by the category of entity being described, the type of the returned value, the name of this particular entity, and its arguments, if any.

For example,

```
@deftypefn {Library Function} int foobar
    (int @var{foo}, float @var{bar})
...
@end deftypefn
```

(where the text before the "...", shown above as two lines, would actually be a single line in a real Texinfo file) produces the following in Info:

```
-- Library Function: int foobar (int FOO, float BAR)
...
```

In a printed manual, it produces:

> **int foobar** (int *foo*, float *bar*)   Library Function
> ...

This means that `foobar` is a "library function" that returns an `int`, and its arguments are *foo* (an `int`) and *bar* (a `float`).

The argument names that you write in `@deftypefn` are not subject to an implicit `@var`—since the actual names of the arguments in `@deftypefn` are typically scattered among data type names and keywords, Texinfo cannot find them without help. Instead, you must write `@var` explicitly around the argument names. In the example above, the argument names are 'foo' and 'bar'.

The template for `@deftypefn` is:

```
@deftypefn category data-type name arguments ...
body-of-description
@end deftypefn
```

Note that if the *category* or *data type* is more than one word then it must be enclosed in braces to make it a single argument.

If you are describing a procedure in a language that has packages, such as Ada, you might consider using `@deftypefn` in a manner somewhat contrary to the convention described in the preceding paragraphs.

For example:

```
@deftypefn stacks private push
          (@var{s}:in out stack;
          @var{n}:in integer)
...
@end deftypefn
```

(The `@deftypefn` arguments are shown split into three lines, but would be a single line in a real Texinfo file.)

In this instance, the procedure is classified as belonging to the package `stacks` rather than classified as a 'procedure' and its data type is described as `private`. (The name of the procedure is `push`, and its arguments are *s* and *n*.)

`@deftypefn` creates an entry in the index of functions for *name*.

`@deftypefun` *data-type name arguments*...

The `@deftypefun` command is the specialized definition command for functions in typed languages. The command is equivalent to '`@deftypefn Function ...`'.

Thus,

```
@deftypefun int foobar (int @var{foo}, float @var{bar})
...
@end deftypefun
```

produces the following in Info:

```
-- Function: int foobar (int FOO, float BAR)
...
```

and the following in a printed manual:

int **foobar** (int *foo*, float *bar*)   Function
...

The template is:

```
@deftypefun type name arguments...
body-of-description
@end deftypefun
```

`@deftypefun` creates an entry in the index of functions for *name*.

16.4.4 Variables in Typed Languages

Variables in typed languages are handled in a manner similar to functions in typed languages. See Section 16.4.3 [Typed Functions], page 132. The general definition command `@deftypevr` corresponds to `@deftypefn` and the specialized definition command `@deftypevar` corresponds to `@deftypefun`.

`@deftypevr` *category data-type name*

The `@deftypevr` command is the general definition command for something like a variable in a typed language—an entity

Chapter 16: Definition Commands   135

that records a value. You must choose a term to describe the
category of the entity being defined; for example, "Variable"
could be used if the entity is a variable.

The `@deftypevr` command is written at the beginning of a line
and is followed on the same line by the category of the entity
being described, the data type, and the name of this particular
entity.

For example:

```
@deftypevr {Global Flag} int enable
...
@end deftypevr
```

produces the following in Info:

```
-- Global Flag: int enable
...
```

and the following in a printed manual:

> **int enable**   Global Flag
> ...

The template is:

```
@deftypevr category data-type name
body-of-description
@end deftypevr
```

`@deftypevr` creates an entry in the index of variables for *name*.

`@deftypevar` *data-type name*

The `@deftypevar` command is the specialized definition command for variables in typed languages. `@deftypevar` is equivalent to '`@deftypevr Variable ...`'.

For example:

```
@deftypevar int fubar
...
@end deftypevar
```

produces the following in Info:

```
-- Variable: int fubar
...
```

and the following in a printed manual:

> **int fubar**   Variable
> ...

The template is:

> `@deftypevar` *data-type name*
> *body-of-description*
> `@end deftypevar`

`@deftypevar` creates an entry in the index of variables for *name*.

16.4.5 Object-Oriented Programming

Here are the commands for formatting descriptions about abstract objects, such as are used in object-oriented programming. A class is a defined type of abstract object. An instance of a class is a particular object that has the type of the class. An instance variable is a variable that belongs to the class but for which each instance has its own value.

In a definition, if the name of a class is truly a name defined in the programming system for a class, then you should write an `@code` around it. Otherwise, it is printed in the usual text font.

`@defcv` *category class name*

> The `@defcv` command is the general definition command for variables associated with classes in object-oriented programming. The `@defcv` command is followed by three arguments: the category of thing being defined, the class to which it belongs, and its name. Thus,
>
> > `@defcv {Class Option} Window border-pattern`
> > `...`
> > `@end defcv`
>
> illustrates how you would write the first line of a definition of the `border-pattern` class option of the class `Window`.
>
> The template is
>
> > `@defcv` *category class name*
> > `...`
> > `@end defcv`
>
> `@defcv` creates an entry in the index of variables.

`@defivar` *class name*

> The `@defivar` command is the definition command for instance variables in object-oriented programming. `@defivar` is equivalent to '`@defcv {Instance Variable} ...`'
>
> The template is:
>
> > `@defivar` *class instance-variable-name*
> > *body-of-definition*
> > `@end defivar`

Chapter 16: Definition Commands

@defivar creates an entry in the index of variables.

@defop *category class name arguments...*

The **@defop** command is the general definition command for entities that may resemble methods in object-oriented programming. These entities take arguments, as functions do, but are associated with particular classes of objects.

For example, some systems have constructs called *wrappers* that are associated with classes as methods are, but that act more like macros than like functions. You could use **@defop Wrapper** to describe one of these.

Sometimes it is useful to distinguish methods and *operations*. You can think of an operation as the specification for a method. Thus, a window system might specify that all window classes have a method named **expose**; we would say that this window system defines an **expose** operation on windows in general. Typically, the operation has a name and also specifies the pattern of arguments; all methods that implement the operation must accept the same arguments, since applications that use the operation do so without knowing which method will implement it.

Often it makes more sense to document operations than methods. For example, window application developers need to know about the **expose** operation, but need not be concerned with whether a given class of windows has its own method to implement this operation. To describe this operation, you would write:

> **@defop Operation windows expose**

The **@defop** command is written at the beginning of a line and is followed on the same line by the overall name of the category of operation, the name of the class of the operation, the name of the operation, and its arguments, if any.

The template is:

> **@defop** *category class name arguments...*
> *body-of-definition*
> **@end defop**

@defop creates an entry, such as '**expose** on **windows**', in the index of functions.

@defmethod *class name arguments...*

The **@defmethod** command is the definition command for methods in object-oriented programming. A method is a kind of function that implements an operation for a particular class of objects and its subclasses. In the Lisp Machine, methods actually were functions, but they were usually defined with `defmethod`.

`@defmethod` is equivalent to '`@defop Method` ...'. The command is written at the beginning of a line and is followed by the name of the class of the method, the name of the method, and its arguments, if any.

For example,

```
@defmethod bar-class bar-method argument
...
@end defmethod
```

illustrates the definition for a method called `bar-method` of the class `bar-class`. The method takes an argument.

The template is:

```
@defmethod class method-name arguments...
body-of-definition
@end defmethod
```

`@defmethod` creates an entry, such as '`bar-method` on `bar-class`', in the index of functions.

16.4.6 Data Types

Here is the command for data types:

`@deftp` *category name attributes...*

> The `@deftp` command is the generic definition command for data types. The command is written at the beginning of a line and is followed on the same line by the category, by the name of the type (which is a word like `int` or `float`), and then by names of attributes of objects of that type. Thus, you could use this command for describing `int` or `float`, in which case you could use `data type` as the category. (A data type is a category of certain objects for purposes of deciding which operations can be performed on them.)
>
> In Lisp, for example, *pair* names a particular data type, and an object of that type has two slots called the CAR and the CDR. Here is how you would write the first line of a definition of `pair`.
>
> ```
> @deftp {Data type} pair car cdr
> ...
> @end deftp
> ```

The template is:

    @deftp category name-of-type attributes...
    body-of-definition
    @end deftp

`@deftp` creates an entry in the index of data types.

16.5 Conventions for Writing Definitions

When you write a definition using `@deffn`, `@defun`, or one of the other definition commands, please take care to use arguments that indicate the meaning, as with the *count* argument to the `forward-word` function. Also, if the name of an argument contains the name of a type, such as *integer*, take care that the argument actually is of that type.

16.6 A Sample Function Definition

A function definition uses the `@defun` and `@end defun` commands. The name of the function follows immediately after the `@defun` command and it is followed, on the same line, by the parameter list.

Here is a definition from *The GNU Emacs Lisp Reference Manual*. (See section "Calling Functions" in *The GNU Emacs Lisp Reference Manual*.)

> **apply** *function* &rest *arguments*   Function
>
> > `apply` calls *function* with *arguments*, just like `funcall` but with one difference: the last of *arguments* is a list of arguments to give to *function*, rather than a single argument. We also say that this list is *appended* to the other arguments.
> >
> > `apply` returns the result of calling *function*. As with `funcall`, *function* must either be a Lisp function or a primitive function; special forms and macros do not make sense in `apply`.
>
> >   (setq f 'list)
> >   ⇒ list
> >   (apply f 'x 'y 'z)
> >   error Wrong type argument: listp, z
> >   (apply '+ 1 2 '(3 4))
> >   ⇒ 10
> >   (apply '+ '(1 2 3 4))
> >   ⇒ 10
> >
> >   (apply 'append '((a b c) nil (x y z) nil))
> >   ⇒ (a b c x y z)

> An interesting example of using `apply` is found in the description of `mapcar`.

In the Texinfo source file, this example looks like this:

```
@defun apply function &rest arguments

@code{apply} calls @var{function} with
@var{arguments}, just like @code{funcall} but with one
difference: the last of @var{arguments} is a list of
arguments to give to @var{function}, rather than a single
argument.  We also say that this list is @dfn{appended}
to the other arguments.

@code{apply} returns the result of calling
@var{function}.  As with @code{funcall},
@var{function} must either be a Lisp function or a
primitive function; special forms and macros do not make
sense in @code{apply}.

@example
(setq f 'list)
     @result{} list
(apply f 'x 'y 'z)
@error{} Wrong type argument: listp, z
(apply '+ 1 2 '(3 4))
     @result{} 10
(apply '+ '(1 2 3 4))
     @result{} 10

(apply 'append '((a b c) nil (x y z) nil))
     @result{} (a b c x y z)
@end example

An interesting example of using @code{apply} is found
in the description of @code{mapcar}.@refill
@end defun
```

In this manual, this function is listed in the Command and Variable Index under `apply`.

Ordinary variables and user options are described using a format like that for functions except that variables do not take arguments.

17 Footnotes

A *footnote* is for a reference that documents or elucidates the primary text.[1]

In Texinfo, footnotes are created with the `@footnote` command. This command is followed immediately by a left brace, then by the text of the footnote, and then by a terminating right brace. The template is:

> `@footnote{`*text*`}`

Footnotes may be of any length, but are usually short.

For example, this clause is followed by a sample footnote[2]; in the Texinfo source, it looks like this:

```
...a sample footnote @footnote{Here is the sample
footnote.}; in the Texinfo source...
```

In a printed manual or book, the reference mark for a footnote is a small, superscripted number; the text of the footnote is written at the bottom of the page, below a horizontal line.

In Info, the reference mark for a footnote is a pair of parentheses with the footnote number between them, like this: '(1)'.

Info has two footnote styles, which determine where the text of the footnote is located:

- In the 'End' node style, all the footnotes for a single node are placed at the end of that node. The footnotes are separated from the rest of the node by a line of dashes with the word '**Footnotes**' within it. Each footnote begins with an '(*n*)' reference mark.

  Here is an example of a single footnote in the end of node style:

  ```
  --------- Footnotes ---------

  (1)   Here is a sample footnote.
  ```

- In the 'Separate' node style, all the footnotes for a single node are placed in an automatically constructed node of their own. In this style, a "footnote reference" follows each '(*n*)' reference mark in the body of the node. The footnote reference is actually a cross reference which you use to reach the footnote node.

  The name of the node containing the footnotes is constructed by appending '-Footnotes' to the name of the node that contains the footnotes. (Consequently, the footnotes' node for the '**Footnotes**' node is

---

[1] A footnote should complement or expand upon the primary text, but a reader should not need to read a footnote to understand the primary text. For a thorough discussion of footnotes, see *The Chicago Manual of Style*, which is published by the University of Chicago Press.

[2] Here is the sample footnote.

'Footnotes-Footnotes'!) The footnotes' node has an 'Up' node pointer that leads back to its parent node.

Here is how the first footnote in this manual looks after being formatted for Info in the separate node style:

```
File: texinfo.info  Node: Overview-Footnotes, Up: Overview

(1) Note that the first syllable of "Texinfo" is
pronounced like "speck", not "hex". ...
```

A Texinfo file may be formatted into an Info file with either footnote style.

Use the `@footnotestyle` command to specify an Info file's footnote style. Write this command at the beginning of a line followed by an argument, either 'end' for the end node style or '**separate**' for the separate node style.

For example,

`@footnotestyle end`

or

`@footnotestyle separate`

Write an `@footnotestyle` command before or shortly after the end-of-header line at the beginning of a Texinfo file. (If you include the `@footnotestyle` command between the start-of-header and end-of-header lines, the region formatting commands will format footnotes as specified.)

If you do not specify a footnote style, the formatting commands use their default style. Currently, `texinfo-format-buffer` and `texinfo-format-region` use the 'separate' style and `makeinfo` uses the 'end' style.

This chapter contains two footnotes.

18 Conditionally Visible Text

Sometimes it is good to use different text for a printed manual and its corresponding Info file. In this case, you can use the *conditional commands* to specify which text is for the printed manual and which is for the Info file.

`@ifinfo` begins segments of text that should be ignored by TeX when it typesets the printed manual. The segment of text appears only in the Info file. The `@ifinfo` command should appear on a line by itself; end the Info-only text with a line containing `@end ifinfo` by itself. At the beginning of a Texinfo file, the Info permissions are contained within a region marked by `@ifinfo` and `@end ifinfo`. (See Section 3.3 [Info Summary and Permissions], page 37.)

The `@iftex` and `@end iftex` commands are similar to the `@ifinfo` and `@end ifinfo` commands, except that they specify text that will appear in the printed manual but not in the Info file.

For example,

```
@iftex
This text will appear only in the printed manual.
@end iftex

@ifinfo
However, this text will appear only in Info.
@end ifinfo
```

The preceding example produces the following line:

This text will appear only in the printed manual.

Note how you only see one of the two lines, depending on whether you are reading the Info version or the printed version of this manual.

The `@titlepage` command is a special variant of `@iftex` that is used for making the title and copyright pages of the printed manual. (See Section 3.4.1 [`@titlepage`], page 38.)

18.1 Using Ordinary TeX Commands

Inside a region delineated by `@iftex` and `@end iftex`, you can embed some PlainTeX commands. Info will ignore these commands since they are only in that part of the file which is seen by TeX. You can write the TeX commands as you would write them in a normal TeX file, except that you must replace the '\' used by TeX with an '@'. For example, in the `@titlepage` section of a Texinfo file, you can use the TeX command `@vskip` to format the copyright page. (The `@titlepage` command causes Info to ignore the region automatically, as it does with the `@iftex` command.)

However, many features of PlainTeX will not work, as they are overridden by features of Texinfo.

You can enter PlainTeX completely, and use '\' in the TeX commands, by delineating a region with the `@tex` and `@end tex` commands. (The `@tex` command also causes Info to ignore the region, like the `@iftex` command.)

For example, here is a mathematical expression written in PlainTeX:

```
@tex
$$ \chi^2 = \sum_{i=1}^N
         \left (y_i - (a + b x_i)
         \over \sigma_i\right)^2 $$
@end tex
```

The output of this example will appear only in a printed manual. If you are reading this in Info, you will not see anything after this paragraph. In a printed manual, the above expression looks like this:

$$\chi^2 = \sum_{i=1}^N \left(\frac{y_i - (a + bx_i)}{\sigma_i} \right)^2$$

18.2 `@set`, `@clear`, and `@value`

You can direct the Texinfo formatting commands to format or ignore parts of a Texinfo file with the `@set`, `@clear`, `@ifset`, and `@ifclear` commands.

In addition, you can use the `@set` *flag* command to set the value of *flag* to a string of characters; and use `@value{`*flag*`}` to insert that string. You can use `@set`, for example, to set a date and use `@value` to insert the date in several places in the Texinfo file.

18.2.1 `@ifset` and `@ifclear`

When a *flag* is set, the Texinfo formatting commands format text between subsequent pairs of `@ifset` *flag* and `@end ifset` commands. When the *flag* is cleared, the Texinfo formatting commands do *not* format the text.

Use the `@set` *flag* command to turn on, or *set*, a *flag*; a *flag* can be any single word. The format for the command looks like this:

```
@set flag
```

Write the conditionally formatted text between `@ifset` *flag* and `@end ifset` commands, like this:

```
@ifset flag
conditional-text
@end ifset
```

Chapter 18: Conditionally Visible Text

For example, you can create one document that has two variants, such as a manual for a 'large' and 'small' model:

```
You can use this machine to dig up shrubs
without hurting them.

@set large

@ifset large
It can also dig up fully grown trees.
@end ifset

Remember to replant promptly ...
```

In the example, the formatting commands will format the text between `@ifset large` and `@end ifset` because the `large` flag is set.

Use the `@clear` *flag* command to turn off, or *clear*, a flag. Clearing a flag is the opposite of setting a flag. The command looks like this:

`@clear` *flag*

Write the command on a line of its own.

When *flag* is cleared, the Texinfo formatting commands do *not* format the text between `@ifset` *flag* and `@end ifset`; that text is ignored and does not appear in either printed or Info output.

For example, if you clear the flag of the preceding example by writing an `@clear large` command after the `@set large` command (but before the conditional text), then the Texinfo formatting commands ignore the text between the `@ifset large` and `@end ifset` commands. In the formatted output, that text does not appear; in both printed and Info output, you see only the lines that say, "You can use this machine to dig up shrubs without hurting them. Remember to replant promptly ...".

If a flag is cleared with an `@clear` *flag* command, then the formatting commands format text between subsequent pairs of `@ifclear` and `@end ifclear` commands. But if the flag is set with `@set` *flag*, then the formatting commands do *not* format text between an `@ifclear` and an `@end ifclear` command; rather, they ignore that text. An `@ifclear` command looks like this:

`@ifclear` *flag*

In brief, the commands are:

`@set` *flag*   Tell the Texinfo formatting commands that *flag* is set.

`@clear` *flag*

        Tell the Texinfo formatting commands that *flag* is cleared.

@ifset *flag*
> If *flag* is set, tell the Texinfo formatting commands to format the text up to the following `@end ifset` command.
>
> If *flag* is cleared, tell the Texinfo formatting commands to ignore text up to the following `@end ifset` command.

@ifclear *flag*
> If *flag* is set, tell the Texinfo formatting commands to ignore the text up to the following `@end ifclear` command.
>
> If *flag* is cleared, tell the Texinfo formatting commands to format the text up to the following `@end ifclear` command.

18.2.2 @value

You can use the `@set` command to specify a value for a flag, which is expanded by the `@value` command. The value is a string a characters.

Write the `@set` command like this:

`@set foo This is a string.`

This sets the value of `foo` to "This is a string."

The Texinfo formatters replace an `@value{`*flag*`}` command with the string to which *flag* is set.

Thus, when `foo` is set as shown above, the Texinfo formatters convert

`@value{foo}`

to

`This is a string.`

You can write an `@value` command within a paragraph; but you must write an `@set` command on a line of its own.

If you write the `@set` command like this:

`@set foo`

without specifying a string, the value of `foo` is an empty string.

If you clear a previously set flag with an `@clear` *flag* command, a subsequent `@value{flag}` command is invalid and the string is replaced with an error message that says '`{No value for "`*flag*`"}`'.

For example, if you set `foo` as follows:

`@set how-much very, very, very`

then the formatters transform

`It is a @value{how-much} wet day.`

into

`It is a very, very, very wet day.`

If you write

Chapter 18: Conditionally Visible Text

```
@clear how-much
```
then the formatters transform
```
    It is a @value{how-much} wet day.
```
into
```
    It is a {No value for "how-much"} wet day.
```

18.2.3 @value Example

You can use the `@value` command to limit the number of places you need to change when you record an update to a manual. Here is how it is done in *The GNU Make Manual*:
Set the flags:
```
@set EDITION 0.35 Beta
@set VERSION 3.63 Beta
@set UPDATED 14 August 1992
@set UPDATE-MONTH August 1992
```
Write text for the first `@ifinfo` section, for people reading the Texinfo file:
```
This is Edition @value{EDITION},
last updated @value{UPDATED},
of @cite{The GNU Make Manual},
for @code{make}, Version @value{VERSION}.
```
Write text for the title page, for people reading the printed manual:
```
@title GNU Make
@subtitle A Program for Directing Recompilation
@subtitle Edition @value{EDITION}, ...
@subtitle @value{UPDATE-MONTH}
```
(On a printed cover, a date listing the month and the year looks less fussy than a date listing the day as well as the month and year.)

Write text for the Top node, for people reading the Info file:
```
This is Edition @value{EDITION}
of the @cite{GNU Make Manual},
last updated @value{UPDATED}
for @code{make} Version @value{VERSION}.
```
After you format the manual, the text in the first `@ifinfo` section looks like this:
```
This is Edition 0.35 Beta, last updated 14 August 1992,
of 'The GNU Make Manual', for 'make', Version 3.63 Beta.
```
When you update the manual, change only the values of the flags; you do not need to rewrite the three sections.

19 Format and Print Hardcopy

There are three major shell commands for making a printed manual from a Texinfo file: one for converting the Texinfo file into a file that will be printed, a second for sorting indices, and a third for printing the formatted document. When you use the shell commands, you can either work directly in the operating system shell or work within a shell inside GNU Emacs.

If you are using GNU Emacs, you can use commands provided by Texinfo mode instead of shell commands. In addition to the three commands to format a file, sort the indices, and print the result, Texinfo mode offers key bindings for commands to recenter the output buffer, show the print queue, and delete a job from the print queue.

The typesetting program called TeX is used for formatting a Texinfo file. TeX is a very powerful typesetting program and, if used right, does an exceptionally good job. See Appendix J [How to Obtain TeX], page 227, for information on how to obtain TeX.

The `makeinfo`, `texinfo-format-region`, and `texinfo-format-buffer` commands read the very same @-commands in the Texinfo file as does TeX, but process them differently to make an Info file; see Chapter 20 [Create an Info File], page 159.

19.1 Format using `tex` and `texindex`

Format the Texinfo file with the shell command `tex` followed by the name of the Texinfo file. This command produces a formatted DVI file as well as several auxiliary files containing indices, cross references, etc. The DVI file (for *DeVice Independent* file) can be printed on a wide variety of printers.

The `tex` formatting command itself does not sort the indices; it writes an output file of unsorted index data. This is a misfeature of TeX. (The `texi2dvi` command automatically generates indices; see Section 19.2 [Format using `texi2dvi`], page 150.) To generate a printed index after running the `tex` command, you first need a sorted index to work from. The `texindex` command sorts indices. (The source file 'texindex.c' comes as part of the standard GNU distribution and is usually installed when Emacs is installed.)

The `tex` formatting command outputs unsorted index files under names that obey a standard convention. These names are the name of your main input file to the `tex` formatting command, with everything after the first period thrown away, and the two letter names of indices added at the end. For example, the raw index output files for the input file 'foo.texinfo' would be 'foo.cp', 'foo.vr', 'foo.fn', 'foo.tp', 'foo.pg' and 'foo.ky'. Those are exactly the arguments to give to `texindex`.

Or else, you can use '??' as "wild-cards" and give the command in this form:

```
texindex foo.??
```

This command will run `texindex` on all the unsorted index files, including any that you have defined yourself using `@defindex` or `@defcodeindex`. (You may execute 'texindex foo.??' even if there are similarly named files with two letter extensions that are not index files, such as 'foo.el'. The `texindex` command reports but otherwise ignores such files.)

For each file specified, `texindex` generates a sorted index file whose name is made by appending 's' to the input file name. The `@printindex` command knows to look for a file of that name. `texindex` does not alter the raw index output file.

After you have sorted the indices, you need to rerun the `tex` formatting command on the Texinfo file. This regenerates a formatted DVI file with up-to-date index entries.[1]

To summarize, this is a three step process:

1. Run the `tex` formatting command on the Texinfo file. This generates the formatted DVI file as well as the raw index files with two letter extensions.
2. Run the shell command `texindex` on the raw index files to sort them. This creates the corresponding sorted index files.
3. Rerun the `tex` formatting command on the Texinfo file. This regenerates a formatted DVI file with the index entries in the correct order. This second run also corrects the page numbers for the cross references. (The tables of contents are always correct.)

You need not run `texindex` each time after you run the `tex` formatting. If you do not, on the next run, the `tex` formatting command will use whatever sorted index files happen to exist from the previous use of `texindex`. This is usually OK while you are debugging.

19.2 Format using `texi2dvi`

The `texi2dvi` command is a shell script that automatically runs both `tex` and `texindex` as needed to produce a DVI file with up-to-date, sorted

---

[1] If you use more than one index and have cross references to an index other than the first, you must run `tex` *three times* to get correct output: once to generate raw index data; again (after `texindex`) to output the text of the indices and determine their true page numbers; and a third time to output correct page numbers in cross references to them. However, cross references to indices are rare.

indices. It simplifies the `tex`—`texindex`—`tex` sequence described in the previous section.

The syntax for `texi2dvi` is like this (where '`%`' is the shell prompt):

```
% texi2dvi filename...
```

19.3 Shell Print Using `lpr -d`

You can print a DVI file with the DVI print command. The precise printing command to use depends on your system; '`lpr -d`' is common. The DVI print command may require a file name without any extension or with a '`.dvi`' extension.

The following commands, for example, sort the indices, format, and print the *Bison Manual* (where '`%`' is the shell prompt):

```
% tex bison.texinfo
% texindex bison.??
% tex bison.texinfo
% lpr -d bison.dvi
```

(Remember that the shell commands may be different at your site; but these are commonly used versions.)

Using the `texi2dvi` shell script, you simply need type:

```
% texi2dvi bison.texinfo
% lpr -d bison.dvi
```

19.4 From an Emacs Shell ...

You can give formatting and printing commands from a shell within GNU Emacs. To create a shell within Emacs, type **`M-x shell`**. In this shell, you can format and print the document. See Chapter 19 [Format and Print Hardcopy], page 149, for details.

You can switch to and from the shell buffer while `tex` is running and do other editing. If you are formatting a long document on a slow machine, this can be very convenient.

You can also use `texi2dvi` from an Emacs shell. For example, here is how to use `texi2dvi` to format and print *Using and Porting GNU CC* from a shell within Emacs (where '`%`' is the shell prompt):

```
% texi2dvi gcc.texinfo
% lpr -d gcc.dvi
```

19.5 Formatting and Printing in Texinfo Mode

Texinfo mode provides several predefined key commands for TeX formatting and printing. These include commands for sorting indices, looking at the printer queue, killing the formatting job, and recentering the display of the buffer in which the operations occur.

`C-c C-t C-b`
`M-x texinfo-tex-buffer`
> Run `texi2dvi` on the current buffer.

`C-c C-t C-r`
`M-x texinfo-tex-region`
> Run TeX on the current region.

`C-c C-t C-i`
`M-x texinfo-texindex`
> Sort the indices of a Texinfo file formatted with `texinfo-tex-region`.

`C-c C-t C-p`
`M-x texinfo-tex-print`
> Print a DVI file that was made with `texinfo-tex-region` or `texinfo-tex-buffer`.

`C-c C-t C-q`
`M-x tex-show-print-queue`
> Show the print queue.

`C-c C-t C-d`
`M-x texinfo-delete-from-print-queue`
> Delete a job from the print queue; you will be prompted for the job number shown by a preceding `C-c C-t C-q` command (`texinfo-show-tex-print-queue`).

`C-c C-t C-k`
`M-x tex-kill-job`
> Kill the currently running TeX job started by `texinfo-tex-region` or `texinfo-tex-buffer`, or any other process running in the Texinfo shell buffer.

`C-c C-t C-x`
`M-x texinfo-quit-job`
> Quit a TeX formatting job that has stopped because of an error by sending an X to it. When you do this, TeX preserves a record of what it did in a '.log' file.

`C-c C-t C-l`
`M-x tex-recenter-output-buffer`
> Redisplay the shell buffer in which the TeX printing and formatting commands are run to show its most recent output.

Chapter 19: Format and Print Hardcopy 153

Thus, the usual sequence of commands for formatting a buffer is as follows (with comments to the right):

C-c C-t C-b	Run `texi2dvi` on the buffer.
C-c C-t C-p	Print the DVI file.
C-c C-t C-q	Display the printer queue.

The Texinfo mode TeX formatting commands start a subshell in Emacs called the '`*tex-shell*`'. The `texinfo-tex-command`, `texinfo-texindex-command`, and `tex-dvi-print-command` commands are all run in this shell.

You can watch the commands operate in the '`*tex-shell*`' buffer, and you can switch to and from and use the '`*tex-shell*`' buffer as you would any other shell buffer.

The formatting and print commands depend on the values of several variables. The default values are:

Variable	Default value
`texinfo-texi2dvi-command`	`"texi2dvi"`
`texinfo-tex-command`	`"tex"`
`texinfo-texindex-command`	`"texindex"`
`texinfo-delete-from-print-queue-command`	`"lprm"`
`texinfo-tex-trailer`	`"@bye"`
`tex-start-of-header`	`"%**start"`
`tex-end-of-header`	`"%**end"`
`tex-dvi-print-command`	`"lpr -d"`
`tex-show-queue-command`	`"lpq"`

You can change the values of these variables with the `M-x edit-options` command (see section "Editing Variable Values" in *The GNU Emacs Manual*), with the `M-x set-variable` command (see section "Examining and Setting Variables" in *The GNU Emacs Manual*), or with your '`.emacs`' initialization file (see section "Init File" in *The GNU Emacs Manual*).

19.6 Using the Local Variables List

Yet another way to apply the TeX formatting command to a Texinfo file is to put that command in a *local variables list* at the end of the Texinfo file. You can then specify the `tex` or `texi2dvi` commands as a `compile-command` and have Emacs run it by typing `M-x compile`. This creates a special shell called the '`*compilation*`' buffer in which Emacs runs the compile command. For example, at the end of the '`gdb.texinfo`' file, after the `@bye`, you could put the following:

```
@c Local Variables:
@c compile-command: "texi2dvi gdb.texinfo"
@c End:
```

This technique is most often used by programmers who also compile programs this way; see section "Compilation" in *The GNU Emacs Manual*.

19.7 TeX Formatting Requirements Summary

Every Texinfo file that is to be input to TeX must begin with a `\input` command and contain an `@settitle` command:

```
\input texinfo
@settitle name-of-manual
```

The first command instructs TeX to load the macros it needs to process a Texinfo file and the second command specifies the title of printed manual.

Every Texinfo file must end with a line that terminates TeX processing and forces out unfinished pages:

```
@bye
```

Strictly speaking, these three lines are all a Texinfo file needs for TeX, besides the body. (The `@setfilename` line is the only line that a Texinfo file needs for Info formatting.)

Usually, the file's first line contains an '`@c -*-texinfo-*-`' comment that causes Emacs to switch to Texinfo mode when you edit the file. In addition, the beginning usually includes an `@setfilename` for Info formatting, an `@setchapternewpage` command, a title page, a copyright page, and permissions. Besides an `@bye`, the end of a file usually includes indices and a table of contents.

For more information, see Section 3.2.5 [`@setchapternewpage`], page 35, Appendix F [Page Headings], page 207, Section 3.4 [Titlepage & Copyright Page], page 38, Section 4.1 [Printing Indices & Menus], page 47, and Section 4.2 [Contents], page 48.

19.8 Preparing to Use TeX

TeX needs to know where to find the '`texinfo.tex`' file that you have told it to input with the '`\input texinfo`' command at the beginning of the first line. The '`texinfo.tex`' file tells TeX how to handle @-commands. ('`texinfo.tex`' is included in the standard GNU distributions.)

Usually, the '`texinfo.tex`' file is put in the default directory that contains TeX macros (the '`/usr/lib/tex/macros`' directory) when GNU Emacs or other GNU software is installed. In this case, TeX will find the file and you do not need to do anything special. Alternatively, you can put '`texinfo.tex`'

Chapter 19: Format and Print Hardcopy   155

in the directory in which the Texinfo source file is located, and TeX will find
it there.

However, you may want to specify the location of the \input file yourself.
One way to do this is to write the complete path for the file after the \input
command. Another way is to set the TEXINPUTS environment variable in
your '.cshrc' or '.profile' file. The TEXINPUTS environment variable will
tell TeX where to find the 'texinfo.tex' file and any other file that you
might want TeX to use.

Whether you use a '.cshrc' or '.profile' file depends on whether you
use csh, sh, or bash for your shell command interpreter. When you use csh,
it looks to the '.cshrc' file for initialization information, and when you use
sh or bash, it looks to the '.profile' file.

In a '.cshrc' file, you could use the following csh command sequence:

    setenv TEXINPUTS .:/usr/me/mylib:/usr/lib/tex/macros

In a '.profile' file, you could use the following sh command sequence:

    TEXINPUTS=.:/usr/me/mylib:/usr/lib/tex/macros
    export TEXINPUTS

This would cause TeX to look for '\input' file first in the current directory,
indicated by the '.', then in a hypothetical user's 'me/mylib' directory, and
finally in the system library.

19.9 Overfull "hboxes"

TeX is sometimes unable to typeset a line without extending it into the
right margin. This can occur when TeX comes upon what it interprets as
a long word that it cannot hyphenate, such as an electronic mail network
address or a very long title. When this happens, TeX prints an error message
like this:

    Overfull \hbox (20.76302pt too wide)

(In TeX, lines are in "horizontal boxes", hence the term, "hbox". The backslash, '\', is the TeX equivalent of '@'.)

TeX also provides the line number in the Texinfo source file and the text
of the offending line, which is marked at all the places that TeX knows how to
hyphenate words. See Section G.2 [Catching Errors with TeX Formatting],
page 215, for more information about typesetting errors.

If the Texinfo file has an overfull hbox, you can rewrite the sentence so
the overfull hbox does not occur, or you can decide to leave it. A small
excursion into the right margin often does not matter and may not even be
noticeable.

However, unless told otherwise, TeX will print a large, ugly, black rectangle beside the line that contains the overful hbox. This is so you will notice the location of the problem if you are correcting a draft.

To prevent such a monstrosity from marring your final printout, write the following in the beginning of the Texinfo file on a line of its own, before the @titlepage command:

    @finalout

19.10 Printing "Small" Books

By default, TeX typesets pages for printing in an 8.5 by 11 inch format. However, you can direct TeX to typeset a document in a 7 by 9.25 inch format that is suitable for bound books by inserting the following command on a line by itself at the beginning of the Texinfo file, before the title page:

    @smallbook

(Since regular sized books are often about 7 by 9.25 inches, this command might better have been called the @regularbooksize command, but it came to be called the @smallbook command by comparison to the 8.5 by 11 inch format.)

If you write the @smallbook command between the start-of-header and end-of-header lines, the Texinfo mode TeX region formatting command, texinfo-tex-region, will format the region in "small" book size (see Section 3.2.2 [Start of Header], page 33).

The Free Software Foundation distributes printed copies of *The GNU Emacs Manual* and other manuals in the "small" book size. See Section 10.6 [@smallexample and @smalllisp], page 95, for information about commands that make it easier to produce examples for a smaller manual.

19.11 Printing on A4 Paper

You can tell TeX to typeset a document for printing on European size A4 paper with the @afourpaper command. Write the command on a line by itself between @iftex and @end iftex lines near the beginning of the Texinfo file, before the title page:

For example, this is how you would write the header for this manual:

Chapter 19: Format and Print Hardcopy

```
\input texinfo      @c -*-texinfo-*-
@c %**start of header
@setfilename texinfo
@settitle Texinfo
@syncodeindex vr fn
@iftex
@afourpaper
@end iftex
@c %**end of header
```

19.12 Cropmarks and Magnification

You can attempt to direct TeX to print cropmarks at the corners of pages with the `@cropmarks` command. Write the `@cropmarks` command on a line by itself between `@iftex` and `@end iftex` lines near the beginning of the Texinfo file, before the title page, like this:

```
@iftex
@cropmarks
@end iftex
```

This command is mainly for printers that typeset several pages on one sheet of film; but you can attempt to use it to mark the corners of a book set to 7 by 9.25 inches with the `@smallbook` command. (Printers will not produce cropmarks for regular sized output that is printed on regular sized paper.) Since different printing machines work in different ways, you should explore the use of this command with a spirit of adventure. You may have to redefine the command in the 'texinfo.tex' definitions file.

You can attempt to direct TeX to typeset pages larger or smaller than usual with the `\mag` TeX command. Everything that is typeset is scaled proportionally larger or smaller. (`\mag` stands for "magnification".) This is *not* a Texinfo @-command, but is a PlainTeX command that is prefixed with a backslash. You have to write this command between `@tex` and `@end tex` (see Section 18.1 [Using Ordinary TeX Commands], page 143).

Follow the `\mag` command with an '=' and then a number that is 1000 times the magnification you desire. For example, to print pages at 1.2 normal size, write the following near the beginning of the Texinfo file, before the title page:

```
@tex
\mag=1200
@end tex
```

With some printing technologies, you can print normal-sized copies that look better than usual by using a larger-than-normal master.

Depending on your system, `\mag` may not work or may work only at certain magnifications. Be prepared to experiment.

20 Creating an Info File

`makeinfo` is a utility that converts a Texinfo file into an Info file; `texinfo-format-region` and `texinfo-format-buffer` are GNU Emacs functions that do the same.

A Texinfo file must possess an `@setfilename` line near its beginning, otherwise the Info formatting commands will fail.

For information on installing the Info file in the Info system, see Chapter 21 [Install an Info File], page 167.

The `makeinfo` utility creates an Info file from a Texinfo source file more quickly than either of the Emacs formatting commands and provides better error messages. We recommend it. `makeinfo` is a C program that is independent of Emacs. You do not need to run Emacs to use `makeinfo`, which means you can use `makeinfo` on machines that are too small to run Emacs. You can run `makeinfo` in any one of three ways: from an operating system shell, from a shell inside Emacs, or by typing a key command in Texinfo mode in Emacs.

The `texinfo-format-region` and the `texinfo-format-buffer` commands are useful if you cannot run `makeinfo`. Also, in some circumstances, they format short regions or buffers more quickly than `makeinfo`.

20.1 Running `makeinfo` from a Shell

To create an Info file from a Texinfo file, type `makeinfo` followed by the name of the Texinfo file. Thus, to create the Info file for Bison, type the following at the shell prompt (where '%' is the prompt):

      % makeinfo bison.texinfo

(You can run a shell inside Emacs by typing `M-x shell`.)

20.2 Options for `makeinfo`

The `makeinfo` command takes a number of options. Most often, options are used to set the value of the fill column and specify the footnote style. Each command line option is a word preceded by '--'[1] or a letter preceded by '-'. You can use abbreviations for the option names as long as they are unique.

For example, you could use the following command to create an Info file for 'bison.texinfo' in which each line is filled to only 68 columns (where '%' is the prompt):

---

[1] '--' has replaced '+', the old introductory character, to maintain POSIX.2 compatibility without losing long-named options.

```
% makeinfo --fill-column=68 bison.texinfo
```

You can write two or more options in sequence, like this:

```
% makeinfo --no-split --fill-column=70 ...
```

This would keep the Info file together as one possibly very long file and would also set the fill column to 70.

If you wish to discover which version of `makeinfo` you are using, type:

```
% makeinfo --version
```

The options are:

-D *var* Cause *var* to be defined. This is equivalent to `@set` *var* in the Texinfo file.

--error-limit *limit*
Set the maximum number of errors that `makeinfo` will report before exiting (on the assumption that continuing would be useless). The default number of errors that can be reported before `makeinfo` gives up is 100.

--fill-column *width*
Specify the maximum number of columns in a line; this is the right-hand edge of a line. Paragraphs that are filled will be filled to this width. (Filling is the process of breaking up and connecting lines so that lines are the same length as or shorter than the number specified as the fill column. Lines are broken between words.) The default value for `fill-column` is 72.

--footnote-style *style*
Set the footnote style to *style*, either 'end' for the end node style or 'separate' for the separate node style. The value set by this option overrides the value set in a Texinfo file by an `@footnotestyle` command. When the footnote style is 'separate', `makeinfo` makes a new node containing the footnotes found in the current node. When the footnote style is 'end', `makeinfo` places the footnote references at the end of the current node.

-I *dir* Add `dir` to the directory search list for finding files that are included using the `@include` command. By default, `makeinfo` searches only the current directory.

--no-headers
Do not include menus or node lines in the output. This results in an ASCII file that you cannot read in Info since it does not contain the requisite nodes or menus; but you can print such a file in a single, typewriter-like font and produce acceptable output.

Chapter 20: Creating an Info File

`--no-split`
: Suppress the splitting stage of `makeinfo`. Normally, large output files (where the size is greater than 70k bytes) are split into smaller subfiles, each one approximately 50k bytes. If you specify '`--no-split`', `makeinfo` will not split up the output file.

`--no-pointer-validate`
`--no-validate`
: Suppress the pointer-validation phase of `makeinfo`. Normally, after a Texinfo file is processed, some consistency checks are made to ensure that cross references can be resolved, etc. See Section 20.3 [Pointer Validation], page 162.

`--no-warn`
: Suppress the output of warning messages. This does *not* suppress the output of error messages, only warnings. You might want this if the file you are creating has examples of Texinfo cross references within it, and the nodes that are referenced do not actually exist.

`--no-number-footnotes`
: Suppress automatic footnote numbering. By default, `makeinfo` numbers each footnote sequentially in a single node, resetting the current footnote number to 1 at the start of each node.

`--output` *file*
`-o` *file*
: Specify that the output should be directed to *file* and not to the file name specified in the `@setfilename` command found in the Texinfo source. *file* can be the special token '-', which specifies standard output.

`--paragraph-indent` *indent*
: Set the paragraph indentation style to *indent*. The value set by this option overrides the value set in a Texinfo file by an `@paragraphindent` command. The value of *indent* is interpreted as follows:

  - If the value of *indent* is '`asis`', do not change the existing indentation at the starts of paragraphs.
  - If the value of *indent* is zero, delete any existing indentation.
  - If the value of *indent* is greater than zero, indent each paragraph by that number of spaces.

`--reference-limit` *limit*
: Set the value of the number of references to a node that `makeinfo` will make without reporting a warning. If a node has more than this number of references in it, `makeinfo` will make the references but also report a warning.

-U *var*   Cause *var* to be undefined. This is equivalent to `@clear` *var* in the Texinfo file.

`--verbose`
: Cause `makeinfo` to display messages saying what it is doing. Normally, `makeinfo` only outputs messages if there are errors or warnings.

`--version`
: Report the version number of this copy of `makeinfo`.

20.3 Pointer Validation

If you do not suppress pointer-validation, `makeinfo` will check the validity of the final Info file. Mostly, this means ensuring that nodes you have referenced really exist. Here is a complete list of what is checked:

1. If a 'Next', 'Previous', or 'Up' node reference is a reference to a node in the current file and is not an external reference such as to '(dir)', then the referenced node must exist.
2. In every node, if the 'Previous' node is different from the 'Up' node, then the 'Previous' node must also be pointed to by a 'Next' node.
3. Every node except the 'Top' node must have an 'Up' pointer.
4. The node referenced by an 'Up' pointer must contain a reference to the current node in some manner other than through a 'Next' reference. This includes menu entries and cross references.
5. If the 'Next' reference of a node is not the same as the 'Next' reference of the 'Up' reference, then the node referenced by the 'Next' pointer must have a 'Previous' pointer that points back to the current node. This rule allows the last node in a section to point to the first node of the next chapter.

20.4 Running `makeinfo` inside Emacs

You can run `makeinfo` in GNU Emacs Texinfo mode by using either the `makeinfo-region` or the `makeinfo-buffer` commands. In Texinfo mode, the commands are bound to `C-c C-m C-r` and `C-c C-m C-b` by default.

`C-c C-m C-r`
`M-x makeinfo-region`
: Format the current region for Info.

`C-c C-m C-b`
`M-x makeinfo-buffer`
: Format the current buffer for Info.

When you invoke either `makeinfo-region` or `makeinfo-buffer`, Emacs prompts for a file name, offering the name of the visited file as the default.

Chapter 20: Creating an Info File

You can edit the default file name in the minibuffer if you wish, before typing `RET` to start the `makeinfo` process.

The Emacs `makeinfo-region` and `makeinfo-buffer` commands run the `makeinfo` program in a temporary shell buffer. If `makeinfo` finds any errors, Emacs displays the error messages in the temporary buffer.

You can parse the error messages by typing `C-x '` (`next-error`). This causes Emacs to go to and position the cursor on the line in the Texinfo source that `makeinfo` thinks caused the error. See section "Running `make` or Compilers Generally" in *The GNU Emacs Manual*, for more information about using the `next-error` command.

In addition, you can kill the shell in which the `makeinfo` command is running or make the shell buffer display its most recent output.

`C-c C-m C-k`
`M-x makeinfo-kill-job`
> Kill the current running `makeinfo` job created by `makeinfo-region` or `makeinfo-buffer`.

`C-c C-m C-l`
`M-x makeinfo-recenter-output-buffer`
> Redisplay the `makeinfo` shell buffer to display its most recent output.

(Note that the parallel commands for killing and recentering a TeX job are `C-c C-t C-k` and `C-c C-t C-l`. See Section 19.5 [Texinfo Mode Printing], page 151.)

You can specify options for `makeinfo` by setting the `makeinfo-options` variable with either the `M-x edit-options` or the `M-x set-variable` command, or by setting the variable in your '`.emacs`' initialization file.

For example, you could write the following in your '`.emacs`' file:

```
(setq makeinfo-options
      "--paragraph-indent=0 --no-split
       --fill-column=70 --verbose")
```

For more information, see Section 20.2 [Options for `makeinfo`], page 159, as well as "Editing Variable Values," "Examining and Setting Variables," and "Init File" in the *The GNU Emacs Manual*.

20.5 The `texinfo-format...` Commands

In GNU Emacs in Texinfo mode, you can format part or all of a Texinfo file with the `texinfo-format-region` command. This formats the current region and displays the formatted text in a temporary buffer called '`*Info Region*`'.

Similarly, you can format a buffer with the `texinfo-format-buffer` command. This command creates a new buffer and generates the Info file in it. Typing `C-x C-s` will save the Info file under the name specified by the `@setfilename` line which must be near the beginning of the Texinfo file.

`C-c C-e C-r`
`texinfo-format-region`
>   Format the current region for Info.

`C-c C-e C-b`
`texinfo-format-buffer`
>   Format the current buffer for Info.

The `texinfo-format-region` and `texinfo-format-buffer` commands provide you with some error checking, and other functions can provide you with further help in finding formatting errors. These procedures are described in an appendix; see Appendix G [Catching Mistakes], page 213. However, the `makeinfo` program is often faster and provides better error checking (see Section 20.4 [makeinfo in Emacs], page 162).

20.6 Batch Formatting

You can format Texinfo files for Info using `batch-texinfo-format` and Emacs Batch mode. You can run Emacs in Batch mode from any shell, including a shell inside of Emacs. (See section "Command Line Switches and Arguments" in *The GNU Emacs Manual*.)

Here is the command to format all the files that end in '`.texinfo`' in the current directory (where '`%`' is the shell prompt):

> `% emacs -batch -funcall batch-texinfo-format *.texinfo`

Emacs processes all the files listed on the command line, even if an error occurs while attempting to format some of them.

Run `batch-texinfo-format` only with Emacs in Batch mode as shown; it is not interactive. It kills the Batch mode Emacs on completion.

`batch-texinfo-format` is convenient if you lack `makeinfo` and want to format several Texinfo files at once. When you use Batch mode, you create a new Emacs process. This frees your current Emacs, so you can continue working in it. (When you run `texinfo-format-region` or `texinfo-format-buffer`, you cannot use that Emacs for anything else until the command finishes.)

20.7 Tag Files and Split Files

If a Texinfo file has more than 30,000 bytes, `texinfo-format-buffer` automatically creates a tag table for its Info file; `makeinfo` always creates a

Chapter 20: Creating an Info File

tag table. With a *tag table*, Info can jump to new nodes more quickly than it can otherwise.

In addition, if the Texinfo file contains more than about 70,000 bytes, `texinfo-format-buffer` and `makeinfo` split the large Info file into shorter *indirect* subfiles of about 50,000 bytes each. Big files are split into smaller files so that Emacs does not need to make a large buffer to hold the whole of a large Info file; instead, Emacs allocates just enough memory for the small, split off file that is needed at the time. This way, Emacs avoids wasting memory when you run Info. (Before splitting was implemented, Info files were always kept short and *include files* were designed as a way to create a single, large printed manual out of the smaller Info files. See Appendix E [Include Files], page 201, for more information. Include files are still used for very large documents, such as *The Emacs Lisp Reference Manual*, in which each chapter is a separate file.)

When a file is split, Info itself makes use of a shortened version of the original file that contains just the tag table and references to the files that were split off. The split off files are called *indirect* files.

The split off files have names that are created by appending '`-1`', '`-2`', '`-3`' and so on to the file name specified by the `@setfilename` command. The shortened version of the original file continues to have the name specified by `@setfilename`.

At one stage in writing this document, for example, the Info file was saved as '`test-texinfo`' and that file looked like this:

```
Info file: test-texinfo,    -*-Text-*-
produced by texinfo-format-buffer
from file: new-texinfo-manual.texinfo

^_
Indirect:
test-texinfo-1: 102
test-texinfo-2: 50422
test-texinfo-3: 101300
^_^L
Tag table:
(Indirect)
Node: overview^?104
Node: info file^?1271
Node: printed manual^?4853
Node: conventions^?6855
...
```

(But '`test-texinfo`' had far more nodes than are shown here.) Each of the split off, indirect files, '`test-texinfo-1`', '`test-texinfo-2`', and 'test-texinfo-3', is listed in this file after the line that says 'Indirect:'. The tag table is listed after the line that says 'Tag table:'.

In the list of indirect files, the number following the file name records the cumulative number of bytes in the preceding indirect files, not counting the file list itself, the tag table, or the permissions text in each file. In the tag table, the number following the node name records the location of the beginning of the node, in bytes from the beginning.

If you are using `texinfo-format-buffer` to create Info files, you may want to run the `Info-validate` command. (The `makeinfo` command does such a good job on its own, you do not need `Info-validate`.) However, you cannot run the `M-x Info-validate` node-checking command on indirect files. For information on how to prevent files from being split and how to validate the structure of the nodes, see Section G.5.1 [Using Info-validate], page 219.

21 Installing an Info File

Info files are usually kept in the 'info' directory. You can read Info files using the standalone Info program or the Info reader built into Emacs. (See Info file 'info', node 'Top', for an introduction to Info.)

For Info to work, the 'info' directory must contain a file that serves as a top level directory for the Info system. By convention, this file is called 'dir'. (You can find the location of this file within Emacs by typing C-h i to enter Info and then typing C-x C-f to see the pathname to the 'info' directory.)

The 'dir' file is itself an Info file. It contains the top level menu for all the Info files in the system. The menu looks like this:

```
* Menu:

* Info:     (info).     Documentation browsing system.
* Emacs:    (emacs).    The extensible, self-documenting
                        text editor.
* Texinfo:  (texinfo).  With one source file, make
                        either a printed manual using
                        TeX or an Info file.
...
```

Each of these menu entries points to the 'Top' node of the Info file that is named in parentheses. (The menu entry does not need to specify the 'Top' node, since Info goes to the 'Top' node if no node name is mentioned. See Section 7.5 [Nodes in Other Info Files], page 70.)

Thus, the 'Info' entry points to the 'Top' node of the 'info' file and the 'Emacs' entry points to the 'Top' node of the 'emacs' file.

In each of the Info files, the 'Up' pointer of the 'Top' node refers back to the dir file. For example, the line for the 'Top' node of the Emacs manual looks like this in Info:

```
File: emacs  Node: Top, Up: (DIR), Next: Distrib
```

(Note that in this case, the 'dir' file name is written in upper case letters—it can be written in either upper or lower case. Info has a feature that it will change the case of the file name to lower case if it cannot find the name as written.)

21.1 Listing a New Info File

To add a new Info file to your system, write a menu entry for it in the menu in the 'dir' file in the 'info' directory. Also, move the new Info file itself to the 'info' directory. For example, if you were adding documentation for GDB, you would write the following new entry:

```
* GDB: (gdb).              The source-level C debugger.
```
The first part of the menu entry is the menu entry name, followed by a colon. The second part is the name of the Info file, in parentheses, followed by a period. The third part is the description.

Conventionally, the name of an Info file has a '.info' extension. Thus, you might list the name of the file like this:
```
* GDB: (gdb.info).         The source-level C debugger.
```
However, Info will look for a file with a '.info' extension if it does not find the file under the name given in the menu. This means that you can refer to the file 'gdb.info' as 'gdb', as shown in the first example. This looks better.

21.2 Info Files in Other Directories

If an Info file is not in the 'info' directory, there are three ways to specify its location:

- Write the pathname in the 'dir' file as the second part of the menu.
- If you are using Emacs, list the name of the file in a second 'dir' file, in its directory; and then add the name of that directory to the `Info-directory-list` variable in your personal or site initialization file.

  This tells Emacs's Info reader reader where to look for 'dir' files. Emacs merges the files named 'dir' from each of the listed directories. (In Emacs Version 18, you can set the `Info-directory` variable to the name of only one directory.)
- Specify the 'info' directory name in an environment variable in your '.profile' or '.cshrc' initialization file. (Only you and others who set this environment variable will be able to find Info files whose location is specified this way.)

For example, to reach a test file in the '~bob/manuals' directory, you could add an entry like this to the menu in the 'dir' file:
```
* Test: (/usr/bob/manuals/info-test).   Bob's own test file.
```
In this case, the absolute file name of the 'info-test' file is written as the second part of the menu entry.

Alternatively, you could write the following in your '.emacs' file:
```
(setq Info-directory-list
      '("/usr/bob/manuals"
        "/usr/local/emacs/info"))
```

This tells Emacs to merge the 'dir' file from the '/usr/bob/manuals' directory with the 'dir' file from the '"/usr/local/emacs/info"' directory. Info will list the '/usr/bob/manuals/info-test' file as a menu entry in the '/usr/bob/manuals/dir' file.

Chapter 21: Installing an Info File

Finally, you can tell Info where to look by setting the `INFOPATH` environment variable in your '.cshrc' or '.profile' file.

If you use **sh** or **bash** for your shell command interpreter, you must set the `INFOPATH` environment variable in the '.profile' initialization file; but if you use **csh**, you must set the variable in the '.cshrc' initialization file. The two files require slightly different command formats.

- In a '.cshrc' file, you could set the `INFOPATH` variable as follows:
    ```
    setenv INFOPATH .:~bob/manuals:/usr/local/emacs/info
    ```
- In a '.profile' file, you would achieve the same effect by writing:
    ```
    INFOPATH=.:~bob/manuals:/usr/local/emacs/info
    export INFOPATH
    ```

The '.' indicates the current directory. Emacs uses the `INFOPATH` environment variable to initialize the value of Emacs's own `Info-directory-list` variable.

Appendix A @-Command List

Here is an alphabetical list of the @-commands in Texinfo. Square brackets, [ ], indicate optional arguments; an ellipsis, '...', indicates repeated text.

@*
    Force a line break. Do not end a paragraph that uses @* with an @refill command. See Section 15.1 [Line Breaks], page 123.

@.
    Stands for a period that really does end a sentence (usually after an end-of-sentence capital letter). See Section 13.1.3 [Controlling Spacing], page 114.

@:
    Indicate to TeX that an immediately preceding period, question mark, exclamation mark, or colon does not end a sentence. Prevent TeX from inserting extra whitespace as it does at the end of a sentence. The command has no effect on the Info file output. See Section 13.1.3 [Controlling Spacing], page 114.

@@
    Stands for '@'. See Section 13.1 [Inserting '@'], page 113.

@{
    Stands for a left-hand brace, '{'.
    See Section 13.1 [Inserting @ braces and periods], page 113.

@}
    Stands for a right-hand brace, '}'.
    See Section 13.1 [Inserting @ braces and periods], page 113.

@appendix *title*
    Begin an appendix. The title appears in the table of contents of a printed manual. In Info, the title is underlined with asterisks. See Section 5.5 [The @unnumbered and @appendix Commands], page 53.

@appendixsec *title*
@appendixsection *title*
    Begin an appendix section within an appendix. The section title appears in the table of contents of a printed manual. In Info, the title is underlined with equal signs. @appendixsection is a longer spelling of the @appendixsec command. See Section 5.8 [Section Commands], page 54.

@appendixsubsec *title*
    Begin an appendix subsection within an appendix. The title appears in the table of contents of a printed manual. In Info, the title is underlined with hyphens. See Section 5.10 [Subsection Commands], page 55.

@appendixsubsubsec *title*
    Begin an appendix subsubsection within a subappendix. The title appears in the table of contents of a printed manual. In

	Info, the title is underlined with periods. See Section 5.11 [The 'subsub' Commands], page 55.
`@asis`	Used following `@table`, `@ftable`, and `@vtable` to print the table's first column without highlighting ("as is"). See Section 11.3 [Making a Two-column Table], page 103.
`@author` *author*	
	Typeset *author* flushleft and underline it. See Section 3.4.3 [The `@title` and `@author` Commands], page 40.
`@b{`*text*`}`	Print *text* in **bold** font. No effect in Info. See Section 9.2.3 [Fonts], page 88.
`@bullet{}`	
	Generate a large round dot, or the closest possible thing to one. See Section 13.3.2 [`@bullet`], page 115.
`@bye`	Stop formatting a file. The formatters do not see the contents of a file following an `@bye` command. See Chapter 4 [Ending a File], page 47.
`@c` *comment*	
	Begin a comment in Texinfo. The rest of the line does not appear in either the Info file or the printed manual. A synonym for `@comment`. See Section 1.5 [Comments], page 8.
`@cartouche`	
	Highlight an example or quotation by drawing a box with rounded corners around it. Pair with `@end cartouche`. No effect in Info. See Section 10.11 [Drawing Cartouches Around Examples], page 97.)
`@center` *line-of-text*	
	Center the line of text following the command. See Section 3.4.2 [`@center`], page 39.
`@lowersections`	
	Change subsequent chapters to sections, sections to subsections, and so on. See Section 5.12 [`@raisesections` and `@lowersections`], page 56.
`@chapheading` *title*	
	Print a chapter-like heading in the text, but not in the table of contents of a printed manual. In Info, the title is underlined with asterisks. See Section 5.6 [`@majorheading` and `@chapheading`], page 53.
`@chapter` *title*	
	Begin a chapter. The chapter title appears in the table of contents of a printed manual. In Info, the title is underlined with asterisks. See Section 5.4 [`@chapter`], page 53.

Appendix A: @-Command List

@cindex *entry*
: Add *entry* to the index of concepts. See Section 12.1 [Defining the Entries of an Index], page 107.

@cite{*reference***}**
: Highlight the name of a book or other reference that lacks a companion Info file. See Section 9.1.8 [`@cite`], page 87.

@clear *flag*
: Unset *flag*, preventing the Texinfo formatting commands from formatting text between subsequent pairs of `@ifset` *flag* and `@end ifset` commands, and preventing `@value{`*flag*`}` from expanding to the value to which *flag* is set. See Section 18.2 [`@set` `@clear` `@value`], page 144.

@code{*sample-code***}**
: Highlight text that is an expression, a syntactically complete token of a program, or a program name. See Section 9.1.1 [`@code`], page 82.

@comment *comment*
: Begin a comment in Texinfo. The rest of the line does not appear in either the Info file or the printed manual. A synonym for `@c`. See Section 1.5 [Comments], page 8.

@contents
: Print a complete table of contents. Has no effect in Info, which uses menus instead. See Section 4.2 [Generating a Table of Contents], page 48.

@copyright{}
: Generate a copyright symbol. See Section 13.4.2 [`@copyright`], page 116.

@defcodeindex *index-name*
: Define a new index and its indexing command. Print entries in an `@code` font. See Section 12.5 [Defining New Indices], page 111.

@defcv *category class name*
: Format a description for a variable associated with a class in object-oriented programming. Takes three arguments: the category of thing being defined, the class to which it belongs, and its name. See Chapter 16 [Definition Commands], page 127.

@deffn *category name arguments...*
: Format a description for a function, interactive command, or similar entity that may take arguments. `@deffn` takes as arguments the category of entity being described, the name of this particular entity, and its arguments, if any. See Chapter 16 [Definition Commands], page 127.

`@defindex` *index-name*
: Define a new index and its indexing command. Print entries in a roman font. See Section 12.5 [Defining New Indices], page 111.

`@definfoenclose` *new-command, before, after,*
: Create new `@`-command for Info that marks text by enclosing it in strings that precede and follow the text. Write definition inside of `@ifinfo` ... `@end ifinfo`. See Section 9.2.4 [Customized Highlighting], page 89.

`@defivar` *class instance-variable-name*
: This command formats a description for an instance variable in object-oriented programming. The command is equivalent to '`@defcv {Instance Variable}` ...'. See Chapter 16 [Definition Commands], page 127.

`@defmac` *macro-name arguments...*
: Format a description for a macro. The command is equivalent to '`@deffn Macro` ...'. See Chapter 16 [Definition Commands], page 127.

`@defmethod` *class method-name arguments...*
: Format a description for a method in object-oriented programming. The command is equivalent to '`@defop Method` ...'. Takes as arguments the name of the class of the method, the name of the method, and its arguments, if any. See Chapter 16 [Definition Commands], page 127.

`@defop` *category class name arguments...*
: Format a description for an operation in object-oriented programming. `@defop` takes as arguments the overall name of the category of operation, the name of the class of the operation, the name of the operation, and its arguments, if any. See Chapter 16 [Definition Commands], page 127.

`@defopt` *option-name*
: Format a description for a user option. The command is equivalent to '`@defvr {User Option}` ...'. See Chapter 16 [Definition Commands], page 127.

`@defspec` *special-form-name arguments...*
: Format a description for a special form. The command is equivalent to '`@deffn {Special Form}` ...'. See Chapter 16 [Definition Commands], page 127.

`@deftp` *category name-of-type attributes...*
: Format a description for a data type. `@deftp` takes as arguments the category, the name of the type (which is a word like '`int`' or '`float`'), and then the names of attributes of objects of that type. See Chapter 16 [Definition Commands], page 127.

Appendix A: @-Command List

@deftypefn *classification data-type name arguments...*
: Format a description for a function or similar entity that may take arguments and that is typed. @deftypefn takes as arguments the classification of entity being described, the type, the name of the entity, and its arguments, if any. See Chapter 16 [Definition Commands], page 127.

@deftypefun *data-type function-name arguments...*
: Format a description for a function in a typed language. The command is equivalent to '@deftypefn Function ...'. See Chapter 16 [Definition Commands], page 127.

@deftypevr *classification data-type name*
: Format a description for something like a variable in a typed language—an entity that records a value. Takes as arguments the classification of entity being described, the type, and the name of the entity. See Chapter 16 [Definition Commands], page 127.

@deftypevar *data-type variable-name*
: Format a description for a variable in a typed language. The command is equivalent to '@deftypevr Variable ...'. See Chapter 16 [Definition Commands], page 127.

@defun *function-name arguments...*
: Format a description for functions. The command is equivalent to '@deffn Function ...'. See Chapter 16 [Definition Commands], page 127.

@defvar *variable-name*
: Format a description for variables. The command is equivalent to '@defvr Variable ...'. See Chapter 16 [Definition Commands], page 127.

@defvr *category name*
: Format a description for any kind of variable. @defvr takes as arguments the category of the entity and the name of the entity. See Chapter 16 [Definition Commands], page 127.

@dfn{*term*}
: Highlight the introductory or defining use of a term. See Section 9.1.7 [@dfn], page 86.

@display
: Begin a kind of example. Indent text, do not fill, do not select a new font. Pair with @end display. See Section 10.7 [@display], page 95.

@dmn{*dimension*}
: Format a dimension. Cause TeX to insert a narrow space before *dimension*. No effect in Info. Use for writing a number followed

by an abbreviation of a dimension name, such as '12 pt', written as '12@dmn{pt}', with no space between the number and the @dmn command. See Section 13.2 [@dmn], page 114.

`@dots{}` Insert an ellipsis: '...'. See Section 13.3.1 [@dots], page 115.

`@emph{`*text*`}`
Highlight *text*; text is displayed in *italics* in printed output, and surrounded by asterisks in Info. See Section 9.2 [Emphasizing Text], page 87.

`@enumerate` [*number-or-letter*]
Begin a numbered list, using `@item` for each entry. Optionally, start list with *number-or-letter*. Pair with `@end enumerate`. See Section 11.2 [@enumerate], page 101.

`@equiv{}` Indicate to the reader the exact equivalence of two forms with a glyph: '$\equiv$'. See Section 14.5 [Equivalence], page 121.

`@error{}` Indicate to the reader with a glyph that the following text is an error message: 'error'. See Section 14.4 [Error Glyph], page 120.

`@evenfooting` [*left*] @| [*center*] @| [*right*]
Specify page footings for even-numbered (left-hand) pages. Not relevant to Info. See Section F.3 [How to Make Your Own Headings], page 209.

`@evenheading` [*left*] @| [*center*] @| [*right*]
Specify page headings for even-numbered (left-hand) pages. Not relevant to Info. See Section F.3 [How to Make Your Own Headings], page 209.

`@everyfooting` [*left*] @| [*center*] @| [*right*]
Specify page footings for every page. Not relevant to Info. See Section F.3 [How to Make Your Own Headings], page 209.

`@everyheading` [*left*] @| [*center*] @| [*right*]
Specify page headings for every page. Not relevant to Info. See Section F.3 [How to Make Your Own Headings], page 209.

`@example` Begin an example. Indent text, do not fill, and select fixed-width font. Pair with `@end example`. See Section 10.3 [@example], page 92.

`@exdent` *line-of-text*
Remove any indentation a line might have. See Section 10.9 [Undoing the Indentation of a Line], page 96.

`@expansion{}`
Indicate the result of a macro expansion to the reader with a special glyph: '$\mapsto$'. See Section 14.2 [$\mapsto$ Indicating an Expansion], page 119.

Appendix A: @-Command List

@file{*filename***}**
>Highlight the name of a file, buffer, node, or directory. See Section 9.1.6 [@file], page 86.

@finalout
>Prevent TeX from printing large black warning rectangles beside over-wide lines. See Section 19.9 [Overfull hboxes], page 155.

@findex *entry*
>Add *entry* to the index of functions. See Section 12.1 [Defining the Entries of an Index], page 107.

@flushleft
>Left justify every line but leave the right end ragged. Leave font as is. Pair with **@end flushleft**. See Section 10.10 [@flushleft and @flushright], page 96.

@flushright
>Right justify every line but leave the left end ragged. Leave font as is. Pair with **@end flushright**. See Section 10.10 [@flushleft and @flushright], page 96.

@footnote{*text-of-footnote***}**
>Enter a footnote. Footnote text is printed at the bottom of the page by TeX; Info may format in either 'End' node or 'Separate' node style. See Chapter 17 [Footnotes], page 141.

@footnotestyle *style*
>Specify an Info file's footnote style, either '**end**' for the end node style or '**separate**' for the separate node style. See Chapter 17 [Footnotes], page 141.

@format
>Begin a kind of example. Like **@example** or **@display**, but do not narrow the margins and do not select the fixed-width font. Pair with **@end format**. See Section 10.3 [@example], page 92.

@ftable *formatting-command*
>Begin a two-column table, using **@item** for each entry. Automatically enter each of the items in the first column into the index of functions. Pair with **@end ftable**. The same as **@table**, except for indexing. See Section 11.3.1 [@ftable and @vtable], page 104.

@group
>Hold text together that must appear on one printed page. Pair with **@end group**. Not relevant to Info. See Section 15.5 [@group], page 125.

@heading *title*
>Print an unnumbered section-like heading in the text, but not in the table of contents of a printed manual. In Info, the title is un-

derlined with equal signs. See Section 5.8 [Section Commands], page 54.

`@headings` *on-off-single-double*
: Turn page headings on or off, or specify single-sided or double-sided page headings for printing. `@headings on` is synonymous with `@headings double`. See Section 3.4.6 [The `@headings` Command], page 42.

`@i{`*text*`}`
: Print *text* in *italic* font. No effect in Info. See Section 9.2.3 [Fonts], page 88.

`@ifclear` *flag*
: If *flag* is cleared, the Texinfo formatting commands format text between `@ifclear` *flag* and the following `@end ifclear` command. See Section 18.2 [`@set @clear @value`], page 144.

`@ifinfo`
: Begin a stretch of text that will be ignored by TeX when it typesets the printed manual. The text appears only in the Info file. Pair with `@end ifinfo`. See Chapter 18 [Conditionally Visible Text], page 143.

`@ifset` *flag*
: If *flag* is set, the Texinfo formatting commands format text between `@ifset` *flag* and the following `@end ifset` command. See Section 18.2 [`@set @clear @value`], page 144.

`@iftex`
: Begin a stretch of text that will not appear in the Info file, but will be processed only by TeX. Pair with `@end iftex`. See Chapter 18 [Conditionally Visible Text], page 143.

`@ignore`
: Begin a stretch of text that will not appear in either the Info file or the printed output. Pair with `@end ignore`. See Section 1.5 [Comments and Ignored Text], page 8.

`@include` *filename*
: Incorporate the contents of the file *filename* into the Info file or printed document. See Appendix E [Include Files], page 201.

`@inforef{`*node-name*, [*entry-name*], *info-file-name*`}`
: Make a cross reference to an Info file for which there is no printed manual. See Section 8.7 [Cross references using `@inforef`], page 80.

`\input` *macro-definitions-file*
: Use the specified macro definitions file. This command is used only in the first line of a Texinfo file to cause TeX to make use of the 'texinfo' macro definitions file. The backslash in `\input` is used instead of an `@` because TeX does not properly recognize `@` until after it has read the definitions file. See Section 3.2 [The Texinfo File Header], page 33.

Appendix A: @-Command List

`@item`
: Indicate the beginning of a marked paragraph for `@itemize` and `@enumerate`; indicate the beginning of the text of a first column entry for `@table`, `@ftable`, and `@vtable`. See Chapter 11 [Lists and Tables], page 99.

`@itemize` *mark-generating-character-or-command*
: Produce a sequence of indented paragraphs, with a mark inside the left margin at the beginning of each paragraph. Pair with `@end itemize`. See Section 11.1 [`@itemize`], page 100.

`@itemx`
: Like `@item` but do not generate extra vertical space above the item text. See Section 11.3.2 [`@itemx`], page 104.

`@kbd{`*keyboard-characters*`}`
: Indicate text that consists of characters of input to be typed by users. See Section 9.1.2 [`@kbd`], page 83.

`@key{`*key-name*`}`
: Highlight *key-name*, a conventional name for a key on a keyboard. See Section 9.1.3 [`@key`], page 84.

`@kindex` *entry*
: Add *entry* to the index of keys. See Section 12.1 [Defining the Entries of an Index], page 107.

`@global@let`*new-command*=*existing-command*
: Equate a new highlighting command with an existing one. Only for TeX. Write definition inside of `@iftex` ... `@end iftex`. See Section 9.2.4 [Customized Highlighting], page 89.

`@lisp`
: Begin an example of Lisp code. Indent text, do not fill, and select fixed-width font. Pair with `@end lisp`. See Section 10.5 [`@lisp`], page 94.

`@majorheading` *title*
: Print a chapter-like heading in the text, but not in the table of contents of a printed manual. Generate more vertical whitespace before the heading than the `@chapheading` command. In Info, the chapter heading line is underlined with asterisks. See Section 5.6 [`@majorheading` and `@chapheading`], page 53.

`@math{`*mathematical-expression*`}`
: Format a mathematical expression. See Section 13.6 [`@math`: Inserting Mathematical Expressions], page 116.

`@menu`
: Mark the beginning of a menu of nodes in Info. No effect in a printed manual. Pair with `@end menu`. See Chapter 7 [Menus], page 67.

`@minus{}`
: Generate a minus sign. See Section 13.5 [`@minus`], page 116.

@need *n*
: Start a new page in a printed manual if fewer than *n* mils (thousandths of an inch) remain on the current page. See Section 15.6 [@need], page 125.

@node *name, next, previous, up*
: Define the beginning of a new node in Info, and serve as a locator for references for TeX. See Section 6.2 [@node], page 61.

@noindent
: Prevent text from being indented as if it were a new paragraph. See Section 10.4 [@noindent], page 93.

@oddfooting [*left*] @| [*center*] @| [*right*]
: Specify page footings for odd-numbered (right-hand) pages. Not relevant to Info. See Section F.3 [How to Make Your Own Headings], page 209.

@oddheading [*left*] @| [*center*] @| [*right*]
: Specify page headings for odd-numbered (right-hand) pages. Not relevant to Info. See Section F.3 [How to Make Your Own Headings], page 209.

@page
: Start a new page in a printed manual. No effect in Info. See Section 15.4 [@page], page 124.

@paragraphindent *indent*
: Indent paragraphs by *indent* number of spaces; delete indentation if the value of *indent* is 0; and do not change indentation if *indent* is `asis`. See Section 3.2.6 [Paragraph Indenting], page 36.

@pindex *entry*
: Add *entry* to the index of programs. See Section 12.1 [Defining the Entries of an Index], page 107.

@point{}
: Indicate the position of point in a buffer to the reader with a glyph: '★'. See Section 14.6 [Indicating Point in a Buffer], page 121.

@print{}
: Indicate printed output to the reader with a glyph: '⊣'. See Section 14.3 [Print Glyph], page 120.

@printindex *index-name*
: Print an alphabetized two-column index in a printed manual or generate an alphabetized menu of index entries for Info. See Section 4.1 [Printing Indices & Menus], page 47.

@pxref{*node-name*, [*entry*], [*topic-or-title*], [*info-file*], [*manual*]}
: Make a reference that starts with a lower case 'see' in a printed manual. Use within parentheses only. Do not follow command with a punctuation mark. The Info formatting commands automatically insert terminating punctuation as needed, which is

Appendix A: @-Command List 181

why you do not need to insert punctuation. Only the first argument is mandatory. See Section 8.6 [@pxref], page 79.

@quotation
Narrow the margins to indicate text that is quoted from another real or imaginary work. Write command on a line of its own. Pair with @end quotation. See Section 10.2 [@quotation], page 92.

@r{text} Print text in roman font. No effect in Info. See Section 9.2.3 [Fonts], page 88.

@raisesections
Change subsequent sections to chapters, subsections to sections, and so on. See Section 5.12 [@raisesections and @lowersections], page 56.

@ref{node-name, [entry], [topic-or-title], [info-file], [manual]}
Make a reference. In a printed manual, the reference does not start with a 'See'. Follow command with a punctuation mark. Only the first argument is mandatory. See Section 8.5 [@ref], page 78.

@refill   In Info, refill and indent the paragraph after all the other processing has been done. No effect on TeX, which always refills. This command is no longer needed, since all formatters now automatically refill. See Appendix H [Refilling Paragraphs], page 223.

@result{}
Indicate the result of an expression to the reader with a special glyph: '⇒'. See Section 14.1 [@result], page 119.

@samp{text}
Highlight text that is a literal example of a sequence of characters. Used for single characters, for statements, and often for entire shell commands. See Section 9.1.4 [@samp], page 84.

@sc{text} Set text in a printed output in THE SMALL CAPS FONT and set text in the Info file in uppercase letters. See Section 9.2.2 [Smallcaps], page 88.

@section title
Begin a section within a chapter. In a printed manual, the section title is numbered and appears in the table of contents. In Info, the title is underlined with equal signs. See Section 5.7 [@section], page 54.

@set flag [string]
Make flag active, causing the Texinfo formatting commands to format text between subsequent pairs of @ifset flag and @end

`ifset` commands. Optionally, set value of *flag* to *string*. See Section 18.2 [`@set @clear @value`], page 144.

`@setchapternewpage` *on-off-odd*
: Specify whether chapters start on new pages, and if so, whether on odd-numbered (right-hand) new pages. See Section 3.2.5 [`@setchapternewpage`], page 35.

`@setfilename` *info-file-name*
: Provide a name to be used by the Info file. See Section 3.2.3 [`@setfilename`], page 34.

`@settitle` *title*
: Provide a title for page headers in a printed manual. See Section 3.2.4 [`@settitle`], page 34.

`@shortcontents`
: Print a short table of contents. Not relevant to Info, which uses menus rather than tables of contents. A synonym for `@summarycontents`. See Section 4.2 [Generating a Table of Contents], page 48.

`@smallbook`
: Cause TeX to produce a printed manual in a 7 by 9.25 inch format rather than the regular 8.5 by 11 inch format. See Section 19.10 [Printing Small Books], page 156. Also, see Section 10.6 [`@smallexample` and `@smalllisp`], page 95.

`@smallexample`
: Indent text to indicate an example. Do not fill, select fixed-width font. In `@smallbook` format, print text in a smaller font than with `@example`. Pair with `@end smallexample`. See Section 10.6 [`@smallexample` and `@smalllisp`], page 95.

`@smalllisp`
: Begin an example of Lisp code. Indent text, do not fill, select fixed-width font. In `@smallbook` format, print text in a smaller font. Pair with `@end smalllisp`. See Section 10.6 [`@smallexample` and `@smalllisp`], page 95.

`@sp` *n*
: Skip *n* blank lines. See Section 15.3 [`@sp`], page 124.

`@strong` *text*
: Emphasize *text* by typesetting it in a **bold** font for the printed manual and by surrounding it with asterisks for Info. See Section 9.2.1 [Emphasizing Text], page 87.

`@subheading` *title*
: Print an unnumbered subsection-like heading in the text, but not in the table of contents of a printed manual. In Info, the title is

Appendix A: @-Command List

underlined with hyphens. See Section 5.10 [@unnumberedsubsec @appendixsubsec @subheading], page 55.

@subsection *title*

Begin a subsection within a section. In a printed manual, the subsection title is numbered and appears in the table of contents. In Info, the title is underlined with hyphens. See Section 5.9 [@subsection], page 55.

@subsubheading *title*

Print an unnumbered subsubsection-like heading in the text, but not in the table of contents of a printed manual. In Info, the title is underlined with periods. See Section 5.11 [The 'subsub' Commands], page 55.

@subsubsection *title*

Begin a subsection within a subsection. In a printed manual, the subsubsection title is numbered and appears in the table of contents. In Info, the title is underlined with periods. See Section 5.11 [The 'subsub' Commands], page 55.

@subtitle *title*

In a printed manual, set a subtitle in a normal sized font flush to the right-hand side of the page. Not relevant to Info, which does not have title pages. See Section 3.4.3 [@title @subtitle and @author Commands], page 40.

@summarycontents

Print a short table of contents. Not relevant to Info, which uses menus rather than tables of contents. A synonym for @shortcontents. See Section 4.2 [Generating a Table of Contents], page 48.

@syncodeindex *from-index into-index*

Merge the index named in the first argument into the index named in the second argument, printing the entries from the first index in @code font. See Section 12.4 [Combining Indices], page 110.

@synindex *from-index into-index*

Merge the index named in the first argument into the index named in the second argument. Do not change the font of *from-index* entries. See Section 12.4 [Combining Indices], page 110.

@t{*text***}** Print *text* in a `fixed-width`, typewriter-like font. No effect in Info. See Section 9.2.3 [Fonts], page 88.

@table *formatting-command*

Begin a two-column table, using @item for each entry. Write each first column entry on the same line as @item. First column entries are printed in the font resulting from *formatting-command*. Pair with `@end table`. See Section 11.3 [Making a Two-column Table], page 103. Also see Section 11.3.1 [`@ftable` and `@vtable`], page 104, and Section 11.3.2 [`@itemx`], page 104.

`@TeX{}`   Insert the logo TeX. See Section 13.4 [Inserting TeX and ©], page 116.

`@tex`   Enter TeX completely. Pair with `@end tex`. See Section 18.1 [Using Ordinary TeX Commands], page 143.

`@thischapter`
In a heading or footing, stands for the number and name of the current chapter, in the format 'Chapter 1: Title'. See Section F.3 [How to Make Your Own Headings], page 209.

`@thischaptername`
In a heading or footing, stands for the name of the current chapter. See Section F.3 [How to Make Your Own Headings], page 209.

`@thisfile`
In a heading or footing, stands for the name of the current `@include` file. Does not insert anything if not within an `@include` file. See Section F.3 [How to Make Your Own Headings], page 209.

`@thispage`
In a heading or footing, stands for the current page number. See Section F.3 [How to Make Your Own Headings], page 209.

`@thistitle`
In a heading or footing, stands for the name of the document, as specified by the `@settitle` command. See Section F.3 [How to Make Your Own Headings], page 209.

`@tindex` *entry*
Add *entry* to the index of data types. See Section 12.1 [Defining the Entries of an Index], page 107.

`@title` *title*
In a printed manual, set a title flush to the left-hand side of the page in a larger than normal font and underline it with a black rule. Not relevant to Info, which does not have title pages. See Section 3.4.3 [The `@title` `@subtitle` and `@author` Commands], page 40.

`@titlefont{`*text*`}`
In a printed manual, print *text* in a larger than normal font. Not relevant to Info, which does not have title pages. See

Appendix A: @-Command List 185

Section 3.4.2 [The @titlefont @center and @sp Commands], page 39.

@titlepage
Indicate to Texinfo the beginning of the title page. Write command on a line of its own. Pair with @end titlepage. Nothing between @titlepage and @end titlepage appears in Info. See Section 3.4.1 [@titlepage], page 38.

@today{}
Insert the current date, in '1 Jan 1900' style. See Section F.3 [How to Make Your Own Headings], page 209.

@top *title*
In a Texinfo file to be formatted with makeinfo, identify the topmost @node line in the file, which must be written on the line immediately preceding the @top command. Used for makeinfo's node pointer insertion feature. The title is underlined with asterisks. Both the @node line and the @top line normally should be enclosed by @ifinfo and @end ifinfo. In TeX and texinfo-format-buffer, the @top command is merely a synonym for @unnumbered. See Section 6.3 [Creating Pointers with makeinfo], page 65.

@unnumbered *title*
In a printed manual, begin a chapter that appears without chapter numbers of any kind. The title appears in the table of contents of a printed manual. In Info, the title is underlined with asterisks. See Section 5.5 [@unnumbered and @appendix], page 53.

@unnumberedsec *title*
In a printed manual, begin a section that appears without section numbers of any kind. The title appears in the table of contents of a printed manual. In Info, the title is underlined with equal signs. See Section 5.8 [Section Commands], page 54.

@unnumberedsubsec *title*
In a printed manual, begin an unnumbered subsection within a chapter. The title appears in the table of contents of a printed manual. In Info, the title is underlined with hyphens. See Section 5.10 [@unnumberedsubsec @appendixsubsec @subheading], page 55.

@unnumberedsubsubsec *title*
In a printed manual, begin an unnumbered subsubsection within a chapter. The title appears in the table of contents of a printed manual. In Info, the title is underlined with periods. See Section 5.11 [The 'subsub' Commands], page 55.

@value{*flag*}
: Replace *flag* with the value to which it is set by @set *flag*. See Section 18.2 [@set @clear @value], page 144.

@var{*metasyntactic-variable*}
: Highlight a metasyntactic variable, which is something that stands for another piece of text. See Section 9.1.5 [Indicating Metasyntactic Variables], page 85.

@vindex *entry*
: Add *entry* to the index of variables. See Section 12.1 [Defining the Entries of an Index], page 107.

@vskip *amount*
: In a printed manual, insert whitespace so as to push text on the remainder of the page towards the bottom of the page. Used in formatting the copyright page with the argument 'Opt plus 1filll'. (Note spelling of 'filll'.) @vskip may be used only in contexts ignored for Info. See Section 3.4.4 [The Copyright Page and Printed Permissions], page 40.

@vtable *formatting-command*
: Begin a two-column table, using @item for each entry. Automatically enter each of the items in the first column into the index of variables. Pair with @end vtable. The same as @table, except for indexing. See Section 11.3.1 [@ftable and @vtable], page 104.

@w{*text*}
: Prevent *text* from being split across two lines. Do not end a paragraph that uses @w with an @refill command. In the Texinfo file, keep *text* on one line. See Section 15.2 [@w], page 124.

@xref{*node-name*, [*entry*], [*topic-or-title*], [*info-file*], [*manual*]}
: Make a reference that starts with 'See' in a printed manual. Follow command with a punctuation mark. Only the first argument is mandatory. See Section 8.3 [@xref], page 73.

Appendix B Tips and Hints

Here are some tips for writing Texinfo documentation:

- Write in the present tense, not in the past or the future.

- Write actively! For example, write "We recommend that ..." rather than "It is recommended that ...".

- Use 70 or 72 as your fill column. Longer lines are hard to read.

- Include a copyright notice and copying permissions.

Index, index, index!

Write many index entries, in different ways. Readers like indices; they are helpful and convenient.

Although it is easiest to write index entries as you write the body of the text, some people prefer to write entries afterwards. In either case, write an entry before the paragraph to which it applies. This way, an index entry points to the first page of a paragraph that is split across pages.

Here are more hints we have found valuable:

- Write each index entry differently, so each entry refers to a different place in the document. The index of an Info file lists only one location for each entry.

- Write index entries only where a topic is discussed significantly. For example, it is not useful to index "debugging information" in a chapter on reporting bugs. Someone who wants to know about debugging information will certainly not find it in that chapter.

- Consistently capitalize the first word of every concept index entry, or else consistently use lower case. Terse entries often call for lower case; longer entries for capitalization. Whichever case convention you use, please use one or the other consistently! Mixing the two styles looks bad.

- Always capitalize or use upper case for those words in an index for which this is proper, such as names of countries or acronyms. Always use the appropriate case for case-sensitive names, such as those in C or Lisp.

- Write the indexing commands that refer to a whole section immediately after the section command, and write the indexing commands that refer to the paragraph before the paragraph.

  In the example that follows, a blank line comes after the index entry for "Leaping":

```
@section The Dog and the Fox
@cindex Jumping, in general
@cindex Leaping

@cindex Dog, lazy, jumped over
@cindex Lazy dog jumped over
@cindex Fox, jumps over dog
@cindex Quick fox jumps over dog
The quick brown fox jumps over the lazy dog.
```

(Note that the example shows entries for the same concept that are written in different ways—'Lazy dog', and 'Dog, lazy'—so readers can look up the concept in different ways.)

Blank lines

- Insert a blank line between a sectioning command and the first following sentence or paragraph, or between the indexing commands associated with the sectioning command and the first following sentence or paragraph, as shown in the tip on indexing. Otherwise, a formatter may fold title and paragraph together.
- Always insert a blank line before an @table command and after an @end table command; but never insert a blank line after an @table command or before an @end table command.

For example,

```
Types of fox:

@table @samp
@item Quick
Jump over lazy dogs.

@item Brown
Also jump over lazy dogs.
@end table

@noindent
On the other hand, ...
```

Insert blank lines before and after @itemize ... @end itemize and @enumerate ... @end enumerate in the same way.

Complete phrases

Complete phrases are easier to read than ...

- Write entries in an itemized list as complete sentences; or at least, as complete phrases. Incomplete expressions ... awkward ... like this.

Appendix B: Tips and Hints

- Write the prefatory sentence or phrase for a multi-item list or table as a complete expression. Do not write "You can set:"; instead, write "You can set these variables:". The former expression sounds cut off.

Editions, dates and versions

Write the edition and version numbers and date in three places in every manual:

1. In the first @ifinfo section, for people reading the Texinfo file.
2. In the @titlepage section, for people reading the printed manual.
3. In the 'Top' node, for people reading the Info file.

Also, it helps to write a note before the first @ifinfo section to explain what you are doing.

For example:

```
@c ===> NOTE! <==
@c Specify the edition and version numbers and date
@c in *three* places:
@c   1. First ifinfo section  2. title page  3. top node
@c To find the locations, search for !!set

@ifinfo
@c !!set edition, date, version
This is Edition 4.03, January 1992,
of the @cite{GDB Manual} for GDB Version 4.3.
...
```

—or use @set and @value (see Section 18.2.3 [@value Example], page 147).

Definition Commands

Definition commands are @deffn, @defun, @defmac, and the like, and enable you to write descriptions in a uniform format.

- Write just one definition command for each entity you define with a definition command. The automatic indexing feature creates an index entry that leads the reader to the definition.
- Use @table ... @end table in an appendix that contains a summary of functions, not @deffn or other definition commands.

Capitalization

- Capitalize 'Texinfo'; it is a name. Do not write the 'x' or 'i' in upper case.
- Capitalize 'Info'; it is a name.

- Write TeX using the `@TeX{}` command. Note the uppercase 'T' and 'X'. This command causes the formatters to typeset the name according to the wishes of Donald Knuth, who wrote TeX.

Spaces

Do not use spaces to format a Texinfo file, except inside of `@example` ... `@end example` and similar commands.

For example, TeX fills the following:

```
@kbd{C-x v}
@kbd{M-x vc-next-action}
    Perform the next logical operation
    on the version-controlled file
    corresponding to the current buffer.
```

so it looks like this:

`C-x v` `M-x vc-next-action` Perform the next logical operation on the version-controlled file corresponding to the current buffer.

In this case, the text should be formatted with `@table`, `@item`, and `@itemx`, to create a table.

@code, @samp, @var, and '---'

- Use `@code` around Lisp symbols, including command names. For example,

    `The main function is @code{vc-next-action}, ...`

- Avoid putting letters such as 's' immediately after an '`@code`'. Such letters look bad.
- Use `@var` around meta-variables. Do not write angle brackets around them.
- Use three hyphens in a row, '`---`', to indicate a long dash. TeX typesets these as a long dash and the Info formatters reduce three hyphens to two.

Periods Outside of Quotes

Place periods and other punctuation marks *outside* of quotations, unless the punctuation is part of the quotation. This practice goes against convention, but enables the reader to distinguish between the contents of the quotation and the whole passage.

For example, you should write the following sentence with the period outside the end quotation marks:

`Evidently, 'au' is an abbreviation for ''author''.`

Appendix B: Tips and Hints

since 'au' does *not* serve as an abbreviation for 'author.' (with a period following the word).

Introducing New Terms

- Introduce new terms so that a user who does not know them can understand them from context; or write a definition for the term.

  For example, in the following, the terms "check in", "register" and "delta" are all appearing for the first time; the example sentence should be rewritten so they are understandable.

  > The major function assists you in checking in a file to your version control system and registering successive sets of changes to it as deltas.

- Use the **@dfn** command around a word being introduced, to indicate that the user should not expect to know the meaning already, and should expect to learn the meaning from this passage.

@pxref

Absolutely never use **@pxref** except in the special context for which it is designed: inside parentheses, with the closing parenthesis following immediately after the closing brace. One formatter automatically inserts closing punctuation and the other does not. This means that the output looks right both in printed output and in an Info file, but only when the command is used inside parentheses.

Invoking from a Shell

You can invoke programs such as Emacs, GCC, and GAWK from a shell. The documentation for each program should contain a section that describes this. Unfortunately, if the node names and titles for these sections are all different, readers find it hard to search for the section.

Name such sections with a phrase beginning with the word 'Invoking ...', as in 'Invoking Emacs'; this way users can find the section easily.

ANSI C Syntax

When you use **@example** to describe a C function's calling conventions, use the ANSI C syntax, like this:

```
void dld_init (char *@var{path});
```

And in the subsequent discussion, refer to the argument values by writing the same argument names, again highlighted with **@var**.

Avoid the obsolete style that looks like this:

```
#include <dld.h>

dld_init (path)
char *path;
```

Also, it is best to avoid writing `#include` above the declaration just to indicate that the function is declared in a header file. The practice may give the misimpression that the `#include` belongs near the declaration of the function. Either state explicitly which header file holds the declaration or, better yet, name the header file used for a group of functions at the beginning of the section that describes the functions.

Bad Examples

Here are several examples of bad writing to avoid:

In this example, say, " ... you must `@dfn{check in}` the new version." That flows better.

> When you are done editing the file, you must perform a `@dfn{check in}`.

In the following example, say, "... makes a unified interface such as VC mode possible."

> SCCS, RCS and other version-control systems all perform similar functions in broadly similar ways (it is this resemblance which makes a unified control mode like this possible).

And in this example, you should specify what 'it' refers to:

> If you are working with other people, it assists in coordinating everyone's changes so they do not step on each other.

And Finally ...

- Pronounce TeX as if the 'X' were a Greek 'chi', as the last sound in the name 'Bach'. But pronounce Texinfo as in 'speck': '`teckinfo`'.
- Write notes for yourself at the very end of a Texinfo file after the `@bye`. None of the formatters process text after the `@bye`; it is as if the text were within `@ignore` ... `@end ignore`.

Appendix C A Sample Texinfo File

Here is a complete, short sample Texinfo file, without any commentary. You can see this file, with comments, in the first chapter. See Section 1.8 [A Short Sample Texinfo File], page 10.

```
\input texinfo   @c -*-texinfo-*-
@c %**start of header
@setfilename sample.info
@settitle Sample Document
@c %**end of header

@setchapternewpage odd

@ifinfo
This is a short example of a complete Texinfo file.

Copyright 1990 Free Software Foundation, Inc.
@end ifinfo

@titlepage
@sp 10
@comment The title is printed in a large font.
@center @titlefont{Sample Title}

@c The following two commands start the copyright page.
@page
@vskip 0pt plus 1filll
Copyright @copyright{} 1990 Free Software Foundation, Inc.
@end titlepage

@node    Top,       First Chapter, (dir),    (dir)
@comment node-name, next,          previous, up

@menu
* First Chapter::    The first chapter is the
                     only chapter in this sample.
* Concept Index::    This index has two entries.
@end menu

@node    First Chapter, Concept Index, Top,      Top
@comment node-name,     next,          previous, up
@chapter First Chapter
```

```
@cindex Sample index entry

This is the contents of the first chapter.
@cindex Another sample index entry

Here is a numbered list.

@enumerate
@item
This is the first item.

@item
This is the second item.
@end enumerate

The @code{makeinfo} and @code{texinfo-format-buffer}
commands transform a Texinfo file such as this into
an Info file; and @TeX{} typesets it for a printed
manual.

@node     Concept Index,    ,  First Chapter, Top
@comment node-name,     next,   previous,     up
@unnumbered Concept Index

@printindex cp

@contents
@bye
```

Appendix D Sample Permissions

Texinfo files should contain sections that tell the readers that they have the right to copy and distribute the Texinfo file, the Info file, and the printed manual.

Also, if you are writing a manual about software, you should explain that the software is free and either include the GNU General Public License (GPL) or provide a reference to it. See section "Distribution" in *The GNU Emacs Manual*, for an example of the text that could be used in the software "Distribution", "General Public License", and "NO WARRANTY" sections of a document. See [Texinfo Copying Conditions], page 1, for an example of a brief explanation of how the copying conditions provide you with rights.

In a Texinfo file, the first **@ifinfo** section usually begins with a line that says what the file documents. This is what a person reading the unprocessed Texinfo file or using the advanced Info command g * sees first. See Info file 'info', node 'Expert', for more information. (A reader using the regular Info commands usually starts reading at the first node and skips this first section, which is not in a node.)

In the **@ifinfo** section, the summary sentence is followed by a copyright notice and then by the copying permission notice. One of the copying permission paragraphs is enclosed in **@ignore** and **@end ignore** commands. This paragraph states that the Texinfo file can be processed through TeX and printed, provided the printed manual carries the proper copying permission notice. This paragraph is not made part of the Info file since it is not relevant to the Info file; but it is a mandatory part of the Texinfo file since it permits people to process the Texinfo file in TeX and print the results.

In the printed manual, the Free Software Foundation copying permission notice follows the copyright notice and publishing information and is located within the region delineated by the **@titlepage** and **@end titlepage** commands. The copying permission notice is exactly the same as the notice in the **@ifinfo** section except that the paragraph enclosed in **@ignore** and **@end ignore** commands is not part of the notice.

To make it simple to insert a permission notice into each section of the Texinfo file, sample permission notices for each section are reproduced in full below.

Note that you may need to specify the correct name of a section mentioned in the permission notice. For example, in *The GDB Manual*, the name of the section referring to the General Public License is called the "GDB General Public License", but in the sample shown below, that section is referred to generically as the "GNU General Public License". If the Texinfo file does not carry a copy of the General Public License, leave out the reference to it, but be sure to include the rest of the sentence.

D.1 'ifinfo' Copying Permissions

In the @ifinfo section of a Texinfo file, the standard Free Software Foundation permission notice reads as follows:

    This file documents ...

    Copyright 1992 Free Software Foundation, Inc.

    Permission is granted to make and distribute verbatim
    copies of this manual provided the copyright notice and
    this permission notice are preserved on all copies.

    @ignore
    Permission is granted to process this file through TeX
    and print the results, provided the printed document
    carries a copying permission notice identical to this
    one except for the removal of this paragraph (this
    paragraph not being relevant to the printed manual).

    @end ignore
    Permission is granted to copy and distribute modified
    versions of this manual under the conditions for
    verbatim copying, provided also that the sections
    entitled ``Copying'' and ``GNU General Public License''
    are included exactly as in the original, and provided
    that the entire resulting derived work is distributed
    under the terms of a permission notice identical to this
    one.

    Permission is granted to copy and distribute
    translations of this manual into another language,
    under the above conditions for modified versions,
    except that this permission notice may be stated in a
    translation approved by the Free Software Foundation.

D.2 Titlepage Copying Permissions

In the @titlepage section of a Texinfo file, the standard Free Software Foundation copying permission notice follows the copyright notice and publishing information. The standard phrasing is as follows:

    Permission is granted to make and distribute verbatim
    copies of this manual provided the copyright notice and
    this permission notice are preserved on all copies.

Appendix D: Sample Permissions

Permission is granted to copy and distribute modified versions of this manual under the conditions for verbatim copying, provided also that the sections entitled ``Copying'' and ``GNU General Public License'' are included exactly as in the original, and provided that the entire resulting derived work is distributed under the terms of a permission notice identical to this one.

Permission is granted to copy and distribute translations of this manual into another language, under the above conditions for modified versions, except that this permission notice may be stated in a translation approved by the Free Software Foundation.

Appendix E Include Files

When TEX or an Info formatting command sees an `@include` command in a Texinfo file, it processes the contents of the file named by the command and incorporates them into the DVI or Info file being created. Index entries from the included file are incorporated into the indices of the output file.

Include files let you keep a single large document as a collection of conveniently small parts.

E.1 How to Use Include Files

To include another file within a Texinfo file, write the `@include` command at the beginning of a line and follow it on the same line by the name of a file to be included. For example:

    @include buffers.texi

An included file should simply be a segment of text that you expect to be included as is into the overall or *outer* Texinfo file; it should not contain the standard beginning and end parts of a Texinfo file. In particular, you should not start an included file with a line saying '`\input texinfo`'; if you do, that phrase is inserted into the output file as is. Likewise, you should not end an included file with an `@bye` command; nothing after `@bye` is formatted.

In the past, you were required to write an `@setfilename` line at the beginning of an included file, but no longer. Now, it does not matter whether you write such a line. If an `@setfilename` line exists in an included file, it is ignored.

Conventionally, an included file begins with an `@node` line that is followed by an `@chapter` line. Each included file is one chapter. This makes it easy to use the regular node and menu creating and updating commands to create the node pointers and menus within the included file. However, the simple Emacs node and menu creating and updating commands do not work with multiple Texinfo files. Thus you cannot use these commands to fill in the 'Next', 'Previous', and 'Up' pointers of the `@node` line that begins the included file. Also, you cannot use the regular commands to create a master menu for the whole file. Either you must insert the menus and the 'Next', 'Previous', and 'Up' pointers by hand, or you must use the GNU Emacs Texinfo mode command, `texinfo-multiple-files-update`, that is designed for `@include` files.

E.2 `texinfo-multiple-files-update`

GNU Emacs Texinfo mode provides the `texinfo-multiple-files-update` command. This command creates or updates 'Next', 'Previous', and 'Up' pointers of included files as well as those in the outer or overall

Texinfo file, and it creates or updates a main menu in the outer file. Depending whether you call it with optional arguments, the command updates only the pointers in the first `@node` line of the included files or all of them:

`M-x texinfo-multiple-files-update`
: Called without any arguments:
    - Create or update the 'Next', 'Previous', and 'Up' pointers of the first `@node` line in each file included in an outer or overall Texinfo file.
    - Create or update the 'Top' level node pointers of the outer or overall file.
    - Create or update a main menu in the outer file.

`C-u M-x texinfo-multiple-files-update`
: Called with `C-u` as a prefix argument:
    - Create or update pointers in the first `@node` line in each included file.
    - Create or update the 'Top' level node pointers of the outer file.
    - Create and insert a master menu in the outer file. The master menu is made from all the menus in all the included files.

`C-u 8 M-x texinfo-multiple-files-update`
: Called with a numeric prefix argument, such as `C-u 8`:
    - Create or update **all** the 'Next', 'Previous', and 'Up' pointers of all the included files.
    - Create or update **all** the menus of all the included files.
    - Create or update the 'Top' level node pointers of the outer or overall file.
    - And then create a master menu in the outer file. This is similar to invoking `texinfo-master-menu` with an argument when you are working with just one file.

Note the use of the prefix argument in interactive use: with a regular prefix argument, just `C-u`, the `texinfo-multiple-files-update` command inserts a master menu; with a numeric prefix argument, such as `C-u 8`, the command updates **every** pointer and menu in **all** the files and then inserts a master menu.

E.3 Include File Requirements

If you plan to use the `texinfo-multiple-files-update` command, the outer Texinfo file that lists included files within it should contain nothing

Appendix E: Include Files

but the beginning and end parts of a Texinfo file, and a number of `@include` commands listing the included files. It should not even include indices, which should be listed in an included file of their own.

Moreover, each of the included files must contain exactly one highest level node (conventionally, `@chapter` or equivalent), and this node must be the first node in the included file. Furthermore, each of these highest level nodes in each included file must be at the same hierarchical level in the file structure. Usually, each is an `@chapter`, an `@appendix`, or an `@unnumbered` node. Thus, normally, each included file contains one, and only one, chapter or equivalent-level node.

The outer file should contain only *one* node, the 'Top' node. It should *not* contain any nodes besides the single 'Top' node. The `texinfo-multiple-files-update` command will not process them.

E.4 Sample File with `@include`

Here is an example of a complete outer Texinfo file with `@include` files within it before running `texinfo-multiple-files-update`, which would insert a main or master menu:

```
\input texinfo @c -*-texinfo-*-
@setfilename   include-example.info
@settitle Include Example

@setchapternewpage odd
@titlepage
@sp 12
@center @titlefont{Include Example}
@sp 2
@center by Whom Ever

@page
@vskip 0pt plus 1filll
Copyright @copyright{} 1990 Free Software Foundation, Inc.
@end titlepage

@ifinfo
@node Top, First, (dir), (dir)
@top Master Menu
@end ifinfo

@include foo.texinfo
@include bar.texinfo
@include concept-index.texinfo
```

```
@summarycontents
@contents

@bye
```

An included file, such as 'foo.texinfo', might look like this:

```
@node First, Second, , Top
@chapter First Chapter

Contents of first chapter ...
```

The full contents of 'concept-index.texinfo' might be as simple as this:

```
@node Concept Index, , Second, Top
@unnumbered Concept Index

@printindex cp
```

The outer Texinfo source file for *The GNU Emacs Lisp Reference Manual* is named 'elisp.texi'. This outer file contains a master menu with 417 entries and a list of 41 `@include` files.

E.5 Evolution of Include Files

When Info was first created, it was customary to create many small Info files on one subject. Each Info file was formatted from its own Texinfo source file. This custom meant that Emacs did not need to make a large buffer to hold the whole of a large Info file when someone wanted information; instead, Emacs allocated just enough memory for the small Info file that contained the particular information sought. This way, Emacs could avoid wasting memory.

References from one file to another were made by referring to the file name as well as the node name. (See Section 7.5 [Referring to Other Info Files], page 70. Also, see Section 8.3.4 [`@xref` with Four and Five Arguments], page 76.)

Include files were designed primarily as a way to create a single, large printed manual out of several smaller Info files. In a printed manual, all the references were within the same document, so TeX could automatically determine the references' page numbers. The Info formatting commands used include files only for creating joint indices; each of the individual Texinfo files had to be formatted for Info individually. (Each, therefore, required its own `@setfilename` line.)

However, because large Info files are now split automatically, it is no longer necessary to keep them small.

Nowadays, multiple Texinfo files are used mostly for large documents, such as *The GNU Emacs Lisp Reference Manual*, and for projects in which several different people write different sections of a document simultaneously.

In addition, the Info formatting commands have been extended to work with the `@include` command so as to create a single large Info file that is split into smaller files if necessary. This means that you can write menus and cross references without naming the different Texinfo files.

Appendix F Page Headings

Most printed manuals contain headings along the top of every page except the title and copyright pages. Some manuals also contain footings. (Headings and footings have no meaning to Info, which is not paginated.)

Texinfo provides standard page heading formats for manuals that are printed on one side of each sheet of paper and for manuals that are printed on both sides of the paper. Usually, you will use one or other of these formats, but you can specify your own format, if you wish.

In addition, you can specify whether chapters should begin on a new page, or merely continue the same page as the previous chapter; and if chapters begin on new pages, you can specify whether they must be odd-numbered pages.

By convention, a book is printed on both sides of each sheet of paper. When you open a book, the right-hand page is odd-numbered, and chapters begin on right-hand pages—a preceding left-hand page is left blank if necessary. Reports, however, are often printed on just one side of paper, and chapters begin on a fresh page immediately following the end of the preceding chapter. In short or informal reports, chapters often do not begin on a new page at all, but are separated from the preceding text by a small amount of whitespace.

The `@setchapternewpage` command controls whether chapters begin on new pages, and whether one of the standard heading formats is used. In addition, Texinfo has several heading and footing commands that you can use to generate your own heading and footing formats.

In Texinfo, headings and footings are single lines at the tops and bottoms of pages; you cannot create multiline headings or footings. Each header or footer line is divided into three parts: a left part, a middle part, and a right part. Any part, or a whole line, may be left blank. Text for the left part of a header or footer line is set flushleft; text for the middle part is centered; and, text for the right part is set flushright.

F.1 Standard Heading Formats

Texinfo provides two standard heading formats, one for manuals printed on one side of each sheet of paper, and the other for manuals printed on both sides of the paper.

By default, nothing is specified for the footing of a Texinfo file, so the footing remains blank.

The standard format for single-sided printing consists of a header line in which the left-hand part contains the name of the chapter, the central part is blank, and the right-hand part contains the page number.

A single-sided page looks like this:

```
-----------------------
|                     |
| chapter   page number |
|                     |
| Start of text ...   |
| ...                 |
|                     |
```

The standard format for two-sided printing depends on whether the page number is even or odd. By convention, even-numbered pages are on the left- and odd-numbered pages are on the right. (TeX will adjust the widths of the left- and right-hand margins. Usually, widths are correct, but during double-sided printing, it is wise to check that pages will bind properly—sometimes a printer will produce output in which the even-numbered pages have a larger right-hand margin than the odd-numbered pages.)

In the standard double-sided format, the left part of the left-hand (even-numbered) page contains the page number, the central part is blank, and the right part contains the title (specified by the **@settitle** command). The left part of the right-hand (odd-numbered) page contains the name of the chapter, the central part is blank, and the right part contains the page number.

Two pages, side by side as in an open book, look like this:

```
-----------------------     -----------------------
|                     |     |                     |
| page number   title |     | chapter   page number |
|                     |     |                     |
| Start of text ...   |     | More text ...       |
| ...                 |     | ...                 |
|                     |     |                     |
```

The chapter name is preceded by the word 'Chapter', the chapter number and a colon. This makes it easier to keep track of where you are in the manual.

F.2 Specifying the Type of Heading

TeX does not begin to generate page headings for a standard Texinfo file until it reaches the **@end titlepage** command. Thus, the title and copyright pages are not numbered. The **@end titlepage** command causes TeX to begin to generate page headings according to a standard format specified by the **@setchapternewpage** command that precedes the **@titlepage** section.

Appendix F: Page Headings

There are four possibilities:

No @setchapternewpage command
: Cause TeX to specify the single-sided heading format, with chapters on new pages. This is the same as @setchapternewpage on.

@setchapternewpage on
: Specify the single-sided heading format, with chapters on new pages.

@setchapternewpage off
: Cause TeX to start a new chapter on the same page as the last page of the preceding chapter, after skipping some vertical whitespace. Also cause TeX to typeset for single-sided printing. (You can override the headers format with the @headings double command; see Section 3.4.6 [The @headings Command], page 42.)

@setchapternewpage odd
: Specify the double-sided heading format, with chapters on new pages.

Texinfo lacks an @setchapternewpage even command.

F.3 How to Make Your Own Headings

You can use the standard headings provided with Texinfo or specify your own.

Texinfo provides six commands for specifying headings and footings. The @everyheading command and @everyfooting command generate page headers and footers that are the same for both even- and odd-numbered pages. The @evenheading command and @evenfooting command generate headers and footers for even-numbered (left-hand) pages; and the @oddheading command and @oddfooting command generate headers and footers for odd-numbered (right-hand) pages.

Write custom heading specifications in the Texinfo file immediately after the @end titlepage command. Enclose your specifications between @iftex and @end iftex commands since the texinfo-format-buffer command may not recognize them. Also, you must cancel the predefined heading commands with the @headings off command before defining your own specifications.

Here is how to tell TeX to place the chapter name at the left, the page number in the center, and the date at the right of every header for both even- and odd-numbered pages:

```
@iftex
@headings off
@everyheading @thischapter @| @thispage @| @today{}
@end iftex
```

You need to divide the left part from the central part and the central part from the right had part by inserting '`@|`' between parts. Otherwise, the specification command will not be able to tell where the text for one part ends and the next part begins.

Each part can contain text or `@`-commands. The text is printed as if the part were within an ordinary paragraph in the body of the page. The `@`-commands replace themselves with the page number, date, chapter name, or whatever.

Here are the six heading and footing commands:

`@everyheading` *left* `@|` *center* `@|` *right*
`@everyfooting` *left* `@|` *center* `@|` *right*

> The 'every' commands specify the format for both even- and odd-numbered pages. These commands are for documents that are printed on one side of each sheet of paper, or for documents in which you want symmetrical headers or footers.

`@evenheading` *left* `@|` *center* `@|` *right*
`@oddheading` *left* `@|` *center* `@|` *right*
`@evenfooting` *left* `@|` *center* `@|` *right*
`@oddfooting` *left* `@|` *center* `@|` *right*

> The 'even' and 'odd' commands specify the format for even-numbered pages and odd-numbered pages. These commands are for books and manuals that are printed on both sides of each sheet of paper.

Use the '`@this...`' series of `@`-commands to provide the names of chapters and sections and the page number. You can use the '`@this...`' commands in the left, center, or right portions of headers and footers, or anywhere else in a Texinfo file so long as they are between `@iftex` and `@end iftex` commands.

Here are the '`@this...`' commands:

`@thispage`
> Expands to the current page number.

`@thischaptername`
> Expands to the name of the current chapter.

Appendix F: Page Headings

@thischapter
> Expands to the number and name of the current chapter, in the format 'Chapter 1: Title'.

@thistitle
> Expands to the name of the document, as specified by the `@settitle` command.

@thisfile
> For `@include` files only: expands to the name of the current `@include` file. If the current Texinfo source file is not an `@include` file, this command has no effect. This command does *not* provide the name of the current Texinfo source file unless it is an `@include` file. (See Appendix E [Include Files], page 201, for more information about `@include` files.)

You can also use the `@today{}` command, which expands to the current date, in '1 Jan 1900' format.

Other @-commands and text are printed in a header or footer just as if they were in the body of a page. It is useful to incorporate text, particularly when you are writing drafts:

```
@iftex
@headings off
@everyheading @emph{Draft!} @| @thispage @| @thischapter
@everyfooting @| @| Version: 0.27: @today{}
@end iftex
```

Beware of overlong titles: they may overlap another part of the header or footer and blot it out.

Appendix G Formatting Mistakes

Besides mistakes in the content of your documentation, there are two kinds of mistake you can make with Texinfo: you can make mistakes with @-commands, and you can make mistakes with the structure of the nodes and chapters.

Emacs has two tools for catching the @-command mistakes and two for catching structuring mistakes.

For finding problems with @-commands, you can run TeX or a region formatting command on the region that has a problem; indeed, you can run these commands on each region as you write it.

For finding problems with the structure of nodes and chapters, you can use C-c C-s (`texinfo-show-structure`) and the related `occur` command and you can use the `M-x Info-validate` command.

The `makeinfo` program does an excellent job of catching errors and reporting them—far better than `texinfo-format-region` or `texinfo-format-buffer`. In addition, the various functions for automatically creating and updating node pointers and menus remove many opportunities for human error.

If you can, use the updating commands to create and insert pointers and menus. These prevent many errors. Then use `makeinfo` (or its Texinfo mode manifestations, `makeinfo-region` and `makeinfo-buffer`) to format your file and check for other errors. This is the best way to work with Texinfo. But if you cannot use `makeinfo`, or your problem is very puzzling, then you may want to use the tools described in this appendix.

G.1 Catching Errors with Info Formatting

After you have written part of a Texinfo file, you can use the `texinfo-format-region` or the `makeinfo-region` command to see whether the region formats properly.

Most likely, however, you are reading this section because for some reason you cannot use the `makeinfo-region` command; therefore, the rest of this section presumes that you are using `texinfo-format-region`.

If you have made a mistake with an @-command, `texinfo-format-region` will stop processing at or after the error and display an error message. To see where in the buffer the error occurred, switch to the '*Info Region*' buffer; the cursor will be in a position that is after the location of the error. Also, the text will not be formatted after the place where the error occurred (or more precisely, where it was detected).

For example, if you accidentally end a menu with the command `@end menus` with an 's' on the end, instead of with `@end menu`, you will see an error message that says:

    @end menus is not handled by texinfo

The cursor will stop at the point in the buffer where the error occurs, or not long after it. The buffer will look like this:

```
---------- Buffer: *Info Region* ----------
* Menu:

* Using texinfo-show-structure::   How to use
                                   'texinfo-show-structure'
                                   to catch mistakes.
* Running Info-Validate::          How to check for
                                   unreferenced nodes.
@end menus
*
---------- Buffer: *Info Region* ----------
```

The `texinfo-format-region` command sometimes provides slightly odd error messages. For example, the following cross reference fails to format:

    (@xref{Catching Mistakes, for more info.)

In this case, `texinfo-format-region` detects the missing closing brace but displays a message that says 'Unbalanced parentheses' rather than 'Unbalanced braces'. This is because the formatting command looks for mismatches between braces as if they were parentheses.

Sometimes `texinfo-format-region` fails to detect mistakes. For example, in the following, the closing brace is swapped with the closing parenthesis:

    (@xref{Catching Mistakes), for more info.}

Formatting produces:

    (*Note for more info.: Catching Mistakes)

The only way for you to detect this error is to realize that the reference should have looked like this:

    (*Note Catching Mistakes::, for more info.)

Incidentally, if you are reading this node in Info and type `f RET` (Info-follow-reference), you will generate an error message that says:

    No such node: "Catching Mistakes) The only way ...

This is because Info perceives the example of the error as the first cross reference in this node and if you type a RET immediately after typing the Info `f` command, Info will attempt to go to the referenced node. If you type `f catch TAB RET`, Info will complete the node name of the correctly written

Appendix G: Formatting Mistakes

example and take you to the 'Catching Mistakes' node. (If you try this, you can return from the 'Catching Mistakes' node by typing l (`Info-last`).)

G.2 Catching Errors with TeX Formatting

You can also catch mistakes when you format a file with TeX.

Usually, you will want to do this after you have run `texinfo-format-buffer` (or, better, `makeinfo-buffer`) on the same file, because `texinfo-format-buffer` sometimes displays error messages that make more sense than TeX. (See Section G.1 [Debugging with Info], page 213, for more information.)

For example, TeX was run on a Texinfo file, part of which is shown here:

```
---------- Buffer: texinfo.texi ----------
name of the Texinfo file as an extension.  The
@samp{??} are 'wildcards' that cause the shell to
substitute all the raw index files.  (@xref{sorting
indices, for more information about sorting
indices.)@refill
---------- Buffer: texinfo.texi ----------
```

(The cross reference lacks a closing brace.) TeX produced the following output, after which it stopped:

```
---------- Buffer: *tex-shell* ----------
Runaway argument?
{sorting indices, for more information about sorting
indices.) @refill @ETC.
! Paragraph ended before @xref was complete.
<to be read again>
                    @par
l.27

?
---------- Buffer: *tex-shell* ----------
```

In this case, TeX produced an accurate and understandable error message:

Paragraph ended before @xref was complete.

'@par' is an internal TeX command of no relevance to Texinfo. 'l.27' means that TeX detected the problem on line 27 of the Texinfo file. The '?' is the prompt TeX uses in this circumstance.

Unfortunately, TeX is not always so helpful, and sometimes you must truly be a Sherlock Holmes to discover what went wrong.

In any case, if you run into a problem like this, you can do one of three things.

1. You can tell TeX to continue running and ignore just this error by typing RET at the '?' prompt.

2. You can tell TeX to continue running and to ignore all errors as best it can by typing r RET at the '?' prompt.

   This is often the best thing to do. However, beware: the one error may produce a cascade of additional error messages as its consequences are felt through the rest of the file. (To stop TeX when it is producing such an avalanche of error messages, type C-d (or C-c C-d, if you are running a shell inside Emacs.))

3. You can tell TeX to stop this run by typing x RET at the '?' prompt.

Please note that if you are running TeX inside Emacs, you need to switch to the shell buffer and line at which TeX offers the '?' prompt.

Sometimes TeX will format a file without producing error messages even though there is a problem. This usually occurs if a command is not ended but TeX is able to continue processing anyhow. For example, if you fail to end an itemized list with the **@end itemize** command, TeX will write a DVI file that you can print out. The only error message that TeX will give you is the somewhat mysterious comment that

```
(@end occurred inside a group at level 1)
```

However, if you print the DVI file, you will find that the text of the file that follows the itemized list is entirely indented as if it were part of the last item in the itemized list. The error message is the way TeX says that it expected to find an **@end** command somewhere in the file; but that it could not determine where it was needed.

Another source of notoriously hard-to-find errors is a missing **@end group** command. If you ever are stumped by incomprehensible errors, look for a missing **@end group** command first.

If the Texinfo file lacks header lines, TeX may stop in the beginning of its run and display output that looks like the following. The '*' indicates that TeX is waiting for input.

```
This is TeX, Version 2.0 for Berkeley UNIX
(preloaded format=plain-cm 87.10.25)
(test.texinfo [1])
*
```

In this case, simply type \end RET after the asterisk. Then write the header lines in the Texinfo file and run the TeX command again. (Note the use of the backslash, '\'. TeX uses '\' instead of '@'; and in this circumstance, you are working directly with TeX, not with Texinfo.)

G.3 Using `texinfo-show-structure`

It is not always easy to keep track of the nodes, chapters, sections, and subsections of a Texinfo file. This is especially true if you are revising or adding to a Texinfo file that someone else has written.

In GNU Emacs, in Texinfo mode, the `texinfo-show-structure` command lists all the lines that begin with the @-commands that specify the structure: `@chapter`, `@section`, `@appendix`, and so on. With an argument (C-u as prefix argument, if interactive), the command also shows the `@node` lines. The `texinfo-show-structure` command is bound to C-c C-s in Texinfo mode, by default.

The lines are displayed in a buffer called the '*Occur*' buffer, indented by hierarchical level. For example, here is a part of what was produced by running `texinfo-show-structure` on this manual:

```
Lines matching "^@\\(chapter \\|sect\\|subs\\|subh\\|
unnum\\|major\\|chapheading \\|heading \\|appendix\\)"
in buffer texinfo.texi.
...
4177:@chapter Nodes
4198:    @heading Two Paths
4231:    @section Node and Menu Illustration
4337:    @section The @code{@@node} Command
4393:        @subheading Choosing Node and Pointer Names
4417:        @subsection How to Write an @code{@@node} Line
4469:        @subsection @code{@@node} Line Tips
...
```

This says that lines 4337, 4393, and 4417 of 'texinfo.texi' begin with the `@section`, `@subheading`, and `@subsection` commands respectively. If you move your cursor into the '*Occur*' window, you can position the cursor over one of the lines and use the C-c C-c command (`occur-mode-goto-occurrence`), to jump to the corresponding spot in the Texinfo file. See section "Using Occur" in *The GNU Emacs Manual*, for more information about `occur-mode-goto-occurrence`.

The first line in the '*Occur*' window describes the *regular expression* specified by *texinfo-heading-pattern*. This regular expression is the pattern that `texinfo-show-structure` looks for. See section "Using Regular Expressions" in *The GNU Emacs Manual*, for more information.

When you invoke the `texinfo-show-structure` command, Emacs will display the structure of the whole buffer. If you want to see the structure of just a part of the buffer, of one chapter, for example, use the C-x n n (`narrow-to-region`) command to mark the region. (See section "Narrowing" in *The GNU Emacs Manual*.) This is how the example used above was generated. (To see the whole buffer again, use C-x n w (`widen`).)

If you call `texinfo-show-structure` with a prefix argument by typing
`C-u C-c C-s`, it will list lines beginning with `@node` as well as the lines beginning with the `@`-sign commands for `@chapter`, `@section`, and the like.

You can remind yourself of the structure of a Texinfo file by looking at the list in the '`*Occur*`' window; and if you have mis-named a node or left out a section, you can correct the mistake.

G.4 Using `occur`

Sometimes the `texinfo-show-structure` command produces too much information. Perhaps you want to remind yourself of the overall structure of a Texinfo file, and are overwhelmed by the detailed list produced by `texinfo-show-structure`. In this case, you can use the `occur` command directly. To do this, type

    M-x occur

and then, when prompted, type a *regexp*, a regular expression for the pattern you want to match. (See section "Regular Expressions" in *The GNU Emacs Manual*.) The `occur` command works from the current location of the cursor in the buffer to the end of the buffer. If you want to run `occur` on the whole buffer, place the cursor at the beginning of the buffer.

For example, to see all the lines that contain the word '`@chapter`' in them, just type '`@chapter`'. This will produce a list of the chapters. It will also list all the sentences with '`@chapter`' in the middle of the line.

If you want to see only those lines that start with the word '`@chapter`', type '`^@chapter`' when prompted by `occur`. If you want to see all the lines that end with a word or phrase, end the last word with a '`$`'; for example, '`catching mistakes$`'. This can be helpful when you want to see all the nodes that are part of the same chapter or section and therefore have the same 'Up' pointer.

See section "Using Occur" in *The GNU Emacs Manual*, for more information.

G.5 Finding Badly Referenced Nodes

You can use the `Info-validate` command to check whether any of the 'Next', 'Previous', 'Up' or other node pointers fail to point to a node. This command checks that every node pointer points to an existing node. The `Info-validate` command works only on Info files, not on Texinfo files.

The `makeinfo` program validates pointers automatically, so you do not need to use the `Info-validate` command if you are using `makeinfo`. You only may need to use `Info-validate` if you are unable to run `makeinfo` and instead must create an Info file using `texinfo-format-region` or `texinfo-format-buffer`, or if you write an Info file from scratch.

Appendix G: Formatting Mistakes 217

G.5.1 Running Info-validate

To use `Info-validate`, visit the Info file you wish to check and type:

`M-x Info-validate`

(Note that the `Info-validate` command requires an upper case 'I'. You may also need to create a tag table before running `Info-validate`. See Section G.5.3 [Tagifying], page 220.)

If your file is valid, you will receive a message that says "File appears valid". However, if you have a pointer that does not point to a node, error messages will be displayed in a buffer called '`*problems in info file*`'.

For example, `Info-validate` was run on a test file that contained only the first node of this manual. One of the messages said:

`In node "Overview", invalid Next: Texinfo Mode`

This meant that the node called '`Overview`' had a 'Next' pointer that did not point to anything (which was true in this case, since the test file had only one node in it).

Now suppose we add a node named '`Texinfo Mode`' to our test case but we do not specify a 'Previous' for this node. Then we will get the following error message:

`In node "Texinfo Mode", should have Previous: Overview`

This is because every 'Next' pointer should be matched by a 'Previous' (in the node where the 'Next' points) which points back.

`Info-validate` also checks that all menu entries and cross references point to actual nodes.

Note that `Info-validate` requires a tag table and does not work with files that have been split. (The `texinfo-format-buffer` command automatically splits large files.) In order to use `Info-validate` on a large file, you must run `texinfo-format-buffer` with an argument so that it does not split the Info file; and you must create a tag table for the unsplit file.

G.5.2 Creating an Unsplit File

You can run `Info-validate` only on a single Info file that has a tag table. The command will not work on the indirect subfiles that are generated when a master file is split. If you have a large file (longer than 70,000 bytes or so), you need to run the `texinfo-format-buffer` or `makeinfo-buffer` command in such a way that it does not create indirect subfiles. You will also need to create a tag table for the Info file. After you have done this, you can run `Info-validate` and look for badly referenced nodes.

The first step is to create an unsplit Info file. To prevent `texinfo-format-buffer` from splitting a Texinfo file into smaller Info files, give a prefix to the `M-x texinfo-format-buffer` command:

```
C-u M-x texinfo-format-buffer
```
or else
```
C-u C-c C-e C-b
```
When you do this, Texinfo will not split the file and will not create a tag table for it.

G.5.3 Tagifying a File

After creating an unsplit Info file, you must create a tag table for it. Visit the Info file you wish to tagify and type:
```
M-x Info-tagify
```
(Note the upper case I in `Info-tagify`.) This creates an Info file with a tag table that you can validate.

The third step is to validate the Info file:
```
M-x Info-validate
```
(Note the upper case I in `Info-validate`.) In brief, the steps are:
```
C-u M-x texinfo-format-buffer
M-x Info-tagify
M-x Info-validate
```
After you have validated the node structure, you can rerun `texinfo-format-buffer` in the normal way so it will construct a tag table and split the file automatically, or you can make the tag table and split the file manually.

G.5.4 Splitting a File Manually

You should split a large file or else let the `texinfo-format-buffer` or `makeinfo-buffer` command do it for you automatically. (Generally you will let one of the formatting commands do this job for you. See Chapter 20 [Create an Info File], page 159.)

The split-off files are called the indirect subfiles.

Info files are split to save memory. With smaller files, Emacs does not have make such a large buffer to hold the information.

If an Info file has more than 30 nodes, you should also make a tag table for it. See Section G.5.1 [Using Info-validate], page 219, for information about creating a tag table. (Again, tag tables are usually created automatically by the formatting command; you only need to create a tag table yourself if you are doing the job manually. Most likely, you will do this for a large, unsplit file on which you have run `Info-validate`.)

Visit the Info file you wish to tagify and split and type the two commands:

Appendix G: Formatting Mistakes

M-x Info-tagify
M-x Info-split

(Note that the 'I' in 'Info' is upper case.)

When you use the `Info-split` command, the buffer is modified into a (small) Info file which lists the indirect subfiles. This file should be saved in place of the original visited file. The indirect subfiles are written in the same directory the original file is in, with names generated by appending '-' and a number to the original file name.

The primary file still functions as an Info file, but it contains just the tag table and a directory of subfiles.

Appendix H Refilling Paragraphs

The `@refill` command refills and, optionally, indents the first line of a paragraph.[1] The `@refill` command is no longer important, but we describe it here because you once needed it. You will see it in many old Texinfo files.

Without refilling, paragraphs containing long `@`-constructs may look bad after formatting because the formatter removes `@`-commands and shortens some lines more than others. In the past, neither the `texinfo-format-region` command nor the `texinfo-format-buffer` command refilled paragraphs automatically. The `@refill` command had to be written at the end of every paragraph to cause these formatters to fill them. (Both TeX and `makeinfo` have always refilled paragraphs automatically.) Now, all the Info formatters automatically fill and indent those paragraphs that need to be filled and indented.

The `@refill` command causes `texinfo-format-region` and `texinfo-format-buffer` to refill a paragraph in the Info file *after* all the other processing has been done. For this reason, you can not use `@refill` with a paragraph containing either `@*` or `@w{ ... }` since the refilling action will override those two commands.

The `texinfo-format-region` and `texinfo-format-buffer` commands now automatically append `@refill` to the end of each paragraph that should be filled. They do not append `@refill` to the ends of paragraphs that contain `@*` or `@w{ ...}` and therefore do not refill or indent them.

---

[1] Perhaps the command should have been called the `@refillandindent` command, but `@refill` is shorter and the name was chosen before indenting was possible.

Appendix I @-Command Syntax

The character '@' is used to start special Texinfo commands. (It has the same meaning that '\' has in PlainTeX.) Texinfo has four types of @-command:

1. Non-alphabetic commands.

    These commands consist of an @ followed by a punctuation mark or other character that is not part of the alphabet. Non-alphabetic commands are almost always part of the text within a paragraph, and never take any argument. The two characters (@ and the other one) are complete in themselves; none is followed by braces. The non-alphabetic commands are: @., @:, @*, @@, @{, and @}.

2. Alphabetic commands that do not require arguments.

    These commands start with @ followed by a word followed by left- and right-hand braces. These commands insert special symbols in the document; they do not require arguments. For example, @dots{} ⇒ '...', @equiv{} ⇒ '≡', @TeX{} ⇒ 'TeX', and @bullet{} ⇒ '•'.

3. Alphabetic commands that require arguments within braces.

    These commands start with @ followed by a letter or a word, followed by an argument within braces. For example, the command @dfn indicates the introductory or defining use of a term; it is used as follows: 'In Texinfo, @@-commands are @dfn{mark-up} commands.'

4. Alphabetic commands that occupy an entire line.

    These commands occupy an entire line. The line starts with @, followed by the name of the command (a word); for example, @center or @cindex. If no argument is needed, the word is followed by the end of the line. If there is an argument, it is separated from the command name by a space. Braces are not used.

Thus, the alphabetic commands fall into classes that have different argument syntaxes. You cannot tell to which class a command belongs by the appearance of its name, but you can tell by the command's meaning: if the command stands for a glyph, it is in class 2 and does not require an argument; if it makes sense to use the command together with other text as part of a paragraph, the command is in class 3 and must be followed by an argument in braces; otherwise, it is in class 4 and uses the rest of the line as its argument.

The purpose of having a different syntax for commands of classes 3 and 4 is to make Texinfo files easier to read, and also to help the GNU Emacs paragraph and filling commands work properly. There is only one exception to this rule: the command `@refill`, which is always used at the end of a paragraph immediately following the final period or other punctuation character. `@refill` takes no argument and does *not* require braces. `@refill` never confuses the Emacs paragraph commands because it cannot appear at the beginning of a line.

Appendix J How to Obtain TeX

TeX is freely redistributable. You can obtain TeX for Unix systems via anonymous ftp or on tape or CD-ROM. The core material consists of Karl Berry's `web2c` TeX package.

On-line retrieval instructions are in `ftp.cs.umb.edu` [158.121.104.33] in 'pub/tex/unixtex.ftp'

The Free Software Foundation provides a core distribution on its Source Code CD-ROM; the University of Washington maintains and supports a tape distribution.

For the FSF Source Code CD-ROM, please contact:

Free Software Foundation, Inc.
675 Massachusetts Avenue
Cambridge, MA   02139-3309
USA

Telephone: +1-617-876-3296
Fax: (including Japan) +1-617-492-9057
Free Dial Fax (in Japan):
  0031-13-2473 (KDD)
  0066-3382-0158 (IDC)
Electronic mail: `gnu@prep.ai.mit.edu`

To order a full distribution from the University of Washington on either a 1/4 inch 4-track QIC-24 cartridge or a 4 mm DAT cartridge, send $210.00 to:

Pierre A. MacKay
Department of Classics
DH-10, Denny Hall 218
University of Washington
Seattle, WA   98195
USA

Telephone: +1-206-543-2268
Electronic mail: `mackay@cs.washington.edu`

Please make checks payable to the University of Washington. Checks must be in U.S. dollars, drawn on a U.S. bank.

Prepaid orders are the only orders that can now be handled. Overseas sites: please add to the base cost, if desired, $20.00 for shipment via air parcel post, or $30.00 for shipment via courier.

Please check with the above for current prices and formats.

Appendix K Second Edition Features

The second edition of the Texinfo manual describes more than 20 new Texinfo mode commands and more than 50 previously undocumented Texinfo @-commands. This edition is more than twice the length of the first edition.

Here is a brief description of the new commands.

K.1 New Texinfo Mode Commands

Texinfo mode provides commands and features especially designed for working with Texinfo files. More than 20 new commands have been added, including commands for automatically creating and updating both nodes and menus. This is a tedious task when done by hand.

The keybindings are intended to be somewhat mnemonic.

Update all nodes and menus

The `texinfo-master-menu` command is the primary command:

`C-c C-u m`
`M-x texinfo-master-menu`
> Create or update a master menu. With `C-u` as a prefix argument, first create or update all nodes and regular menus.

Update Pointers

Create or update 'Next', 'Previous', and 'Up' node pointers.
See Section 2.4 [Updating Nodes and Menus], page 19.

`C-c C-u C-n`
`M-x texinfo-update-node`
> Update a node.

`C-c C-u C-e`
`M-x texinfo-every-node-update`
> Update every node in the buffer.

Update Menus

Create or update menus.
See Section 2.4 [Updating Nodes and Menus], page 19.

`C-c C-u C-m`
`M-x texinfo-make-menu`
> Make or update a menu.

`C-c C-u C-a`
`M-x texinfo-all-menus-update`
> Make or update all the menus in a buffer. With `C-u` as a prefix argument, first update all the nodes.

Insert Title as Description

Insert a node's chapter or section title in the space for the description in a menu entry line; position point so you can edit the insert. (This command works somewhat differently than the other insertion commands, which insert only a predefined string.)

See Section 2.2 [Inserting], page 16.

`C-c C-c C-d`   Insert title.

Format for Info

Provide keybindings both for the Info formatting commands that are written in Emacs Lisp and for `makeinfo` that is written in C.

See Section 2.5 [Info Formatting], page 24.

Use the Emacs lisp `texinfo-format...` commands:

`C-c C-e C-r`   Format the region.

`C-c C-e C-b`   Format the buffer.

Use `makeinfo`:

`C-c C-m C-r`   Format the region.

`C-c C-m C-b`   Format the buffer.

`C-c C-m C-l`   Recenter the `makeinfo` output buffer.

`C-c C-m C-k`   Kill the `makeinfo` formatting job.

Typeset and Print

Typeset and print Texinfo documents from within Emacs.
See Section 2.6 [Formatting and Printing], page 25.

`C-c C-t C-b`   Run `texi2dvi` on the buffer.

`C-c C-t C-r`   Run TeX on the region.

`C-c C-t C-i`   Run `texindex`.

`C-c C-t C-p`   Print the DVI file.

`C-c C-t C-q`   Show the print queue.

Appendix K: Second Edition Features   229

C-c C-t C-d   Delete a job from the print queue.

C-c C-t C-k   Kill the current TeX formatting job.

C-c C-t C-x   Quit a currently stopped TeX formatting job.

C-c C-t C-l   Recenter the output buffer.

Other Updating Commands

The "other updating commands" do not have standard keybindings because they are used less frequently.

See Section 2.4.2 [Other Updating Commands], page 23.

M-x texinfo-insert-node-lines
: Insert missing @node lines using section titles as node names.

M-x texinfo-multiple-files-update
: Update a multi-file document. With a numeric prefix, such as C-u 8, update **every** pointer and menu in **all** the files and then insert a master menu.

M-x texinfo-indent-menu-description
: Indent descriptions in menus.

M-x texinfo-sequential-node-update
: Insert node pointers in strict sequence.

K.2 New Texinfo @-Commands

The second edition of the Texinfo manual describes more than 50 commands that were not described in the first edition. A third or so of these commands existed in Texinfo but were not documented in the manual; the others are new. Here is a listing, with brief descriptions of them:

Indexing

Create your own index, and merge indices.

See Chapter 12 [Indices], page 107.

@defindex *index-name*
: Define a new index and its indexing command. See also the @defcodeindex command.

@synindex *from-index into-index*
: Merge the *from-index* index into the *into-index* index. See also the @syncodeindex command.

Definitions

Describe functions, variables, macros, commands, user options, special forms, and other such artifacts in a uniform format.

See Chapter 16 [Definition Commands], page 127.

`@deffn` *category name arguments...*
        Format a description for functions, interactive commands, and similar entities.

`@defvr, @defop, ...`
        15 other related commands.

Glyphs

Indicate the results of evaluation, expansion, printed output, an error message, equivalence of expressions, and the location of point.

See Chapter 14 [Glyphs], page 119.

`@equiv{}`
≡   Equivalence:

`@error{}`
`error`   Error message

`@expansion{}`
↦   Macro expansion

`@point{}`
⋆   Position of point

`@print{}`
⊣   Printed output

`@result{}`
⇒   Result of an expression

Page Headings

Customize page headings.

See Appendix F [Headings], page 207.

`@headings` *on-off-single-double*
        Headings on or off, single, or double-sided.

`@evenfooting` [*left*] `@|` [*center*] `@|` [*right*]
        Footings for even-numbered (left-hand) pages.

`@evenheading, @everyheading, @oddheading, ...`
        Five other related commands.

Appendix K: Second Edition Features 231

`@thischapter`
    Insert name of chapter and chapter number.

`@thischaptername`, `@thisfile`, `@thistitle`, `@thispage`
    Related commands.

Formatting

Format blocks of text.

See Chapter 10 [Quotations and Examples], page 91, and Chapter 11 [Making Lists and Tables], page 99.

`@cartouche`   Draw rounded box surrounding text (not in Info).

`@enumerate` *optional-arg*
    Enumerate a list with letters or numbers.

`@exdent` *line-of-text*
    Remove indentation.

`@flushleft`   Left justify.

`@flushright` Right justify.

`@format`   Do not narrow nor change font.

`@ftable` *formatting-command*
`@vtable` *formatting-command*
    Two-column table with indexing.

`@lisp`   For an example of Lisp code.

`@smallexample`
`@smalllisp`   Like `@table` and `@lisp` but for `@smallbook`.

Conditionals

Conditionally format text.
See Section 18.2 [`@set` `@clear` `@value`], page 144.

`@set` *flag* [*string*]
    Set a flag. Optionally, set value of *flag* to *string*.

`@clear` *flag*   Clear a flag.

`@value{`*flag*`}` Replace with value to which *flag* is set.

`@ifset` *flag*   Format, if *flag* is set.

`@ifclear` *flag*
    Ignore, if *flag* is set.

@heading series for Titles

Produce unnumbered headings that do not appear in a table of contents.
See Chapter 5 [Structuring], page 51.

`@heading` *title*
>   Unnumbered section-like heading not listed in the table of contents of a printed manual.

`@chapheading`, `@majorheading`, `@subheading`, `@subsubheading`
>   Related commands.

Font commands

See Section 9.2.2 [Smallcaps], page 88, and
Section 9.2.3 [Fonts], page 88.

`@r{`*text*`}`   Print in roman font.

`@sc{`*text*`}`   Print in SMALL CAPS font.

Miscellaneous

See Section 3.4.3 [`@title` `@subtitle` and `@author` Commands], page 40,
see Section 9.2.4 [Customized Highlighting], page 89,
see Section 19.9 [Overfull hboxes], page 155,
see Chapter 17 [Footnotes], page 141,
see Section 13.2 [Format a Dimension], page 114,
see Section 5.12 [`@raisesections` and `@lowersections`], page 56,
see Section 13.6 [`@math`: Inserting Mathematical Expressions], page 116,
see Section 13.5 [Inserting a Minus Sign], page 116,
see Section 3.2.6 [Paragraph Indenting], page 36,
see Section 8.1 [Cross Reference Commands], page 71,
see Section 3.4.3 [`@title` `@subtitle` and `@author`], page 40, and
see Section F.3 [How to Make Your Own Headings], page 209.

`@author` *author*
>   Typeset author's name.

`@definfoenclose` *new-command, before, after,*
>   Define a highlighting command for Info. (Info only.)

`@finalout`   Produce cleaner printed output.

`@footnotestyle` *end-or-separate*
>   Specify footnote style.

`@dmn{`*dimension*`}`
>   Format a dimension.

Appendix K: Second Edition Features 233

@global@let *new-cmd=existing-cmd*
: Define a highlighting command for TeX. (TeX only.)

@lowersections
: Reduce hierarchical level of sectioning commands.

@math{*mathematical-expression*}
: Format a mathematical expression.

@minus{}   Generate a minus sign.

@paragraphindent *asis-or-number*
: Specify paragraph indentation.

@raisesections
: Raise hierarchical level of sectioning commands.

@ref{*node-name*, [*entry*], [*topic-or-title*], [*info-file*], [*manual*]}
: Make a reference. In the printed manual, the reference does not start with the word 'see'.

@title *title*   Typeset *title* in the alternative title page format.

@subtitle *subtitle*
: Typeset *subtitle* in the alternative title page format.

@today{}   Insert the current date.

Command and Variable Index

This is an alphabetical list of all the @-commands and several variables. To make the list easier to use, the commands are listed without their preceding '@'.

*
* (force line break) 123

.
. (true end of sentence) 114

:
: (suppress widening) 114

@
@ (single '@') 113
@definfoenclose 89
@lowersections 56
@raisesections 56

{
{ (single '{') 113

}
} (single '}') 113

A
afourpaper 156
appendix 53
appendixsec 54
appendixsection 54
appendixsubsec 55
appendixsubsubsec 55
apply 139
author 40

B
b (bold font) 88
buffer-end 128
bullet 115
bye 47, 49

C
c (comment) 9
cartouche 97
center 39
chapheading 53
chapter 53
cindex 109
cite 87
clear 145
code 82
comment 9
contents 48
copyright 41, 116
cropmarks 157

D
defcodeindex 111
defcv 136
deffn 130
deffnx 129
defindex 111
defivar 136
defmac 131
defmethod 137
defop 137
defopt 132
defspec 131
deftp 138
deftypefn 132
deftypefun 134
deftypevar 135
deftypevr 135
defun 131
defvar 132
defvr 131
dfn 86
display 95
dmn 114
dots 115

E

`emph`	87
`enable`	135
`end`	91, 99
`end titlepage`	41
`enumerate`	101
`evenfooting`	210
`evenheading`	210
`everyfooting`	210
`everyheading`	210
`example`	92
`exdent`	96

F

`file`	86
`filll`	41
`finalout`	156
`findex`	109
`flushleft`	96
`flushright`	96
`foobar`	129, 133, 134
`footnote`	141
`footnotestyle`	142
`format`	96
`forward-word`	127
`ftable`	104
`fubar`	135

G

`group`	125

H

`heading`	54
`headings`	42

I

`i` (italic font)	88
`ifclear`	145
`ifinfo`	143
`ifset`	144
`iftex`	143
`ignore`	9
`include`	201
`Info-directory-list`	168
`Info-validate`	218
`INFOPATH`	168

`inforef`	80
`input` (TeX command)	9
`isearch-backward`	129
`isearch-forward`	129
`item`	100, 103
`itemize`	100
`itemx`	104

K

`kbd`	83
`key`	84
`kindex`	109

L

`lisp`	94
`lpr` (DVI print command)	151

M

`mag` (TeX command)	157
`majorheading`	53
`makeinfo-buffer`	162
`makeinfo-kill-job`	163
`makeinfo-recenter-output-buffer`	163
`makeinfo-region`	162
`math`	116
`menu`	67
`minus`	116

N

`need`	125
`next-error`	163
`noindent`	93

O

`occur`	218
`occur-mode-goto-occurrence`	18
`oddfooting`	210
`oddheading`	210

P

`page`	124
`page-delimiter`	19
`paragraphindent`	36
`pindex`	109
`printindex`	47
`pxref`	79

Command and Variable Index

Q
quotation 92

R
r (Roman font) 88
ref 78
refill 223

S
samp 84
sc (small caps font) 88
section 54
set 144
setchapternewpage 35
setfilename 34
settitle 34
shortcontents 48
smallbook 156
smallexample 95
smalllisp 95
sp (line spacing) 124
sp (titlepage line spacing) 39
strong 87
subheading 55
subsection 55
subsubheading 55
subsubsection 55
subtitle 40
summarycontents 48
syncodeindex 110
synindex 111

T
t (typewriter font) 88
table 103
tex 144
tex (command) 116
texi2dvi (shell script) 150
texindex 149
texinfo-all-menus-update 21
texinfo-every-node-update 21
texinfo-format-buffer 24, 163, 164
texinfo-format-region 24, 163, 164
texinfo-indent-menu-description ... 24
texinfo-insert-@code 16
texinfo-insert-@dfn 16
texinfo-insert-@end 16
texinfo-insert-@example 17
texinfo-insert-@item 16
texinfo-insert-@kbd 16
texinfo-insert-@node 16
texinfo-insert-@noindent 17
texinfo-insert-@samp 17
texinfo-insert-@table 17
texinfo-insert-@var 17
texinfo-insert-braces 17
texinfo-insert-node-lines 23
texinfo-make-menu 21
texinfo-master-menu 20
texinfo-multiple-files-update 201
texinfo-multiple-files-update (in brief) 23
texinfo-sequential-node-update 24
texinfo-show-structure 18, 217
texinfo-start-menu-description 17
texinfo-tex-buffer 25
texinfo-tex-print 26
texinfo-tex-region 25
texinfo-update-node 21
TEXINPUTS 154
thischapter 210
thischaptername 210
thisfile 211
thispage 210
thistitle 211
tindex 109
title 40
titlefont 39
titlepage 38
today 211
top (@-command) 64

U
unnumbered 53
unnumberedsec 54
unnumberedsubsec 55
unnumberedsubsubsec 55
up-list 17

V
value 146
var 85
vindex 109
vskip 41

vtable 104

W

w (prevent line break) 124

X

xref 73

Concept Index

.

.cshrc initialization file 154
.profile initialization file 154

'

'Enclosure' command for Info 89

@

@-command in nodename 63
@-command list 171
@-command syntax 225
@-commands 6
@include file sample 203
@menu parts 68
@node line writing 62

A

A4 paper, printing on 156
Abbreviations for keys 84
Adding a new info file 167
Alphabetical @-command list 171
Another Info directory 168
Apostrophe in nodename 64
Arguments, repeated and optional 129
Automatic pointer creation with `makeinfo` 65
Automatically insert nodes, menus 19

B

Badly referenced nodes 218
Batch formatting for Info 164
Beginning a Texinfo file 31
Beginning line of a Texinfo file 33
Black rectangle in hardcopy 155
Blank lines 124
Book characteristics, printed 5
Book, printing small 156
Box with rounded corners 97
Braces and argument syntax 225
Braces, inserting 113
Braces, when to use 7
Breaks in a line 123
Buffer formatting and printing 25

Bullets, inserting 115

C

Case in nodename 64
Catching errors with Info formatting .. 213
Catching errors with TeX formatting 215
Catching mistakes 213
Chapter structuring 51
Characteristics, printed books or manuals 5
Checking for badly referenced nodes .. 218
Colon in nodename 64
Combining indices 110
Comma in nodename 64
Command definitions 139
Commands to insert single characters 113
Commands using ordinary TeX 143
Commands, inserting them 16
Comments 9
Compile command for formatting 153
Conditionally visible text 143
Conditions for copying Texinfo 1
Contents, Table of 48
Contents-like outline of file structure .. 18
Conventions for writing definitions ... 139
Conventions, syntactic 8
Copying conditions 1
Copying permissions 197
Copying software 45
Copyright page 40
Correcting mistakes 213
Create nodes, menus automatically ... 19
Creating an Info file 159
Creating an unsplit file 219
Creating index entries 108
Creating indices 107
Creating pointers with `makeinfo` 65
Cropmarks for printing 157
Cross reference parts 72
Cross references 71
Cross references using @inforef 80
Cross references using @pxref 79

Cross references using @ref 78
Cross references using @xref 73
Customized highlighting 89

D

Debugging the Texinfo structure 213
Debugging with Info formatting 213
Debugging with TeX formatting 215
Defining indexing entries 108
Defining new indices 111
Definition commands 127
Definition conventions 139
Definition template 127
Definitions grouped together 129
Description for menu, start 17
Different cross reference commands 71
Dimension formatting 114
'dir' directory for Info installation ... 167
'dir' file listing 167
Display formatting 95
Distribution 45
Dots, inserting 115
Double-colon menu entries 69
DVI file 149

E

Ellipsis, inserting 115
Emacs 15
Emacs shell, format, print from 151
Emphasizing text 87
Emphasizing text, font for 87
'End' node footnote style 141
End of header line 37
End titlepage starts headings 41
Ending a Texinfo file 47
Entries for an index 108
Entries, making index 107
Enumeration 101
Equivalence, indicating it 121
Error message, indicating it 120
Errors, parsing 163
European A4 paper 156
Evaluation glyph 119
Example for a small book 95
Example menu 69
Examples, formatting them 92
Expansion, indicating it 119

F

File beginning 31
File ending 47
File section structure, showing it 18
Filling paragraphs 223
Final output 155
Finding badly referenced nodes 218
First line of a Texinfo file 33
First node 64
Fonts for indices 111
Fonts for printing, not for Info 88
Footings 207
Footnotes 141
Format a dimension 114
Format and print hardcopy 149
Format and print in Texinfo mode.... 151
Format with the compile command ... 153
Format, print from Emacs shell 151
Formatting a file for Info 159
Formatting commands 6
Formatting examples 92
Formatting for Info 24
Formatting for printing 25
Formatting headings and footings 207
Formatting requirements 154
Formatting with tex and texindex ... 149
Frequently used commands, inserting .. 16
Function definitions 139

G

General syntactic conventions 8
Generating menus with indices 47
Glyphs 119
GNU Emacs 15
GNU Emacs shell, format, print from
 151
Going to other Info files' nodes 70
Group (hold text together vertically)
 125
Grouping two definitions together 129

H

Hardcopy, printing it 149
'hboxes', overfull 155
Header for Texinfo files 33
Header of a Texinfo file 33
Headings 207

Concept Index

Headings, page, begin to appear 41
Highlighting text 81
Highlighting, customized 89
Hints 189
Holding text together vertically 125

I

If text conditionally visible 143
'ifinfo' permissions 198
Ignored text 9
Include file requirements 202
Include file sample 203
Include files 201
Indentation undoing 96
Indenting paragraphs 36
Index entries 108
Index entries, making 107
Index entry writing 108
Index font types 109
Indexing commands, predefined 109
Indexing table entries automatically .. 104
Indicating commands, definitions, etc.
.... 81
Indicating evaluation 119
Indices 107
Indices, combining them 110
Indices, defining new 111
Indices, printing and menus 47
Indices, sorting 149
Indices, two letter names 110
Indirect subfiles 165
Info batch formatting 164
Info file installation 167
Info file requires @setfilename 34
Info file, listing new one 167
Info file, splitting manually 220
Info files 4
Info formatting 24
Info installed in another directory 168
Info validating a large file 219
Info, creating an on-line file 159
Info; other files' nodes 70
Initialization file for TeX input 154
Insert nodes, menus automatically 19
Inserting @, braces, and periods 113
Inserting dots 115
Inserting ellipsis 115
Inserting frequently used commands ... 16

Inserting special characters and symbols
.... 113
Installing an Info file 167
Installing Info in another directory ... 168
Introduction, as part of file 45
Itemization 100

K

Keys, recommended names 84

L

Larger or smaller pages 157
Less cluttered menu entry 69
License agreement 45
Line breaks 123
Line breaks, preventing 124
Line spacing 124
Lisp example 94
Lisp example for a small book 95
List of @-commands 171
Listing a new info file 167
Lists and tables, making them 99
Local variables 153
Location of menus 67
Looking for badly referenced nodes ... 218

M

Macro definitions 139
Magnified printing 157
makeinfo inside Emacs 162
makeinfo options 159
Making a printed manual 149
Making a tag table automatically 164
Making a tag table manually 220
Making cross references 71
Making line and page breaks 123
Making lists and tables 99
Manual characteristics, printed 5
Marking text within a paragraph 81
Marking words and phrases 81
Master menu 43
Master menu parts 44
Mathematical expressions 116, 144
Menu description, start 17
Menu entries with two colons 69
Menu example 69
Menu location 67

Menu parts 68
Menu writing 68
Menus 67
Menus generated with indices 47
META key............................ 84
Meta-syntactic chars for arguments... 129
Minimal Texinfo file (requirements)..... 9
Mistakes, catching 213
Mode, using Texinfo.................. 15
Must have in Texinfo file 9

N

Names for indices 110
Names recommended for keys 84
Naming a 'Top' Node in references 77
Need space at page bottom 125
New index defining................... 111
New info file, listing it in 'dir' file.... 167
Node line requirements............... 63
Node line writing 62
Node, 'Top' 43
Node, defined 61
Nodename must be unique 63
Nodename, cannot contain 63
Nodes for menus are short............ 67
Nodes in other Info files.............. 70
Nodes, catching mistakes............. 213
Nodes, checking for badly referenced.. 218

O

Obtaining TEX....................... 227
Occurrences, listing with @occur 218
Optional and repeated arguments 129
Options for makeinfo................ 159
Ordinary TEX commands, using...... 143
Other Info files' nodes................ 70
Outline of file structure, showing it 18
Overfull 'hboxes'..................... 155
Overview of Texinfo 3

P

Page breaks.......................... 124
Page delimiter in Texinfo mode........ 19
Page headings....................... 207
Page numbering..................... 207
Page sizes for books................. 156
Pages, starting odd................... 35

Paper size, European A4............. 156
Paragraph indentation 36
Paragraph, marking text within 81
Parsing errors....................... 163
Part of file formatting and printing.... 25
Parts of a cross reference............. 72
Parts of a master menu 44
Parts of a menu...................... 68
Periods, inserting 113
Permissions.......................... 197
Permissions, printed................. 40
Plain TEX 143
Point, indicating it in a buffer........ 121
Pointer creation with makeinfo........ 65
Pointer validation with makeinfo..... 162
Predefined indexing commands....... 109
Predefined names for indices 110
Preparing to use TEX 154
Preventing line and page breaks...... 123
Print and format in Texinfo mode.... 151
Print, format from Emacs shell....... 151
Printed book and manual characteristics
.... 5
Printed output, indicating it 120
Printed permissions 40
Printing a region or buffer............. 25
Printing an index 47
Printing cropmarks 157
Problems, catching................... 213

Q

Quotations........................... 92

R

Raising and lowering sections.......... 56
Recommended names for keys 84
Rectangle, ugly, black in hardcopy.... 155
References 71
References using @inforef............ 80
References using @pxref............. 79
References using @ref............... 78
References using @xref.............. 73
Referring to other Info files........... 70
Refilling paragraphs.................. 223
Region formatting and printing........ 25
Region printing in Texinfo mode 151
Repeated and optional arguments 129
Required in Texinfo file................. 9

Concept Index   243

Requirements for formatting 154
Requirements for include files 202
Requirements for updating commands
    22
Result of an expression 119
Running an Info formatter 24
Running Info-validate 219
Running `makeinfo` in Emacs 162

S

Sample `@include` file 203
Sample function definition 139
Sample Texinfo file 10
Sample Texinfo file, no comments 195
Section structure of a file, showing it .. 18
Sections, raising and lowering 56
'Separate' footnote style 141
Shell formatting with `tex` and `texindex`
    149
Shell, format, print from 151
Shell, running `makeinfo` in 162
Short nodes for menus 67
Showing the section structure of a file .. 18
Showing the structure of a file 217
Single characters, commands to insert
    113
Size of printed book 156
Small book example 95
Small book size 156
Small caps font 88
Software copying permissions 45
Sorting indices 149
Spaces (blank lines) 124
Special insertions 113
Special typesetting commands 115
Specifying index entries 108
Splitting an Info file manually 220
Start of header line 33
Starting chapters 35
Structure of a file, showing it 18
Structure, catching mistakes in 213
Structuring of chapters 51
Subsection-like commands 55
Subsub commands 55
Syntactic conventions 8
Syntax, optional & repeated arguments
    129

T

Table of contents 48
Tables and lists, making them 99
Tables with indexes 104
Tables, making two-column 103
Tabs; don't use! 8
Tag table, making automatically 164
Tag table, making manually 220
Template for a definition 127
TeX commands, using ordinary 143
TeX index sorting 149
TeX input initialization 154
TeX, how to obtain 227
Texinfo file beginning 31
Texinfo file ending 47
Texinfo file header 33
Texinfo file minimum 9
Texinfo file section structure, showing it
    18
Texinfo mode 15
Texinfo overview 3
Texinfo printed book characteristics 5
`TEXINPUTS` environment variable...... 154
Text, conditionally visible 143
Thin space between number, dimension
    114
Tips 189
Title page 38
Titlepage end starts headings 41
Titlepage permissions 198
'Top' node 43
'Top' node is first 64
'Top' node naming for references 77
'Top' node summary 65
Tree structuring 51
Two 'First' Lines for `@deffn` 129
Two letter names for indices 110
Two named items for `@table` 104
Two part menu entry 69
Typesetting commands for dots, etc... 115

U

Uncluttered menu entry 69
Unique nodename requirement 63
Unprocessed text 9
Unsplit file creation 219
Updating nodes and menus 19
Updating requirements 22

Usage tips 189

V

Validating a large file 219
Validation of pointers 162
Value of an expression, indicating 119
Vertical whitespace ('vskip') 41
Vertically holding text together 125

Visibility of conditional text 143

W

Words and phrases, marking them 81
Writing a menu 68
Writing an @node line 62
Writing index entries 108